Powell's Excavations in the West Plaza of

$69.95 / 9.98   NDJ

Anthropology & Archaeology   117635

Tikal Report No. 17

EXCAVATIONS IN THE WEST PLAZA OF TIKAL

Frontispiece. Excavations in the West Plaza begin, February 1962. The trenches are Op. 19C, D, and E (see Fig. 2).

University Museum Monograph 151

Tikal Report No. 17

EXCAVATIONS IN THE WEST PLAZA OF TIKAL

By William A. Haviland
For Peter D. Harrison

Series Editors
William A. Haviland
Simon Martin

Published by

UNIVERSITY OF PENNSYLVANIA MUSEUM
of Archaeology and Anthropology
Philadelphia
2019

LIBRARY OF CONGRESS CATALOGING-IN-PUBLICATION DATA

Names: Haviland, William A., author. | Harrison, Peter D., 1937-2013, author.
Title: Excavations in the West Plaza of Tikal / by William A. Haviland for
  Peter D. Harrison.
Description: Philadelphia : University of Pennsylvania Museum of Archaeology
  and Anthropology, 2019. | Series: University Museum monograph ; 151 |
  Series: Tikal report ; 17 | Includes bibliographical references.
Identifiers: LCCN 2018058202| ISBN 9781949057010 (hardcover : alk. paper) |
  ISBN 1949057011 (hardcover : alk. paper)

© 2019 by the University of Pennsylvania Museum of Archaeology and Anthropology
Philadelphia, PA
All rights reserved. Published 2019

Distributed for the University of Pennsylvania Museum of Archaeology and Anthropology
by the University of Pennsylvania Press.

Printed in the United States of America on acid-free paper.

DEDICATION

This book is dedicated to the memory of Christopher Jones, the latest fallen member of the Tikal Project. His comradeship in the field, his collaboration as co-editor of these reports, and his contributions to our knowledge will long be remembered.

Table of Contents

FRONTISPIECE...ii
LIST OF TABLES..ix
LIST OF ILLUSTRATIONS..xi
EDITORS' NOTE..xiii
ABBREVIATIONS..xv

I   INTRODUCTION..1

II   ARCHITECTURE..3
    Platform 5D-5..3
    Structure 5D-11 and Burial 77..12
    Structure 5D-15 and Cache 167..16
    Structure 5D-19...26
    Structure 5D-144..27

III STONE MONUMENTS AND ASSOCIATED SPECIAL DEPOSITS.............31
    Introduction...31
    The East Group of Monuments..31
    Stela P30 and Cache 84..31
    Stela P31 and Cache 95..32
    Miscellaneous Stone 38 (Stela P21, Fragment 2), Altar P26, and Cache 94..................33
    General Discussion of East Group Monuments....................34
    The Northwest Group of Monuments...............................34
    Stela 15 and Cache 122..35
    Stela P32..36
    Stela P33..36
    Altar P27..37
    Altar P28..37
    Altar P29..38
    General Discussion of Northwest Monument Group.............38
    Column Altar 1..39

IV CHULTUNS	41
Chultun 5D-2	41
Chultun 5D-3	44
V SUMMARY AND CONCLUSIONS	47
APPENDIX I: Test Pits North of the West Plaza: Locations and Contents	51
APPENDIX II: Report by Robert H. Dyson Jr. and Peter D. Harrison on the West Plaza Resistivity Survey	63
APPENDIX III: A Preliminary Classification of Tikal Chultuns	67
APPENDIX IV: Artifacts from General Excavations in Group 5D-10 Illustrated in Tikal Report 27A and 27B	71
REFERENCES	73
ILLUSTRATIONS	77

Tables

Table 1.1	Chronology	2
Table 2.1	Platform 5D-5: Lot Groups	9
Table 2.2	Platform 5D-5: Time Spans	10
Table 2.3	Structure 5D-11: Lot Groups	16
Table 2.4	Structure 5D-11: Late Occupation Material	17
Table 2.5	Structure 5D-11: Time Spans	18
Table 2.6	Structure 5D-15: Lot Groups	23
Table 2.7	Structure 5D-15: Late Occupation Material	24
Table 2.8	Structure 5D-15: Time Spans	25
Table 2.9	Structure 5D-19: Lot Groups	27
Table 2.10	Structure 5D-19: Late Occupation Material	28
Table 2.11	Structure 5D-19: Time Spans	28
Table 2.12	Structure 5D-144: Time Spans	29
Table 4.1	Chultun 5D-2: Lot Groups	42
Table 4.2	Chultun 5D-2: Artifacts	43
Table 4.3	Chultun 5D-2: Time Spans	43
Table 4.4	Chultun 5D-3: Lot Groups	44
Table 4.5	Chultun 5D-3: Artifacts	45
Table 4.6	Chultun 5D-3: Time Spans	45
Table 5.1	Group 5D-10: Time Spans	48

Illustrations

Figure 1	Group 5D-10: Plan
Figure 2	Overall Plan of West Plaza Excavations
Figure 3	Operation 19E: Section
Figure 4	Operation 19F: Plan (a) and Section (b)
Figure 5	Operation 19G: Section (a); 19H and Stela P32 North-South (b) and East-West (c) Sections
Figure 6	Operation 19I: Section
Figure 7	Operation 19N, Stela P33, and Altar P27: Section
Figure 8	Operation 19J with Stela P32: Section (a) and Operation 19D: Section (b)
Figure 9	Operation 19C and 19L: Plans
Figure 10	Operation 19C and 19L: Section in Main Trench (a) and Trench 1 (b)
Figure 11	Structure 5D-11: Section A-A'
Figure 12	Structure 5D-11: Plan, as Revealed by Surface Clearing
Figure 13	Platform 5D-5 and Structure 5D-11: Section B-B' (a) and Schematic Drawing of Plaza Walls (b)
Figure 14	Peter Harrison's Reconstruction Drawing of Structure 5D-11-1st, Frontal View
Figure 15	Schematic Representation of Structure 5D-11-1st and its Relation to 2nd
Figure 16	Structure 5D-15 and 5D-144: Section A-A'
Figure 17	Structure 5D-15-1st: Plan
Figure 18	Structure 5D-15: Elevation of Rear Substructure Wall Masonry as Seen in Axial Trench
Figure 19	Structure 5D-15: Plan of Basal Row of Masonry in Rear Substructure Wall (a) and Elevation of Unit 18 Masonry (b)
Figure 20	Structure 5D-15: Section B-B'
Figure 21	Structure 5D-15: Elevation of East Stair Wall Face and Profile of Unit 21 Wall
Figure 22	Structure 5D-15: West End of Vault Looking West (a) and Profile of West End Vault, Rear Room (b)
Figure 23	Structure 5D-15: Elevation of North (a) and South (b) Walls in the East End of the Rear Gallery Showing Vault Beam Holes
Figure 24	Structure 5D-15: Elevation Showing West End of Building Facade
Figure 25	Structure 5D-15: Surviving Upper Zone Masonry, West End Exterior
Figure 26	Structure 5D-15: Decorated Stucco Fragments Fallen from Building Facade
Figure 27	Structure 5D-19: Plan
Figure 28	Structure 5D-19: Plan of Southwest Quarter after Surface Clearing
Figure 29	Structure 5D-19: Section A-A'
Figure 30	Structure 5D-19: Section B-B'
Figure 31	Structure 5D-19: Elevation of South Half of Facade

Figure 32	Structure 5D-19: Elevation of South Stair Wall
Figure 33	Structure 5D-19: Reconstruction Drawings of the Front (a) and South End (b)
Figure 34	Burial 77 (a) and Cache 167 (b): Plans
Figure 35	Stelae P30, P31, Miscellaneous Stone 38 (Stela P21, Fragment 2) and Altar P26: Plan (a) and Section A-A′ (b)
Figure 36	Stela P31: Section B-B′ (a) and Reconstruction (b); Miscellaneous Stone 38 (Stela P21, Fragment 2) with Altar P26: Section C-C′ (c)
Figure 37	Stela 15 and Alt. P28: Plan (a) and Section (b) of Excavation; Section of Stela (c)
Figure 38	Stela P32: Fragments as Found (a) and Reconstructed (b); Section through Stela (c)
Figure 39	Stela P33: Fragments as Found (a) and Reconstructed (b); Section of Excavation (c)
Figure 40	Altar P27: Plan (a) and Section (b)
Figure 41	Altar P28: Plan (a), Section of Excavation (b) and Section of Repaired Altar (c)
Figure 42	Altar P29: Section of Excavation (a) and Repaired Altar (b)
Figure 43	Chultun 5D-2: Plan (a) and Section (b)
Figure 44	(a) Structure 5D-11: Before Excavation; (b) Structure 5D-11: Looking West into Axial Trench; (c) Structure 5D-11: Second and Third Steps of 2nd in Axial Trench; (d) Structure 5D-11-1st: West Wall Stripped of Masonry
Figure 45	(a) Structure 5D-11: Exposed Front South of Axis; (b) Clearing of Rubble from Burial 77; (c) Burial 77: Rubble Collapsed into Grave; (d) Burial 77: Bedrock Chamber with skeleton
Figure 46	(a) Burial 77: Hattula Moholy-Nagy Cleaning Large *Spondylus* Shell; (b) Peter Harrison Drawing Burial 77; (c) Burial 77: Skull and Chest of Skeleton; (d) Structure 5D-15: Initial Clearing Operations
Figure 47	(a) Structure 5D-15 after Clearing; (b) Structure 5D-15-3rd: Rear Wall Masonry of Substructure; (c) Structure 5D-15-3rd: Looking South into Axial Trench; (d) Structure 5D-15-6th: Stairway
Figure 48	(a) Structure 5D-15-3rd: Lowest Stairs; (b) Structure 5D-15-3rd: West End Masonry; (c) Structure 5D-15-3rd: Northwest Corner; (d) Structure 5D-15-3rd: Looking East along Front of Supporting Terrace
Figure 49	(a) Structure 5D-15-3rd: Supporting Terrace by West Side of Stairs; (b) Structure 5D-15-3rd, 2nd, and 1st: West Half of Facade; (c) Structure 5D-15-3rd: Section of East End Vault of Rear Gallery, Looking West; (d) Structure 5D-15-3rd: Section of East End Vault of Rear Gallery, Looking East
Figure 50	(a) Structure 5D-15-1st: Partition Added in Rear Gallery That Defines 1st-A; (b) Column Altar 1 as Found; (c) Cache 167; (d) Structure 5D-19 Cleared Before Excavation
Figure 51	(a) Structure 5D-19 Showing Southwest Quarter Excavated; (b) Broken Pottery on Floor of Platform 5D-5 Near Structure 5D-19; (c) Stela 15 as Reset; (d) Stela P32
Figure 52	(a) Stela P33; (b) Altar P27; (c) Altar P28

Editors' Note

Tikal Reports present the results of the University of Pennsylvania excavations from 1956–1969, largely in accord with the projected scheme set out by William R. Coe and William A. Haviland in Tikal Report 12. A great deal of research has taken place at Tikal since those investigations were completed with, in particular, several important projects undertaken by the Instituto Nacional de Antropología e Historia de Guatemala and the Agencia Española de Cooperación Internacional. Since their work has often enlarged upon that conducted by the University of Pennsylvania,—in some cases excavating the same structures—there is a clear opportunity to integrate recent and historical investigations to produce a synthetic treatment. This idea is undoubtedly appealing, but it is one we have resisted for the monograph series. The reasons are threefold. Firstly, consistency of scope and presentation was integral to the original scheme and has been implemented in all the reports published thus far. Secondly, the Tikal Report authors do not have access to the newly produced data to anything like the extent necessary to do that work justice. Thirdly, to produce synthetic treatments of this kind would introduce very considerable delays in publishing future Tikal Reports, hampering the work of those scholars and students who could make immediate use of the data they contain. In acknowledgment of subsequent work, the introduction to each volume in the series will henceforth note where later work has taken place on the same structures and reference the relevant publications. Even without the addition of new data, the Tikal Report series provides needed information on things that can no longer be observed first hand, either because of excavation or continuing destruction by the elements.

William A. Haviland
Simon Martin
Series Editors

Abbreviations

Alt.: Altar
Bu.: Burial
Ca.: Cache
Ch.: Chultun
Chm.: Chamber
Col. Alt.: Column Altar
CS.: Construction Stage
E: East
Fl.: Floor
Frag.: Fragment
Gp.: Group
LG.: Lot Group
MS.: Miscellaneous Stone
MT.: Miscellaneous Text
N: North
Op.: Operation
PD.: Problematical Deposit
Plat.: Platform
S: South
St.: Stela
Str.: Structure
TS.: Time Span
U.: Unit
W: West

I

Introduction

Formally designated Gp. 5D-10, the architecture of the West Plaza group consists of Str. 5D-4, 11, 13, 15, 17, and 19, facing Plat. 5D-5 (the plaza proper; Fig. 1). In size, it is second only to the East Plaza in the epicenter of Tikal and ranks as one of the largest spaces at the site. Although it was of obvious interest to the question of how open plazas relate to the buildings that define them, the group received little attention until Peter D. Harrison's work in 1962. Prior to that, William A. Haviland had excavated around St. 15 in 1959 (as Op. 19A; Fig. 2) and William R. Coe investigated St. P30, P31, and Alt. P26 in 1960 (as Op. 19B, see TR. 11 for location). In that same year, a number of test pits were dug to the N of the group (see Appendix I: Op. 10F, 22I, 22Q–S, and 23G–I). A year later, a resistivity survey conducted by Richard Linnington (Appendix II) across the surface of the plaza prompted the digging of several trenches (Op. 19C–S). They revealed the electromagnetic results to be basically negative, as the buried features were of the same material and consistency as the bedrock.

Attention then shifted to the architecture with Harrison's excavation of Str. 5D-11 (Op. 41), 5D-15 (Op. 42), and 5D-19 (Op. 47). In 1962, Robert Dyson excavated around St. P32, P33, and Alt. P27, P28, and P29. In 1963, Dennis Puleston investigated Ch. 5D-2 and 3 as Op. 66T and 72B. By this time, Harrison had turned his attention to the Central Acropolis, but did return to the West Plaza in 1964 to complete drawings and carry out strategic probes. A year later others carried out small-scale work off the SW corner of Str. 5D-12 (Op. 10F), but with disappointing results. In 1968 Harrison returned briefly to Str. 5D-15 (Op. 42J). His last effort in the group was in 1995, in order to complete a group plan shown here as Figure 1.

Peter Harrison first arrived at Tikal in the summer of 1959, having just received his BA from the University of Toronto. As a member of a crew under the supervision of Ann Chowning, who had worked previously at Mayapan, he participated in the first "housemound" excavations at the site (reported in TR. 19). In 1961, he received a master's degree from Toronto, but did not return to Tikal until 1962. Thereafter, he was a regular member until the end of the University of Pennsylvania Tikal Project. With his PhD in hand in 1970, he went on to other things (Chase and Chase 2014), but over the years, the Central Acropolis at Tikal continued to preoccupy Harrison (see Harrison 2003). In particular, his reconstructions of life in the royal court, and his discovery of how the Maya planned the layout of major architecture, rank as major contributions to our knowledge of the Maya.

Harrison did complete inked drawings of some of his West Plaza excavations. With his untimely death in 2013, these and his original field drawings were gathered up, along with other field records, and sent to Haviland, who worked with these to create the present report. In this, he received assistance from a number of people, most notably Travis Feltman, Virginia Greene, Christopher Jones, Stanley Loten, and Hattula Moholy-Nagy. Special thanks go to Dr. Barbara Hayden for her word processing, editing, and inking of Harrison's drawings. Her assistance was indispensable. Thanks also to Linda

Campbell of Due North Surveying for copying the larger plan and section drawings.

By its very nature, archaeological excavation destroys the remains that are under investigation. Thus, it is important to make available the data recovered in the course of this work. Moreover, natural processes over time are likely to have erased some features that were still visible in the 1960s.

Accordingly, the main purpose of this report is to present the data recovered in the 1960s. Nevertheless, this presentation cannot be entirely free from interpretation. Although Haviland has had to interpret Harrison's records, he has tried as much as possible not to deviate from Harrison's ideas. In the final analysis, however, any flaws in interpretations herein are Haviland's and not Harrison's.

For the most part, this report follows the organization of TR. 14, in order to facilitate reference to neighboring Gp. 5D-2 for those interested in doing so. This report likewise follows the precedent of TR. 14 (pp. 9, 840–841) in use of the terms "Intermediate Classic" and "Late Classic" (see Table 1.1). Abbreviations are those standard for Tikal Reports (see p. xv in this volume and TR. 12: table 2).

TABLE 1.1
Chronology

Period	Long Count	Date	Ceramics
Early Postclassic			Caban
		AD 950	
Terminal Classic			Eznab
	10.2.0.0.0	AD 869	
Late Late Classic			Imix
	9.15.5.0.0	AD 735	
Early Late Classic			Imix
	9.13.0.0.0	AD 692	
Intermediate Classic			Ik
	9.6.0.0.0	AD 554	
Early Classic			Manik
	8.11.0.0.0	AD 250	
Terminal Preclassic			Cimi
		AD 150	
Late Late Preclassic			Cauac
		1 BC	
Early Late Preclassic			Chuen
		350 BC	
Late Middle Preclassic			Tzec
		600 BC	
Early Middle Preclassic			Eb
		800 BC	

II

Architecture

Platform 5D-5

Introduction

Knowledge of Plat. 5D-5, the West Plaza proper, derives from trenches (shown in Fig. 2) designated by operation number, as well as ancillary excavations associated with Str. 5D-11, 15, and 19, and two groups of monuments (see TR. 11). Hence, information is far from complete and what there is has had to be pieced together from disparate exposures, primarily of floor surfaces. The reference point for these floors is their exposure by St. P30, P31, and Alt. P26.

Platform 5D-5-6th

Our only certain knowledge of this earliest plaza is Coe's statement in TR. 14 (p. 168) that "Fl. 4B [of Plat. 5D-1] undoubtedly was laid continuously into the West Plaza." The problem is that our excavations did not go deep enough to encounter this pavement where it might have been present. Deep probes, in Op. 19D and E (Fig. 2, 3, 8b), surely were W of the edge of the plaza. On the other hand, the floor may be one of those seen deep in the Op. 42D trench behind Str. 5D-15 (Fig. 16). Unfortunately, these floors "float" relative to others of the West Plaza, and there are no adequate ceramic samples by which to date them.

That said, if one of the floors deep behind 5D-15 is the equivalent of Great Plaza Fl. 4B, it is the deepest, U. 32. Its elevation is within a centimeter or two of Fl. 4B, where it is seen beneath Str. 5D-2 (TR. 14: fig. 274). As shown in Fig. 16, it is thought to run up to a stairway of Str. 5D-15-6th. Beneath Str. 5D-2, Fl. 4B is 0.65 m below Fl. 4A (TR. 14:169), which compares with the 0.31 m that separates Plat. 5D-5:U. 32 from overlying U. 33. Suspected is that the Preclassic (including Cauac) sherds consistently present in later core material here come from disturbance when the Maya dismantled Str. 5D-15-6th, and/or from other construction that reused this fill.

Unit 32 underwent two resurfacings, each about 4 cm thick, and each laid on the surface of the preceding pavement (Fig. 16:U. 34, 35). Their thinness suggests that they are localized renewals of their predecessors, but absent further excavation, this is not certain.

One other enigmatic feature is U. 36, a wall barely glimpsed in the recovery of Ca. 167 (see Str. 5D-15, "Special Deposits" and Fig. 34b). Its top is close to the elevations of U. 32, 34, and 35, and could relate to those floors. One possibility, though far from certain, is that this is part of a retaining wall. If so, then U. 32 would have been a separate entity N of Plat. 5D-5. Alternatively, it could simply have been a construction wall buried in the fill of 6th.

Platform 5D-5-5th

The earliest surface of Plat. 5D-5 observed in excavations around St. P30, P31, and Alt. P26 is a well-preserved floor, U. 4 (see Part III). This is interpreted as part of Plat. 5D-1:Fl. 4A, its nearest exposure seen in the tunnel beneath Str. 5D-2 (TR. 14:fig. 274). Constructed to modify a marked gradient to the W, Fl. 4A feathered into the original plaster surface of the Great Plaza (TR. 14:169). According to Coe (TR. 14:170), there is little reason to doubt that the original pavement ran W into what later became the West Plaza. Floor 4A slopes down to the W, as do all surfaces of Plat. 5D-1 (TR. 14:fig. 235c), so for that reason, a drop in elevation between that floor beneath Str. 5D-2 and Plat. 5D-5:U. 4 is not deemed significant. More telling is the stratigraphy—like Fl. 4A beneath Str. 5D-2, U. 4 is the third one down beneath the uppermost pavement (Plat. 5D-5:U. 1). Both U. 1 and Plat. 5D-1:Fl. 1 are the sole pavements dated to the era of Ik pottery production, and the next floor down at the West Plaza (U. 2) was identified by Coe (TR. 14:180) as a "match" for Plat. 5D-1:Fl. 2B.

Another candidate for a floor of 5th is U. 17, seen in the S end of the Op. 19F trench (Fig. 4a,b). This occupies the same stratigraphic position, beneath three more recent pavements, as does U. 4. It runs N, to turn up to the base of a wall that runs SE-NW (U. 18, Fig. 4a,b). Total thickness of U. 18 is 0.85 m, which suggests it served as a parapet on the N edge of the plaza. That said, U. 33, 38, and 39, floors seen in the axial trench through Str. 5D-15 (Fig. 16), raise doubts. One of these could be part of the same pavement as U. 17. We suspect, but cannot prove, that this is U. 33. It turns up to the lowest step of Preclassic Str. 5D-15-5th, about halfway up its face. Clearly, the structure was in use sometime before the pavement, but continued in use thereafter. If this interpretation is correct, one can only wonder about previously mentioned U. 18. Could this have been a step up to a higher plaza level to the N?

With so little known, nothing more can be said of this plaza, save that it was part of Plat. 5D-1-4th-B, rather than a separate entity. Although its northern edge may have been detected, how far it extended to the S or W is unknown.

Platform 5D-5-4th

Like the earlier 5th, this iteration of what would later become the West Plaza was really nothing more than the western portion of Plat. 5D-1. Floor 3B of 5D-1 clearly ran beyond where it was seen beneath Str. 5D-2 and is identified by the eastern group of West Plaza monuments as Plat. 5D-5:U. 3. This sloped down to the W, like the other floors of Plat 5D-1, in this case some 0.80 m, from its crest to where it was seen beneath Str. 5D-2 (TR. 14:175). Unit 3 of Plat. 5D-5 was a further 0.23 m below this.

The nearest exposure of plaza surfaces to the W of those just noted is in the Op. 19E trench, which was dug W toward "Str. 5D-4" (actually, not a structure; see Plat. 5D-5-1st). In its E end, a series of three floors, U. 5, 6, and 11 were observed, as shown in Fig. 3. This is a reasonable match with the ground surface and floors in the nearby end of the Op. 19F trench (Fig. 4b), which can be correlated with those around the monuments (see below).

In Op. 19E, U. 11 seems to be at the same elevation as U. 3. Its stratigraphic position, like that of U. 3, is below two later floors. Sherds below U. 11, like those beneath Plat. 5D-1:Fl. 3B (TR. 14:177), were all from Preclassic vessels. Unit 11 could be followed W some 5.20 m, where it had been destroyed in the course of extensive Intermediate Classic reconstruction.

Material placed beneath U. 11 continues W of the floor rip-out, its surface declining to the W (see Fig. 3, 8b) with, as might be expected, Preclassic pottery within it showing mixture with later Manik and a few Ik sherds. Within this deposit are the remains of three walls, U. 12, 13, and 14. Their rough appearance clearly reflects their purpose as construction-retaining walls separating core units. A finished wall must once have stood farther W, probably about 25.40 m W in Op. 20D (Fig. 8b:5, 6), where the Maya removed core material for 4th to a mere 5 cm above bedrock.

For the most part, excavations over the West Plaza were not sufficiently deep to encounter the floor of 4th. One exception is in Op. 19F, where the stratigraphic position of U. 15 (Fig. 4b) suggests that it is the floor of 4th. Its surface is 0.12 m below Early Classic U. 6, and a mere 0.24 m was exposed. It did not extend all the way to U. 7, an apparent expansion S of the original U. 18 structure. Presumably, it once abutted that wall. Alternatively, it may have run up to the earlier U. 18 wall, but if so, it was later torn out for an intrusion of U. 7.

Another exception is the trench through Str. 5D-15 (Fig. 16), where U. 39 was laid 0.14 m above

U. 33. Like the earlier pavement, it abuts the lowest step of Str. 5D-15-5th, in this case about 0.18 m below its tread. Thus, the floor represents a second repaving in front of 15-5th.

A deep probe in the N end of the Op. 19I trench may have encountered this same pavement. Here, it took the form of a plaster surface (U. 16) on which the foundation of U. 6 (the floor of 3rd) was laid. Otherwise, no other traces of this floor were found, even in two deep probes (Op. 19Q, R, 1.90 and 1.10 m deep, respectively) W of Op. 19F and G (Fig. 2).

Platform 5D-5-3rd

Unit 2, around the eastern group of monuments, represents a fourth major paving of the plaza. Although its elevation is 0.15 m below Plat. 5D-1:Fl. 2B (where seen beneath Str. 5D-2), this is evidently the pavement Coe (TR. 14:180) identified as part of that floor. In other excavations around the West Plaza, this surface was identified by its stratigraphic position relative to that of Plat. 5D-5-2nd, and its association with Manik ceramics beneath.

In the S end of the Op. 19F trench (Fig. 4b), a floor (U. 6) some 0.27 m below that of 5D-5-2nd is thought to be the same as U. 2. This spacing compares with the 9 cm that separate Fl. 2B and 1 beneath Str. 5D-2; this is not a great difference, considering the distance between the two exposures. The floor runs up to a badly ruined wall oriented SE-NW, 2.60 m wide (U. 7, Fig. 4a), its N wall that of the earlier U. 18. What this construction represents is not known, but on its N side another pavement is seen abutting its masonry base. This surface rises 0.14 m across an 0.80 m interval to a level equivalent to that of U. 6 and is, therefore, considered the same surface. In the Op. 19G trench (Fig. 5a–c), the floor is so labeled by the excavator, consistent with its stratigraphic position beneath U. 5.

The next exposure of this floor is a probe N of St. P32 (Fig. 5b). Here, its well-preserved surface was uncovered 0.20 m below U. 5, with a body 0.28 m thick. A similar situation was seen in Op. 19I (Fig. 6), where U. 6 is 0.18 m below U. 5, with a thickness, including its foundation, of 0.28 m. Unfortunately, usable sherd samples were not obtained from beneath U. 6, but Manik sherds are consistently present in the stratum between this and Intermediate Classic U. 5. Although scarcely conclusive, some of these likely came from mixing of material where floor surfaces are in poor condition.

Although Manik sherds are plentiful in the Op. 19J and K trenches (Fig. 8a, 11), where excavations penetrated up to 0.60 m below U. 5, no sign of U. 6 was encountered. It appears that this floor was never present here or was ripped out before laying U. 5. It is likely the former, as the W wall of 3rd (see below) ran well E of Str. 5D-11 (Fig. 13b).

Beneath Str. 5D-11 is a thick layer of lime, U. 27 (Fig. 11). This runs W, with a distinct downward slope, ending at a rough retaining wall (U. 28). Ceramics below are predominantly Manik, with some Preclassic. Evidently, this represents an occupation surface W of 3rd.

In Op. 19E, U. 6 could be followed for 5.20 m, beyond which it had been destroyed (see Fig. 3:1). What remained of its underlying material, however, extended farther W. Undoubtedly, the W edge of the plaza was located W of that of Plat. 5D-5-4th. Uninterrupted core material containing abundant Manik sherds extends W in the Op. 19D trench and into the E end of Op. 19C (see Fig. 8a, 10a,b). Here, it ends at a wall, U. 9 (Fig. 13b), its top at roughly the same elevation as U. 6. This was probably the W edge of Plat. 5D-5-3rd, even though Ik sherds were found within it. This area was heavily disturbed when U. 6 was removed, so mixing of earlier and later material is to be expected. What can be said is that Manik sherds were at least as abundant as later ones.

The U. 9 wall was followed N in a series of trenches (Fig. 10–12, 13b) to a point near Str. 5D-11, where as expected U. 5 (the floor of Plat. 5D-5-2nd) overlies it. Throughout its length, the wall had a thickness of 1.36 to 1.44 m and consisted of a rubble core faced on both sides by masonry installed solely as headers.

In the section through Str. 5D-15 (Fig. 16), U. 37 has the same stratigraphic position beneath U. 5 as does U. 6. The two pavements are separated by 0.16 m, close to the separation of U. 6 from U. 5 in the Op. 19I trench. As noted in its discussion (see Str. 5D-15, "Special Deposits"), Ca. 167 (Fig. 34b) dates U. 37 to Early Classic times. In short, we are confident that U. 37 is part of the same floor as U. 6. To the N, U. 37 is thought to turn up to Str. 5D-15-4th (see its discussion).

Between U. 37 and 39 (the floor of 4th) is U. 38, another floor of Plat. 5D-5-3rd. This is the floor through which the pit for Ca. 167 was dug (Fig. 34b). After its placement, packed lime sealed the pit. We interpret U. 38 as the original floor of 3rd and that U. 37 represents a repaving restricted to this part of the plaza. Like U. 37, but unlike preceding U. 39, U. 38 does not run all the way to Str. 5D-15-5th. Like U. 37, it too is thought to have turned up to proposed 5D-15-4th.

Another alteration of the pavement of Plat. 5D-5-3rd eliminated the construction represented by U. 7 and 18. When this was done, a floor patch (U. 10) covering what remained of U. 7/18 was feathered into U. 6, 0.80 m E of U. 7/18 (see Fig. 4b). Unfortunately, upheaval over U. 7, probably from an uprooted tree, destroyed evidence of a suspected feathering back into U. 6 on the S side of U. 7.

Given the reality of these alterations of Plat. 5D-5-3rd, we distinguish between 3rd-B (U. 2, 6, 27, 28, and 38) and 3rd-A (U. 10, 37).

Platform 5D-5-2nd

The U. 1 pavement associated with the eastern group of monuments (see Part III) was part of Fl. 1 of Plat. 5D-1-1st-E. Probably dating sometime between 9.11.0.0.0 and 9.11.5.0.0 (see discussion below of TS. 7), that floor turned up to the walls of little-known Str. 5D-2-2nd which, for the first time, created a separation—albeit not a complete one—between the Great and West Plazas. Over the Great Plaza, Fl. 1 declined gradually to its margins, so it is not surprising that U. 1 is a few centimeters below its elevation beneath Str. 5D-2.

Although badly broken over most of the West Plaza, the pavement was usually traceable, with occasional remnants of finished surface and a consistent presence of Ik ceramics within its body. It is represented by U. 5 in the Op. 19F trench (Fig. 4a,b). Traces of it were picked up in Op. 19G, H, and I (Fig. 5a–c, 6), up to the Op. 19A excavations (see Part III). Going W and S from here in the Op. 19N trench, U. 5 could be followed beyond Alt. P27 to a point (Fig. 7:1) at which all traces of it disappear. Some 1.80 m beyond, a floor surface again appears, at roughly the same elevation as U. 5. This could be traced S up to the Op. 19K trench. From here, remnants of U. 5 could be followed E and picked up again in Op. 19J. In the E end of this trench, the elevation of the pavement is the same as that of U. 5 in the adjacent end of the Op. 19G and H trenches. West of Op. 19K, U. 5 turns up to the first step of Str. 5D-11-2nd.

In the Op. 19P trench (Fig. 2), U. 5, though broken, was still identifiable. It was followed up to Str. 5D-15, rising some 0.27 m over a distance of 4 m. In the Op. 42F trench into the axis of Str. 5D-15, the floor was in "mint condition," owing to protection afforded by overlying construction (Fig. 16). Here, U. 5 has a smooth plaster surface over a body 0.12 m thick, composed of heavy mortar and pebbles over pebble ballast. Beneath this was a dark soil fill that contained a few Manik and Ik sherds.

At elevation 251.10 m, the floor runs N some 0.33 m below the floor on which Str. 5D-15-3rd was built. How far N it runs is not known, as excavations did not penetrate far into 5D-15 fill. It may have run up to a structure presumed to have been served by the floors of Plat. 5D-5-3rd (see its discussion, above).

In the Op. 19E trench (Fig. 3), the excavator's notes record U. 5 at 0.45 m below surface, as compared to 0.18 m below in the nearby end of Op. 19F. Assumed is that the discrepancy is the result of disturbance—especially in Op. 19F—caused by tree growth. Discontinuous remnants of U. 5 were seen running W and were picked up in Op. 19D (Fig. 8b). At this point, the broken surface was followed up to the W end of the trench, above deep deposits loaded with Ik ceramics, though mixed with earlier material. The only Imix sherds were directly beneath U. 5 and are easily explainable as intrusive from above the floor, where such sherds were abundant.

In the Op. 19C trench (Fig. 10a), the stratigraphy is considerably disturbed, and sherd samples badly mixed. In the E end of the trench, it looks as if U. 5 ran over the top of U. 9 to a new wall (U. 20) 0.60 m farther W. Based on a compact layer of lime, Ik sherds seem well represented in material beneath. West of U. 20, the compact lime served as an informal occupation surface. Below it, the latest identifiable sherds are from Ik vessels.

Platform 5D-5-1st

Evidence for this final version of the West Plaza consists of traces of pavement seen at a few places, and reflected in others by "late-looking" altars at elevations significantly above the floor of Plat. 5D-5-2nd. Allowing for post-abandonment humps and dips caused by tree growth and uprooting, not to mention possible deliberate grading when the pavement was laid, relative elevations are reasonably consistent. Moreover, accumulations of Imix sherds are invariably present where evidence of the floor is found.

At the eastern group of monuments (see Part III), there was no actual remnant of the floor. But as noted in its discussion, the underside of Alt. P26 was at an elevation almost 0.20 m above underlying U. 1 (Fig. 35b), in turn representing Plat. 5D-1:Fl. 1 in its extension over the West Plaza. The position of the altar is consistent with the elevations of remnants of pavement for 1st seen elsewhere.

One place where actual remains of this pavement were seen is around the NW group of monuments (see their discussion in Part III). The surface here was badly broken (Fig. 7:3), but in Op. 19I a well-preserved surface above U. 5 (Fig. 6:U. 19) must be the same later floor. In even better condition is U. 30, a floor seen above U. 5 beneath Str. 5D-15 (Fig. 16). Although it has been given a separate number than U. 19, its stratigraphic position and probable Imix sherds beneath identify it as the same floor. Unit 30 has a smooth but uneven surface of plaster 4 cm in thickness, underlain by loose gravel piled directly on U. 5. This is the surface on which Str. 5D-15-3rd was built, but since the pavement runs beneath the stairs of 3rd, it must predate the structure, though by how much we cannot say.

When Str. 5D-15-3rd was built, the plaster on its steps was extended over the plaza in front, directly onto U. 30. Not seen anywhere else, this U. 31 is interpreted as a localized skim coat, with original U. 30 continuing to serve (with U. 19) over the rest of the plaza. Accordingly, U. 31 defines Plat. 5D-5-1st-A, as opposed to a separate architectural development. The original floor, U. 19/30, defines 1st-B.

Other surviving Imix-related construction was seen in the Op. 19C and L trenches (Fig. 9, 10a). Unfortunately, the stratigraphy here is anything but clear, a situation not helped by badly mixed ceramic samples. West of the wall (U. 20) of 2nd, a series of N-S walls (U. 21, 22, and 23) seem to relate to Late Classic activity (Fig. 9, 10a). The first of these, U. 21, appears to be a construction wall within material placed for a Late Classic floor. Retaining a gray-brown soil containing numerous pieces of limestone, both wall and fill were covered by gray, powdery earth containing Imix and earlier sherds. This deposit is retained on the W by piled masonry blocks on which the outer, facing masonry of U. 22 was based. The inner (E) face of this wall, with its core of rubble, was set on the powdery earth. Within the U. 22 core, latest sherds are Imix, even beneath the wall, confirming its Late Classic construction. To the E, more fill was dumped, burying the lowest two courses of U. 22 masonry. This brought the elevation up to where plaza pavement, no longer visible, is presumed to have been. The wall protrudes 0.25 to 0.30 m above this, and must have formed a parapet, rather than the "Str. 5D-4" labeled on the site map (TR. 11).

The presence of a parapet calls into question a statement by Harrison (2012:24) that construction of Str. 5D-11 (see below) would have rendered inoperative a system by which runoff rainwater from the West Plaza was directed into the Temple Reservoir. To the contrary, the parapet running S from 5D-11 would have enhanced the flow of runoff into the reservoir by preventing its spilling over the W edge of the plaza.

Some sort of occupation surface probably once was present at the base of the W-face masonry of U. 22, but was not revealed by excavation. What was seen was another wall, U. 23, like the other ones constructed of two faces of masonry stretchers against a core. Its inner face is 1.25 m beyond previously constructed U. 22, its top at the same elevation as the base of the latter. Accordingly, U. 23 likely served as a lower terrace wall on the W face of Plat. 5D-1-1st. Three successive plaster floors (U. 24, 25, and 26) turned up to its outer face, and Imix sherds were sealed beneath all three. Such sherds, of midden quality, were also abundant between U. 22 and 23, perhaps trash discarded before U. 23 was built. This last wall is assigned as part of Plat. 5D-5-1st-B, but it is not certain that its construction took place at exactly the same time as U. 22.

A 1.90 m wide wall (U. 29; Fig. 13a), with facing masonry against either side of a core, similar to U. 22 and 23, was seen abutting the N end of Str. 5D-11-1st (Fig. 12). From here, it ran N to Str. 5D-12. Like contemporary U. 22 with U. 23, U. 29 defined the W edge of the plaza. Beneath the wall was a floor, U. 40, but how this relates to earlier floors of Plat. 5D-5 is unknown.

In spite of our inability to follow its Late Classic floor over the entire West Plaza, we believe this once covered all of Plat. 5D-5-1st. Surely, it must have abutted that part of Str. 5D-11-2nd that was incorporated into 11-1st. But the exposure of this floor to the elements after Tikal was abandoned, and the shallow depth of soil that accumulated as the forest reclaimed the area, made it particularly vulnerable to destruction. It is remarkable that any traces remain.

It is not precisely known when this final paving operation took place, other than it was after the appearance of Imix ceramics, ca. 9.13.0.0.0. It could not have been soon thereafter, as heavy deposits of Imix sherds beneath the floor imply significant passage of time for broken pottery to accumulate in trash recycled in construction cores. This rules out linkage to Plat. 5D-1:U. 33 (TR. 14:186), a grading floor around Str. 5D-2-1st (Temple II) dating from ca. 9.13.0.0.0, when the temple was built (TR. 14:table 28). A later grading floor, Plat. 5D-1:U. 34, is estimated to date around 9.15.0.0.0 (ibid.), and might have extended into the West Plaza. With the construction 40 years earlier of Temple II and westward extension of the terrace fronting the North Acropolis, however, the West Plaza was all but cut off from the Great Plaza. For the first time, the West Plaza was a completely separate entity. The only direct access was a narrow alleyway between the temple and terrace. Unit 34 was likely a localized repaving between the two. Thus, this final pavement looks to be an exclusively West Plaza surface. Nevertheless, as a "guess date" for the floor, 9.15.0.0.0 is not unreasonable. Some 40 years seems sufficient for abundant Imix ceramics to accumulate in trash destined for use in Plat. 5D-5-1st.

LOT GROUPS

Most of the object lots from Plat. 5D-5 consist of construction core material (see Table 2.1). As such, they are badly mixed, as might be expected; sherds from pottery in vogue at the time of construction are mixed with those from vessels of all preceding complexes, all the way back to Tzec. To complicate matters, more recent material contaminated earlier deposits. This happened where the Maya tore out old construction for new. In addition, poor preservation of floor surfaces in many cases provides less than perfect seals for underlying material. As a consequence, as tree roots have penetrated downward, or have been torn up as trees have been uprooted, later material has worked downward into earlier strata. Obviously, such contamination is unlikely to seriously affect the deepest levels, but most excavations over the plaza did not penetrate very deeply.

Material discarded by people using the plaza probably found its way into successive deposits. If so, it is doubtless well mixed with debris recycled from other places. Surely, the Maya "cast their nets (actually baskets) widely" to amass sufficient material for construction cores. In short, we do not know where this material originated. One exception may be LG. 5c, which has the look of an in situ midden that accumulated in TS. 6 (Table 2.2). Left in place, it was incorporated into the core of 1st. Otherwise, sources included domestic trash, although numerous censer fragments also suggest non-domestic sources.

Trash that accumulated off the W edge of the plaza from use of 1st constitutes LG. 6. Lot Group 7b seems to consist of a scatter of litter left on the NW portion of the plaza at the time of abandonment.

TIME SPANS

Time spans for Plat. 5D-5 are presented in Table 2.2. We begin with TS. 17 and subsequent TS. 16, to allow for construction predating that for 5th beneath U. 4. Such defines Plat. 5D-5-6th and follows from Coe's statement that "Fl. 4B [part of Plat. 5D-1] undoubtedly was laid continuously into the West Plaza" (TR. 14:168). Actual construction was seen only below Str. 5D-15.

With TS. 15 there is firmer evidence for a Plat. 5D-5-5th, which was nothing more than the western portion of Plat. 5D-1-4th-A. Hence, this and succeeding TS. 14 (use of the plaza) are the same as Plat. 5D-1-4th:TS. 2 and 1 (TR. 14:table 23). Similarly, TS. 13 is equivalent to 5D-1-3rd:TS. 4 (TR. 14:table 24), followed by 5D-5:TS. 12 for use. Time Spans 3-1 of 5D-1-3rd would be contemporary.

Time Span 11 of Plat. 5D-5, marked by construction of 3rd-B, was yet another part of Plat. 5D-1, in this case 2nd-B. Hence, it is equivalent to TS. 4 of Plat. 5D-1-2nd (TR. 14:table 26), its TS. 3–1 subsumed within Plat. 5D-5:TS. 10. Partial resurfacing of the plaza (3rd-A) defines TS. 9, with TS. 8 as final use of 3rd-A. Not until Plat. 5D-5:TS. 7 did the West Plaza begin to take on a distinct identity of

TABLE 2.1
Platform 5D-5: Lot Groups

Lot Group	Lot	Provenience	Ceramic Evaluation
1	19B/7; 19E/4-6	Core material of 5th	Tzec, Chuen, Cauac
2	19D/6	Mostly core material of 4th	Tzec, Chuen, Manik; a little Ik
3	19C/17; 19D/5; 19H/4; 41A/20-23; 42F/15,17	Mostly core material of 3rd	Much Manik and Preclassic; possible Ik
4	19B/4; 19C/6-8, 15,16; 19D/3,4; 19E/3; 19F/2,3; 19H/3; 19J/3; 19K/3; 19M/3; 42F/14,16	Mostly core material of 2nd	Heavy Ik with a few Imix; much Manik, Cauac, Tzec
5a	19A/2,3,5; 19C/3,4,10-14; 19E/2; 19L/6,7; 19N/3; 42F/13	Core material of 1st	Some Preclassic; much Manik; heavy Ik, Imix
5b	19L/5,8	Core material of 1st-A	Midden quality Ik, Imix; some Manik
5c	5C/5,9	Intermediate Classic middens in 1st core	Ik; a little Manik
6	19L/2-4	Occupation debris from 1st	Mostly Imix midden; a little Manik
7a	19A/1,4; 19B/1,3; 19C/1,2; 19D/1,2; 19E/1; 19F/1; 19G/1; 19H/1,2; 19I/1-3; 19J/1,2; 19K/1,2; 19L/1; 19M/1;	Surface; probably mostly rooted out, of 1st and 2nd core material	Much Ik, Imix, and Manik; some Preclassic
7b	19N/1,2	Surface; midden scatter mixed with core material	Early Imix; some Manik

TABLE 2.2 (part 1)
Platform 5D-5: Time Spans

Time Span	Architectural Development	Unit	Floor	Special Deposit Cache	Lot Group	Other Data
1						Abandonment and ruin
2					7b (late occupation scatter) 6 (occupation)	Last period of use; possible movement and abandonment of Alt. P26–P29
3	1st-A	25?, 26?, 31			5b	Localized modifications of 1st-B
4						Use of 1st-B
5	1st-B	19, 21, 22–24, 29?, 30, 40?	Floor of 1st	122 (secondary)	5a,c; 7a	Final paving of plaza, setting of St. P32, P33, and resetting of St. 15, possible removal of top of St. P21. Imix pottery in vogue, estimated date of 9.15.0.0.0 or later
6						Use of 2nd. Around 9.13.0.0.0, with construction of Temple II on the Great Plaza and westward extension of the terrace fronting the North Acropolis, separation of the West from the Great Plaza becomes complete
7	2nd	1, 5, 8, 20	Floor of 2nd	84, 94, 95	4 (most)	Fifth plaza-wide paving, setting of St. P21, P30, P31. Partial separation of West and Great Plaza by Str. 5D-2-2nd. Ik pottery in vogue. Equivalent to Plat. 5D-1: TS. 11, dated at ca. 9.11.0.0.0
8						Use of 3rd-A
9	3rd-A	10, 37		167		Localized repairing
10						Use of 3rd-B
11	3rd-B	2, 6, 7?, 9, 27, 28, 38	Floor of 3rd		3 (most)	Fourth plaza-wide paving, an extension of Plat. 5D-1: FL. 2B. Equivalent to TS. 4 of Plat. 5D-1-2nd; Manik pottery in vogue

TABLE 2.2 (part 2)
Platform 5D-5: Time Spans

Time Span	Architectural Development	Unit	Floor	Special Deposit Cache	Lot Group	Other Data
12						Use of 4th
13	4th	3, 7?, 11–16, 39	Floor of 4th		2 (most)	Third plaza-wide paving, an extension of Plat. 5D-1: Fl. 3B. Equivalent to TS. 4 of Plat. 5D-1-3rd. Cauac pottery in vogue
14						Use of 5th
15	5th	4, 17, 18, 33	Floor of 5th		1 (all)	Second plaza-wide paving, an extension of Plat. 5D-1: Fl. 4A. Equivalent to TS. 2 of Plat. 5D-1-4th. Cauac pottery in vogue
16		34, 35				Use of hypothetical 6th; repavings of plaza floor in front of 5D-15-5th
17	6th	32, 36?				First-known construction consists of extension of Plat. 5D-1: Fl. 4B. Equivalent to TS. 4 of Plat. 5D-1-4th. Cauac pottery in vogue

its own. Although its floor was an extension of that for Plat. 5D-1-1st-E, Str. 5D-2-2nd partially separated the two plazas. With this came a set of monuments belonging to the West Plaza, St. P21, P30, and P31, as well as, for the first time, a structure (5D-11-2nd) on its W edge. All of this corresponds with the activity of Plat. 5D-1-1st:TS. 11 (TR. 14:table 28). Originally, Coe (TR. 14:841) thought that this activity was all linked to the interment of the 22nd ruler of Tikal (in Bu. 195), which provided him with a date of ca. 9.8.0.0.0 (see also TR. 14:841, 842, 846, and chart 1). A more recent consideration of the evidence by Jones (2003:212–214), however, would place the date closer to the end of Intermediate Classic times, just before burning activity that took place between Bu. 23 and 24. Coe considered this to have happened roughly 75 years after Bu. 195, which is in the range (9.11.0.0.0–9.12.0.0.0) of a radiocarbon date from Bu. 23 (TR. 14:chart 2, reference 43). The year 9.11.0.0.0 (AD 652) seems about right for the accession of Nuun Ujol Chaak (Shield Skull), the 25th ruler of Tikal, who assumed power some time before AD 657 (Martin 2003:28). He suffered at least two significant defeats in his career, one of which (on 9.11.4.5.14) sent him fleeing from Tikal when it was attacked by Calakmul, and another (on 9.12.6.16.17) at the hands of his probable half-brother, the king of Dos Pilas (ibid., p. 28–29). Nevertheless, the reign of Nuun Ujol Chaak initiated a return of a militarily aggressive Tikal (ibid., p. 30). This was to be more successfully pursued by Nuun Ujol Chaak's son, Jasaw Chan K'awiil.

In view of the above, the construction of Plat. 5D-1-1st-E and Plat. 5D-5-2nd, along with other associated remodeling of the North Acropolis and East Plaza, may reflect Nuun Ujol Chaak's optimism in the early years of his reign, before his disastrous defeat in 9.11.4.5.14.

Time Span 6 of Plat. 5D-5 corresponds with Plat. 5D-1-1st:TS. 10–6, during which interval the separation between the West and Great Plazas became virtually complete. This resulted from the construction of Str. 5D-2-1st (Temple II) and westward extension of the terrace fronting the North Acropolis. What was left was a narrow alleyway between temple and terrace, whereas the main access to the West Plaza was from the S. For access from the Great Plaza, one had to go S of Temple II.

Time Span 5 of the West Plaza saw its last major alteration. Sometime estimated to be around 9.15.0.0.0—perhaps later but not much earlier—its final floor was laid, three more stelae were set up (St. P32, P33, and reset St. 15), and structures on the margins of the plaza were modified. If it was not removed earlier, TS. 6 was probably when the top of St. P21 was broken to be reset on the neighboring Great Plaza.

Time Span 3 saw a final alteration of the W edge of the plaza. It was probably also in the succeeding TS. 2 that the four plain altars (P26, P27, P28, and P29) were left on the last floor of the plaza. We cannot say which came first, but suspect plaza expansion. Time Span 1 is defined by abandonment of the plaza and subsequent reclamation by the forest.

Structure 5D-11 and Burial 77

Introduction

Depicted on the site map (TR. 11) as a square temple, excavation in 1962 explored what was thought to be the E-W axis of Str. 5D-11 (Op. 41A; Fig. 44a,b), although it proved to be slightly N of this (Fig. 12). Nevertheless, deep beneath the structure, an impressive Late Classic chamber burial was encountered. Subsequent probes (Fig. 2:Op. 19S, 41C, E, G, H–K) established the basal outline of the final structure, and helped clarify relations to Plat. 5D-5. Final 5D-11 (1st) was preceded by 5D-11-2nd (Fig. 15), with no earlier structure located here.

Structure 5D-11-2nd

The earliest identified architectural development of Str. 5D-11 (2nd) is represented by three steps with the riser for a fourth (U. 6, Fig. 44c, 45a), a wall (U. 4) to the W, and core material in between (Fig. 11). The riser for the first step is based on Plat. 5D-5:U. 8, a stratum of compact lime and pebbles, at about the same elevation as Plat. 5D-5:U. 5. Ceramics beneath U. 8 are of the Ik Complex. Evidently this stratum was the result of preparation for construction of Str. 5D-11-2nd before U. 5 of the plaza was laid. The plaster of U. 5 turns up to a scratch coat of plaster on the riser of the lowest step. A finish coat was then applied, turning down onto the surface of U. 5. Above, the plaster is continuous over the faces and treads of all three steps, up to the remains of a fourth riser, where the plaster was later torn out. Remains of a turnup survive here, with traces of red paint on it. Riser masonry consists of well-cut square to rectangular blocks set as stretchers in Stair 1, stretchers with one small header in Stair 2, and stretchers in Stair 3.

As the stairs were constructed, a mix of earth, rubble, and trash was dumped behind. Amid the rubble are shaped stones with bits of stucco adhering to them. As this material was built up, masonry for the next risers was set in place. Similar to the masonry of the first step, blocks were set as stretchers, but with occasional headers (Fig. 12). Within the core, pause-lines (not shown in Fig. 11) were observed at roughly the same level as the first two stair treads.

Beneath the tread of the third step is a cap of limestone pebbles (Fig. 11:U. 2) ending at the base of the fourth stair riser, beneath which is another such deposit that continues W, sloping downward. Described by Harrison as an "unplastered floor," this has an E-W groove cut into it. South of the section, this feature was cut by construction of Str. 5D-11-1st. Evidently, this and other pause-lines mark the ends of discreet construction stages.

A remnant of the wall of 2nd is represented by U. 4, which is a battered wall of five courses, missing upper courses having been destroyed during construction of 5D-11-1st. Its original height was probably at the same elevation as the top of the fourth stair riser, but every trace of a surface between the two was destroyed when 1st was built. Two masonry blocks shown in Fig. 11 lying just W of U. 4 would exactly fit the missing part of the wall. Some 0.80 m E of this finished wall is a rough retaining wall, U. 3, which rises to the level of the "unplastered floor," U. 2. This retained core material prior to completion of the finished W wall and fourth stair riser. Both it and U. 4 were built upon the remains of Plat. 5D-5:U. 27. Turning up to the second course of masonry of U. 4 is an exterior plaster floor, U. 1. How far W it once extended is not known, as it was cut through for the grave of Bu. 77. It could have been paving on a lower terrace of 2nd (see Fig. 15).

Summing up, at least four or five construction stages may be recognized for 2nd: five and four for the first two steps, with core material behind, and part of U. 3; CS. 3 for the third step and the rest of U. 3; and CS. 2 for the rear wall (U. 4) and the structure summit. The final stage (CS. 1) would have been the finished plaster on the steps and plaza in front, as well as U. 1 behind.

Structure 5D-11-1st

The first operation in this replacement of 2nd was removal of the summit of 2nd (Fig. 11:U. 5) and excavation of a bedrock chamber for Bu. 77 W of 2nd:U. 4. Following that interment, the chamber was roofed with logs, above which was placed a combination of masonry blocks with stones of irregular size and shape. Mixed in were copious amounts of chert and obsidian debitage. This deposit rose to the level of old U. 4 of 2nd. Above was piled core material for the eastern part of 1st, held in place by concurrently built U. 7, a rough construction wall (Fig. 45b). This was positioned above the W edge of the burial. Core material consisted mostly of a mixture of irregular stones, shaped masonry blocks (originally part of 2nd?), and refuse. The exception was a large pocket (U. 8) of loose earth and rubble where the W wall of 2nd had been torn out.

Excavation did not explore W of U. 7, although a bit of the W face of the structure was exposed (as Op. 41E). All that remained of this back face (U. 9) was rough masonry, without finished facing (Fig. 44d). The base of this rested upon the surface of bedrock, which probably remained exposed to the W. Configuration of the surviving masonry suggests the back of a substructure rising in a series of five levels. These evidently ran the length of the structure (Fig. 12, 14), rather than as terraces around the ends (see below).

Incorporated into the front (E face) of 1st were the first three steps of 2nd and two courses of masonry for a fourth riser. Above this, the front of the old structure was torn out and a new series of three terrace faces built (U. 10–12) running the length of the front. These terrace levels correspond to the top three on the W face (U. 9). The absence of corresponding terraces on the ends is a surprise, given the square footprint of the structure; one would expect them to be present, creating a stepped pyramid. Indeed, Harrison drew a reconstruction of 5D-11-1st that made this assumption (Fig. 14). Yet his plan of surface features (Fig. 12) refutes this, most clearly in the case of U. 12. This upper terrace wall is shown unequivocally to run all the way to the N end of the structure. Though less clear, U. 10 appears to have done so as well. A feature of this wall seems to have been a central outset. Least obvious is U. 11, where extensive disturbance has obscured things. Much of this wall is no longer discernable, with the exception of two separated portions. Now displaced, Fig. 12 shows how these would have been positioned when built.

How the top of the structure was accessed is somewhat confusing; in Fig. 11, the three front steps seem to end at a terrace face 1.10 m in height. To ascend this and the two subsequent levels would have required a scramble. The problem is that the section runs just N of an inset stairway that now lies mostly in ruins (Fig. 12:U. 13). Nevertheless, enough remains to attest to its one-time presence. Unit 6 is the remains of the first inset step, but the section makes it appear as if U. 6 is the base of the terrace wall, which actually was a few centimeters N of the stair. Another of the inset steps is represented by a line of blocks (U. 14) that looks like the remains of a stair riser, not shown in Fig. 10. Perpendicular to its N end is an arrangement of blocks (U. 15) that suggest an end wall of a stairway. Otherwise, the current jumble seems to be the result of an uprooted tree fall.

In addition to identification of the E and W faces of 5D-11-1st, excavation located the NE corner and portions of the N wall base (Fig. 12). Running N from the corner and abutting the structure is a plaza-facing wall, Plat. 5D-5:U. 29 (see discussion of Plat. 5D-5-1st). Evidently, the E wall of the structure incorporated the third stair riser, with its tread continuing beyond the stairs as a surface for a terrace, which extended to the N end. Excavator's notes indicate a similar situation at the SE corner. Set back from the front, U. 10 masonry faced a higher terrace level (Fig. 12). Behind U. 10, U. 11, 12, and 9 ran the full length as did U. 10. Badly eroded masonry of these walls seems to have consisted originally of well-cut blocks, set mostly as stretchers.

To sum up, at least five, if not six, stages of construction seem likely. First (CS.6) was preparation of the site, followed by the burial (CS. 5). Next came construction of U. 7 and the new E face (CS. 4), followed by that (CS. 3) of U. 9 with its fill. Finished facing seems to have been planned as a separate stage (CS. 2), if Coe (TR. 14:865) is correct in his contention that the structure was never completed. Alternatively, as Culbert (1973:74) suggested, CS. 2 was completed, but the finished masonry was later stripped.

No finished floor was found atop 1st, but this is scarcely surprising. In the absence of a masonry building to afford protection, summit floors are especially vulnerable to structural collapse and destruction by tree growth. From the thinness of debris, it is clear that no such building stood here, although one of perishable materials is a distinct possibility (cf. Str. 5D-73; TR. 14:638–639). For this, we postulate a CS. 1.

SPECIAL DEPOSITS

Burial 77

LOCATION

Structure 5D-11, just W of 5D-11-2nd, beneath fill of 11-1st, on its front-rear axis (Fig. 11, 45b). Perhaps it was on the axis of 2nd, but this is pure speculation. Op. 41F/4. See Fig. 34a for plan; Fig. 45c–46c for photos.

GRAVE

The grave consisted of a roughly rectangular chamber dug down 1.20 m into bedrock (Fig. 11) and roofed with wooden beams. These were overlain by a mixture of stone blocks (Fig. 45c) with a large deposit of debitage from the production of chert bifaces and prismatic blades of obsidian (cf. TR. 27B:fig. 69u for one example). The chamber itself remained empty until collapse of its log roof, save for the skeleton and accompanying objects. With a flat floor, the grave measured 3.20 m N-S by 1.17 to 1.60 m E-W, far larger than required to accommodate the interment with its associated objects. Total volume of the chamber was about 5.45 m³.

INDIVIDUAL AND ASSOCIATED MATERIAL

Individual: Adult, probably a female, aged perhaps around 30, laid out in a supine position, head to the N, facing up (Fig. 46c). Elbows were partially flexed, placing hands in the pubic region. Primary burial is certain.

Associated material: 6 Imix pottery vessels (Fig. 34a:1–6), a Palmar Orange Polychrome tripod plate (TR. 25A:fig. 58a) W of (Fig. 34a:2) a Zacatel Cream Polychrome tripod plate (TR. 25A:fig. 58b) from which the feet had been removed and a biconical "kill" hole drilled in its center. This was placed upside down directly N of the individual's head; (Fig. 34a:3), a Chantouri Black-on-orange cylinder (TR. 25A:fig. 57c1) was upright a short distance E of the head. South of and touching this (Fig. 33a:4) was a Zacatel Cream Polychrome bowl (TR. 25A:fig. 58c) containing (Fig. 34a:5) a Palmar Orange Polychrome cylinder (TR. 25A:fig. 57c2) with MT. 339. On its side, touching (vessel 4) on the S and a short distance from the left upper arm of the corpse was (Fig. 34a:6) a Mex Composite cylinder (TR. 25A:fig. 57c3). Between vessels 2 and 3, and overlapping the rim of the former, was a *Spondylus* shell (Fig. 34a:7), interior side up. Set within it were a rectangular jade bead (TR. 27A:fig. 121c; Fig. 34a:8) and pearl (TR. 27A:fig. 152f1). The shell was of the Pacific species, *S. calcifer* and had been perforated for suspension, its edges trimmed, and its white inner lining mostly scraped away.

Other objects with the burial included (Fig. 34a:9) a jade bead (TR. 27A:fig. 121b) in the chest area; a jade pendant with MT. 18 (TR. 27A:fig. 121f) found above the left clavicle (Fig. 34a:10); a pair of composite ear ornaments of jade (TR. 27A:fig. 121d), each with a pearl pendant (TR. 27A:fig. 152f; Fig. 34a:12); 411 jade beads (TR. 27A:fig. 121a), together with 41 *Spondylus* beads (TR. 27A:fig. 155e) by the left wrist (Fig. 33a:13), possibly part of a multistrand bracelet; beneath the skull (Fig. 34a:11, shown in inset) were 36 small jade flares (TR. 27A:fig. 121e), apparently a diadem worn by the deceased. Unspecified as to position were some deer toe bones; 2 pearl pendants; 1 unworked fragment of a fresh water bivalve and 7 jade beads. Thirty-three jaguar toe bones were probably from pelts on which the body lay; they were found in 7 groups, evidently from 2 skins, along the sides of the skeleton. Sprinkled over the head, body, and objects on or near the body was cinnabar pigment.

SKELETAL MATERIAL

Seen in situ (Fig. 46c), it is clear that a whole skeleton, properly articulated, was present, so primary burial is certain. Unfortunately, upon removal, the bones became extremely fragmented, limiting observations. Cranial modification was present, indicated by a flat frontal bone with a slight dip just below the coronal suture. All teeth were present but heavily worn, with exposure of the pulp chambers of the upper incisors. The left upper lateral incisor was barrel-shaped; all others were shoveled. Upper central incisors were diagonally notched (see TR. 30).

Long bones were generally gracile, far more so than those in nearby Imix-related Bu. 116 and 196. Stature was in the realm of 1.67 m, tall for a Tikal female but typical of the ruling elite (including the two burials just mentioned). Nevertheless, the individual was likely a woman, rather than a gracile male.

DISCUSSION

Various aspects of this burial have already been discussed by Coe (TR. 14:865–866), Coggins (1975:585–590), Culbert (1973:74 and TR. 25A: fig 57), Harrison (1963), and Moholy-Nagy (TR. 27A:39, 46, 48, and 59). Of these, the lengthiest is that of Coe, who interpreted the interment as that of a gracile male, presumably the man portrayed on St. 11. He based this on Haviland's original field diagnosis as "female???" and features of the burial shared with the "regal graves" of Gp. 5D-2. Coggins, however, saw the western location of the burial relative to Plat. 5D-5 as more in keeping with a woman's interment. Moholy-Nagy (pers. comm. 2015), on the other hand, points out that carved jade, pearls, and jaguar pelts have otherwise not been found with female burials at Tikal. Subsequent reassessment of the skeletal evidence by Haviland inclines him to see it as more likely than not a female, even if gracile male cannot be entirely ruled out.

Although Coe (TR. 14:865–866) is correct that Bu. 77 does share many characteristics with burials of the ruling elite of Tikal, it is nonetheless deficient in some respects. Despite the presence of some impressive items of jade, it lacks profuse jade beads and *Spondylus* shells on and about the body (TR. 14:866). One might mention as well the skimpy ceramic inclusions, compared with opulent Bu. 116 and 196. Possibly, this reflects interment late in Tikal history, when the city was already in decline. Alternatively, it may merely reflect gender inequality, with the status of women below that of men (see Haviland 1997). In this case, the deceased may have been a royal woman whose status required an opulent interment, but not on the scale accorded a royal man. Could she have been the wife of such a man?

One other observation worth noting pertains to vessel 2 and the *Spondylus* shell (Fig. 46a,b). With respect to the latter, Coe (TR. 14:866) described it as capping the head of the body in the manner of other royal burials. To be sure, its location in the burial as found could have resulted from falling from such a position, but then, what about the two beads found inside it? They appear to have been intentionally placed there. Suggested is the use of a pendant as a container for precious objects, as seen sometimes in caches where pairs of *Spondylus* valves enclosed jade beads, among other objects (Moholy-Nagy, pers. comm. 2015). Furthermore, with the head already crowned with a fancy jade diadem, how could the *Spondylus* shell have been placed? In short, the evidence does not support Coe's interpretation of the shell capping the head.

The placement of vessel 2 behind rather than beneath the skull seems odd. In some other burials, inverted footless plates with kill holes have been found beneath the skull, as a sort of pillow (cf. Bu. 28; TR. 19:130 and Fig. 46a). Perhaps the diadem precluded such an arrangement here, with the plate being placed as close as possible.

SEQUENTIAL POSITION

Time Span 3 of Str. 5D-11, initial to 1st (see Table 2.5).

LOT GROUPS

As expected, samples of core material (Table 2.3:LG. 1, 2) are mixed, but in this case there has been virtually no infiltration of later material. Structure 5D-11-2nd is firmly dated to the era of Ik ceramic production, and 1st by the Imix pottery in Bu. 77. Lot Group 3 is subdivided; material from TS. 2 (Table 2.5) may be in LG. 3a, but most of this is rooted out of the construction core. Lot Group 3b, however, clearly includes significant occupation content, including an Eznab midden over the structure and an Imix midden off the N wall (Lot 41K/4–6). The latter may have been thrown from the plaza, but

TABLE 2.3
Structure 5D-11: Lot Groups

Lot Group	Lot	Provenience	Ceramic Evaluation
1	41A/7-11,13,14	Core material of 2nd	Ik (including late), much Manik, Cimi, Tzec
2	41A/4,5,12,15-17;41D/1,2; 41F/1,2,4	Core material of 1st	Mostly Ik (including late), much Manik, Cimi, Cauac, some Imix
3a	41A/2,3; 41B/1,2; 41C/2-5	Surface (largely core material)	Imix, Ik, Manik, Preclassic
3b	19S/1,2; 41A/1;41C/1; 41G/1,2; 41H/1;41I/1; 41J/1;41K/1-6	Surface (includes material from TS. 2)	Eznab (including midden), mostly Imix (early and late, including a midden), Manik, Preclassic

the former must have been left on the summit of 5D-11-1st.

In TR. 27A (p. 69), LG. 3b was treated as a problematical deposit (PD. 44). The thought was that it might represent some sort of ritual terminating use of Str. 5D-11-1st. The problematical deposit was later vacated, as we have no evidence that the material is anything other than trash left strewn around by those who made use of the structure—that is, an in situ scatter subsequently spread farther as 5D-11 deteriorated.

Although the Eznab midden consists almost exclusively of pottery fragments, the Imix midden includes 14 censer fragments. Although censer fragments are commonly (but not invariably) present in ordinary household trash (TR. 20B:91), they usually occur in small numbers. Looking at all artifacts (most of them fragmentary) from LG. 3b (Table 2.4), despite significant domestic content (TR. 20B:91, 112), again the large number of censer fragments stands out. Nor are bone tubes (cf. TR. 27A:fig. 213; 215s) commonly found outside of civic-ceremonial or range structure groups (TR. 27A:63). Here, then, may be clues to the use of 5D-11.

TIME SPANS

These are defined in Table 2.5 and are quite straightforward. The original structure (2nd) came into being in TS. 5 with the paving of Plat. 5D-5-2nd. This is dated to ca. 9.11.0.0.0 (see Table 2.2). After a period of use (TS. 4), the death of a prominent person, we think a woman, inspired demolition of 2nd and construction of 1st (TS. 3). This happened during the era of Imix ceramic production, long enough before the appearance of Eznab pottery for a significant accumulation of Imix sherds in trash (TS. 2). This final period of use extended some time beyond 10.2.0.0.0, when Eznab pottery came into use. Final TS. 1 covers the period from abandonment up to the mid-twentieth century.

A final issue to address here is the absence of finished masonry on the back wall of 1st. Were facing stones installed, but later removed ("robbed"), or were they never installed? In our opinion, the former is more likely, as it is hard to imagine use of an unfinished structure for perhaps as many as 140 years (see LG. 3b). The most likely time of removal would be at the end of TS. 2.

Structure 5D-15 and Cache 167

Introduction

This imposing building holds pride of place on the N edge of the West Plaza (Fig. 1). Beginning in

TABLE 2.4
Structure 5D-11-1st: Late Occupation Material

Study Category	Object
Pottery Artifacts	4 Figurines 242 Censers 1 Pellet 1 Miscellaneous modeled object 2 Miniature vessels
Flaked Chert Artifacts	4 Flake cores (3 burned) 4 Elongate bifaces 1 Thin biface 1 Prismatic blade 12 Variably retouched flakes 4 Pointed retouched flakes 66 Used flakes (10 burned) 38 Unused flakes (6 burned) 3 Nodules (1 burned)
Flaked Obsidian Artifacts	23 Prismatic blades (3 green) 1 Core preparation flake
Ground, Pecked, and Polished Stone Artifacts	1 Metate 1 Hammer stone 1 Unclassifiable artifact
Bone	1 Awl 2 Bone tubes 1 Carved fragment 1 Worked fragment 16 Unmodified, animal 9 Turtle shell

1962 and continuing in 1964, Peter Harrison carried out excavations in and around what, in its final form, was a range-type structure, or "palace" (Fig. 46d, 47a). This was the culmination of a series of precursors, which may have been "palaces," going all the way back into Preclassic times. In the following description, the basic point of reference is a trench and tunnel, dug into the axis of the structure (Fig. 16, 47b–d). Supplementary information comes from partial clearing of the rooms, clearing of the western half of the front, and trenches at the W end (Fig. 17, 24, 48a–d to 50a).

Structure 5D-15-6th

Little is known of this earliest architecture, encountered deep in the trench behind 15-1st. Evidence consists of a set of stairs, once painted red, which is assumed to descend to an early floor (U. 32) of Plat. 5D-5 (Fig. 47d). Although samples from its core are lacking, it is believed that this construction dates to Preclassic times (see Plat. 5D-5 discussion). What is known is that the Maya demolished whatever architecture there was above the tenth step up, and that Preclassic sherds (Cauac and Cimi included) are common within the cores of later nearby construction. Presumably these derive from the core and/or use of 6th recycled in later architecture.

No data are available concerning the overall form of this structure. It is considered an architectural development of 5D-15 solely because of the sequential stairways at this locus culminating in those of 3rd, 2nd, and 1st. In the last analysis, however,

TABLE 2.5
Structure 5D-11: Time Spans

Time Span	Architectural Development	Construction Stage	Unit	Special Deposit Burial	Lot Group	Other Data
1						Abandonment after 10.2.0.0.0 (Eznab ceramics in vogue), collapse of structure and regrowth of forest
2					3a(part) 3b(most)	Accumulation of Imix midden, ends with Eznab sherds left on summit and probable removal of rear wall veneer
3	1st	1				Construction of pole-and-thatch building (hypothetical)
		2	13			Finished facing installed
		3	9-11, 12?		2,3a(most)	Final fill operations
		4	7,8			First fill operations
		5		77		Interment and closing of grave
		6	5			Preparation of site for construction, partial demolition of 2nd; Imix ceramics in vogue
4						Use
5	2nd	1	1			Exterior plastering completed
		2	4,6			Rear wall and fill completed
		3	2,3		1	Third step and top of U. 3 constructed
		4	3			Second step constructed, with part of U. 3
		5				First step constructed, with base of U. 3; Ik ceramics, ca. 9.11.0.0.0

this stairway might be considered to belong in the structure "sub" series, unrelated to later 5D-15.

Structure 5D-15-5th

This structure is known only from a stairway that replaced that of 6th, and, like its predecessor, it too was painted red. About half of its upper step, and any architecture that stood above, was removed by the Maya, at the same elevation as that of 6th (Fig. 16). The stairs were built on Plat. 5D-5:U. 35, a second refurbishing of the floor that served 6th. Unit 35 may have continued in use in front of 5th, but eventually a new plaza floor (U. 33) was laid, turning up to the first riser of 5th about halfway up its face. Later, a second plaza floor (U. 39) turned up to this same step, a mere 0.20 m below its tread.

In the case of this stair, a sample of core material from behind them exists, unsealed though it is (Table 2.6:LG. 1). Sherds within it are evaluated as Manik and Preclassic, including Cauac. Since the plaza floors that turn up to 5th are thought to be Preclassic (see their discussion), it is suspected that the Manik sherds are intrusive; the sample was, after all, unsealed. It cannot be stated categorically, however, that the structure does not date from Early Classic times.

Structure 5D-15-4th

If evidence of the two preceding structures is limited, that for 4th is nearly nonexistent. Circumstantial evidence, however, seems to call for its existence. The evidence consists of Ca. 167, and an Early Classic plaza floor (Plat. 5D-5:U. 37) that sealed it. As proposed in discussion of the offering, it is believed to be placed on the axis in front of a building contemporary with plaza U. 38, which underlies U. 37. Units 37 and 38 run N beneath Str. 5D-15-3rd (Fig. 16), but where they ended is not known. They clearly did not run as far N as the stairway of 5th. Therefore, somewhere in the unexcavated core of 3rd, there should be traces of currently unseen 4th. Manik sherds, so abundant in later core material, should be recycled material associated with 4th, which is dated to the Early Classic period by Ca. 167. What is likely undisturbed core material of 4th, S of the stairs of 5th (Table 2.6:LG. 2), contains nothing later than early Manik sherds.

Structure 5D-15-3rd

Sometime after the appearance of Imix ceramics, which are present in its core, this structure replaced its predecessor. As seen in the axial trench and tunnel (Fig. 16), the first operation in its construction was preparation of the surface on which it was to stand. This called for demolition of much of postulated 15-4th, completion of which is marked by U. 4, a packed layer of lime. This pause-line capped the remaining core of 4th. North of this, another pauseline (U. 3) capped the older core of 5th.

As material for a lower terrace of the substructure of 3rd was loaded in, rough construction walls were built up, marking successive stages of construction. Two of these, U. 1 and 2, were seen in the Op. 42D excavations (Fig. 47c). The final stage in construction was installation of veneer masonry for the rear wall, concurrent with which was dumping of a mixture of earth, trash, and stones between it and U. 2. Masonry for the rear wall consists of well-cut rectangular blocks, set as a combination of headers and stretchers (see Fig. 18, 19a, 47b, and 47c). The same is true of the W end wall, U. 18, seen in the Op. 42C trench (Fig. 19b, 20, and 48b).

The lower terrace level in back is reconstructed as rising about 3 m above a floor, U. 6, the second of two that was laid to turn up to the wall at its base. A second terrace level, about 2.70 m high, topped the lower level. Its veneer is long gone, but enough of its core remained to prevent collapse of the rear of the building platform, and the building wall above. On the W end, a remnant of the top of the lower level (U. 20) was seen running up to the wall (U. 19) of the upper terrace level (Fig. 48b). Unlike U. 20, the masonry of U. 19 is not as smoothly finished and is installed as stretchers without headers. This, and the fact that it extends below U. 20, suggests that it may have been part of 4th, reused as part of 3rd. Alternatively, it may reflect construction by a different crew. Another possibility, not incompatible with the second, is that a construction wall comparable to U. 1 or 2 was simply continued upward, with reliance on plaster alone to "dress" the surface. Only more digging could provide an answer.

The plaza surface in front of 5D-15 was that of Plat. 5D-5-1st. Although this pavement predates 15-3rd, a skim coat (Plat. 5D-5:U. 31) was run out from the base of the stairway (to which it turns up) to merge with the existing plaza floor (U. 30). Its elevation is well below that of the floor (U. 6) behind the structure, necessitating another terrace level in front. Designated U. 21, this terrace served as a large platform surrounding 5D-15 (Fig. 17, 48c,d, and 49a). Its front wall runs W from the stairs, takes a jog to the N, then resumes its westward course. After a second jog, it appears to join the front of Str. 5D-13, but this was not verified by excavation. East of the stairs, the wall also jogs to the N, but at a greater distance than on the W. Thus, the front was by no means symmetrical. Turning E again, the wall appears to run in front of (unexcavated) Str. 5D-17.

The summit of U. 21 is at the same elevation as U. 6 in back of 5D-15 (Fig. 16), the base of the U. 18 wall (Fig. 20, 48b), and U. 7 (discussed below). Unit 6 appears to be a refurbishing of the original pavement (U. 22) over which U. 6 was laid (see discussion of Str. 5D-144).

As for the stairway, this ascends in a series of eight steps (Fig. 48a) to a landing 2 m deep, before climbing farther. The floor of the landing (U. 7) is 2.50 m above the plaza floor, but allowing for its slight slope, a projection N of its surface is within a few centimeters of U. 22 behind 15-3rd.

A second series of steps continues upwards. Reconstructed as fourteen in number, only the lower six and the tenth survive (Fig. 16). Their projection upward reaches the floor (U. 8) of a second landing, 4.37 m above the lower one. Here, the plaster surface runs at least 1.40 m back, at which point traces of 3rd disappear. Evidently, the Maya tore out an upper set of stairs when they later replaced 5D-15-3rd with 2nd. Using measurements of the lower set of stairs, however, a projection upward of five steps neatly meets the elevation of U. 14, a floor with a smooth plaster surface that runs beneath a building platform. When this platform was built, the plaster on its S face turned out onto U. 14. It appears, then, that the substructure was given a paved summit, on which the building platform was constructed.

The building platform itself was of two levels, lowest in front and highest in back. The front wall of the building was positioned 10 cm back from the front of the building platform. This wall was pierced by nine doorways, giving access to a gallery that ran the length of the building (Fig. 24). Almost nothing is known of the upper zone of the building, save for a bit of its W end (Fig. 25), and that the facade above the doorways was elaborately decorated. This is revealed by several shaped stucco fragments, recovered from debris in front of the building, and illustrated in Fig. 26.

On the front of the rear (highest) level of the building platform stands an interior spine wall, set back in this case 4 cm, separating a rear gallery from the one in front. Three doorways through this gave access to the back room, with the one in the center skewed 6 cm from perfect alignment with the center doorway of the front wall. The other two are 0.26 m from the E wall and 0.30 m from the W wall. Again, these are imperfectly aligned with the end doorways in the front wall (Fig. 17). The chambers were vaulted, as shown in Fig. 16, 22a,b, 23a,b, 49c,d, and 50a.

A probe into the W jamb of the center doorway of the spine wall revealed that, unlike the substructure summit, the building platform was not given a finished paving prior to construction above. Instead, a mixture of mortar and pebbles was laid down, on which the walls were built. When construction was complete, this layer was given a smooth plaster surface that turns up and is continuous with the wall plaster.

Opposite one another in the jambs of the central doorway in the spine wall, midway between the front and back galleries, were holes for cord holders. Excavator's notes make no mention of ceramic inserts or pegs. Each hole was 0.40 m above the floor, 0.40 to 0.50 m deep with a 0.20 m diameter at their openings. Two similar holes, again 0.40 m above the floor, were seen opposite each other in the back and spine walls just W of the central doorway (see Fig. 17 for position). Evidently, not just the central doorway, but the western half of the back gallery could be curtained off. Elsewhere, similar holes were seen 0.74 m above the floor of the back gallery, 3.85 m W of the E doorway (see Fig. 23a).

Structure 5D-15-2nd

For this revision of 5D-15, much of 3rd continued to serve. This includes the substructure with part of the front stairway, as well as the building above. What was new was a lower stairway, built on the floor of Plat. 5D-5-1st, 3.20 m S of the comparable stairs of 3rd. Although the first six steps are well preserved, the situation above this becomes murky. Here, a combination of disturbance caused by construction of a new stairway for 1st, and post-abandonment destruction from natural causes, make it difficult to visualize the rest of 2nd. Suspected is that the lower steps rose to the level of U. 9 (Fig. 16), a remnant of a floor that appears to have deepened the lower landing of 3rd. A peculiar feature of this surface is that it is 2 cm below that of the old U. 7.

From this landing on up, the stairway of 3rd continued in use, but at the upper landing, the old surface, U. 8, was replaced by a new one, U. 11. This, too, is peculiar, in that the paving, rather than being flat, rises from 4 cm above the former U. 8 on the S to 0.20 m where it meets the masonry for another set of stairs (later demolished) leading to the summit.

Eventually, minor alterations were made to 2nd, defining 2nd-A as opposed to original 2nd-B. This consisted of a new pavement for the lower stair landing, of which a substantial portion, U. 10, remains. This probably ran all the way to the top of U. 12, which has the look of masonry for a stair riser. Destruction below and in front, however, prevents certainty about revised steps below.

Structure 5D-15-1st-B

In its final form, 5D-15 retained the old building and substructure of 3rd, but with a new terrace and yet another stairway in front. Almost nothing remains of the latter, so its reconstruction is based as much on logic as anything else. The configuration of its ruin suggests the presence of a deep landing, perhaps of two levels, replacing the earlier ones (U. 7, 9, 10, and 12) of 2nd and 3rd (Fig. 16). At the summit, new paving (U. 13) replaced that of 2nd and 3rd (U. 14) in front of the building platform, to which it turned up. Consisting of a smooth plaster surface over a foundation of mixed plaster and pebbles, it overlay the original floor by 6 cm.

Structure 5D-15-1st-A

After an initial period of use, 5D-15-1st underwent some minor alterations, which define 1st-A. In the back gallery, a thin partition (U. 15) created a separate, small room in the E end (see Fig. 17, 50a). Built of rough, unfinished masonry, the wall abuts the rear and spine walls. Access to the new room was through the E doorway in the spine wall. The height of U. 15 came to within 0.12 m below the vault spring stones, but loose mortar on top suggests it may have stood higher.

Excavator's notes refer to a hole "punched through" the partition 0.25 m above the floor, 0.53 m wide and 0.25 m high. West of the wall, silt eventually accumulated to a depth of 0.40 m, covering much of the hole. On the E side (in the new room), just below the hole, a mere 0.15 m accumulated.

Also in the rear gallery, the floor near the partition was deliberately roughened, as if in preparation for a new coat of plaster, though a new surface was never applied. This suggests that this construction was a late event, never completed.

Three other additions were masonry steps, one (U. 16) in front of the outside center doorway and the other two (U. 17 and 23) in front of the outside E and W doorways. Each consisted of unplastered masonry, set on the surface of U. 13, against the face of the building platform. Unit 16 was the same width as the doorway behind, whereas U. 17 was wider than the doorway behind. Although together these additions define 1st-A, we do not know if all construction happened at the same time.

SPECIAL DEPOSITS

CACHE 167

LOCATION

Beneath the floor of Plat. 5D-5-3rd, 1.44 m W of the axis of later Str. 5D-15-3rd, about 0.73 m S of the stairs of 2nd was found the top of a roughly circular pit with a diameter of 0.70 m, Op. 42F/19. For location, plan, and section, see Fig. 17, 34b, and 50c.

CONTENT AND ARRANGEMENT

The cache included a Balanza Black: Cache-Cylinder Variety, Cylindrical cache vessel, straight-side variety; and a Quintal Unslipped Cylindrical cache vessel cover (TR. 25A:fig. 102e). The exterior base of the vessel is worn, and the cover is heavily weathered. Also included are 3 Class 4 chert eccentrics (2 Type EF-11, 1 Type EF-12; TR. 27A:fig. 8i); 7 Class 2 obsidian eccentrics (1 Type EO-5 illustrated in TR. 27A:fig. 26b); ca. 150 jade mosaic elements and 29 fragments; shell mosaic elements; *Spondylus* chips and fragments; a tiny marine worm fragment; and 2 snake vertebrae.

The jar stood upright, its base 0.35 m above the floor of the pit, beside a large masonry block (Fig. 50c) between it and the deepest part of the pit. Immediately beneath the jar in loose earth were the jade and *Spondylus* pieces. The excavator did not specify the position of other objects.

DISCUSSION

The pit in which the cache was placed was dug through three early plaza floors (U. 33, 38, and 39) to a depth of 1.28 m. About 0.70 m down, the diggers encountered a wall (U. 36), so to compensate, they undercut 0.50 m to the S, cut through part of the wall, and in a very much smaller pit, went down another 0.30 m. Why they did so is a mystery, as the cache was placed above this lower pit.

Once the cache was placed, the pit was filled with stones and loose earth, and capped by a packed layer of lime and small stones level with the cut-through surface of Plat. 5D-5:U. 38. The deposit was further sealed by the laying of a newer floor (U. 37) 0.18 m above.

The cache itself is assigned to the Muul Offertory Complex, which dates it somewhere in the range of about 8.15.0.0.0 (AD 337) and 9.6.0.0.0 (AD 554; TR. 27A:22, 24). This is consistent with the floor that sealed it, beneath which the single identifiable sherd was from a Manik vessel. The offering, then, clearly predates Str. 5D-15-3rd by a considerable period. It seems likely that the cache was in front and on the axis of a structure, any remains of which still lie buried beneath Str. 5D-15-3rd. Since our excavations did not explore within the core of this structure, this must remain pure supposition. It is, however, supported by the presence of two Early Classic floors that run beneath the front of 3rd, but which are not present in the tunnel in back (see Plat. 5D-5-3rd).

SEQUENTIAL POSITION

Platform 5D-5:TS. 9 (Table 2.2). The deposit clearly dates to the Early Classic period, sometime after 8.15.0.0.0.

EVIDENCE OF USE

As discussed below (Table 2.6:LG. 5a–e), trash from late use of 15-1st was relatively abundant, strewn over the front of the stairs and substructure, as well as off the W end. In addition to broken Eznab pottery, objects were of the sort usually associated with domestic structures (TR. 20B:91 and 102).

Along with this trash was a hearth, positioned 0.50 m S of the building platform, in front of the central doorway. Overall, the hearth measured 0.80 m N-S, and 0.60 m E-W. Within it (included in LG. 5c) were 3 chert flakes; a chert core; an unfinished ovate biface; and 7 pieces of a single burned mano (an eighth piece was found in trash just below the hearth). Clearly, this material derives from people living in the structure, even as it was falling into disrepair. For reasons discussed below, however, this does not mean that the original function of 5D-15 was necessarily residential.

LOT GROUPS

Sources of sherds and artifacts found in and around Str. 5D-15 are listed in Table 2.6. Generally, samples from construction cores are mixed, as they are elsewhere from West Plaza sources, but certain conclusions are possible. Despite the presence of Manik sherds, the core material from 15-5th (LG. 1) is considered to be Preclassic. Unit 3 did not completely seal the deposit; moreover, the seal itself was a product of Late Classic activity. Lot Group 2, by contrast, seems more effectively sealed, and contains no material later than what was in use at the time 4th was built. The Preclassic content likely derives from recycled 5th debris.

Lot Group 3a is effectively dated by Imix ceramics, the few Eznab sherds representing later contamination where masonry has fallen away. This is even clearer in LG. 3b, in which later occupation material could not be separated from collapse debris. In any event, LG. 3b samples were small. Notable is the presence of several fragments of a red painted stucco mask in LG. 3a. Suspected is that these came from demolition of 5D-15-4th, if not 5th or 6th.

Surface material in LG. 4 clearly includes some late occupation trash, but this is overwhelmed by core material from structure breakup. By contrast, the subgroupings of LG. 5 are overwhelmingly made up of late occupation debris. Core material is not altogether absent but is relatively insignificant. Lot Groups 5c, 5d, and 5e in particular are properly considered Terminal Classic middens. Table 2.7 lists the artifacts (other than pottery vessels) from these sources. Of note is the presence of ten of the eleven basic domestic artifacts (TR. 20B:91). The eleventh, jar necks (for pot stands), may well have

TABLE 2.6
Structure 5D-15: Lot Groups

Lot Group	Lot	Provenience	Ceramic Evaluation
1	42D/8	Core material, 5th, partially sealed by U. 3	Manik and some Preclassic, including Cauac
2	42D/11	Core material, 4th, sealed by U. 4	Early Manik, Cimi, Tzec
3a	42C/1-3;42D/1-4,6,7,9,10;42F/18	Core material, 3rd, substructure	Eznab, Imix, Ik, much Manik, Cauac, Chuen, Tzec
3b	42A/1,2; 42B/1-3; 42E/1,3; 42F/1-4	Core material, 3rd, building collapse	A few Eznab, Imix, Ik, much Manik, 1 Preclassic
4	42A/3;42C/4; 42E/2,4;42F/5,9-11;42G/3-7;42I/1,2	Surface; largely collapsed and uprooted core material from 1st, 2nd, and 3rd	Some Eznab, Imix, much Manik, Preclassic
5a	42C/5	Off W end	Mostly Eznab, some earlier
5b	42E/5,6	At base of substructure	Heavy Eznab and Imix; some Ik, heavy Manik, some Cauac and Tzec
5c	42F/6-8,12	Hearth, surface below over stairs, and terrace W of stairs	Eznab, some Ik and/or Imix, heavy Manik, a little Preclassic
5d	42G/1,2	In front of S terrace, down to floor of Plat. 5D-5-2nd	Much Eznab and Imix, much Manik, little Preclassic
5e	42H/1-3;42I/3	Surface to floor in front of building platform	Heavy Eznab, some Manik

been present, but were not separated out. Four of the six types commonly (but not invariably) found around houses (TR. 20B:91, 112) are also present. As for the remaining objects, the bone splinters and spindle whorl are certainly household items, and the other five items are not out of place in such a context. The one possible exception is the eccentric vessel.

TIME SPANS

Time spans for Str. 5D-15 are defined in Table 2.8. The earliest construction (TS. 17) seems to have been associated with the earliest floor of the West Plaza, actually part of Plat. 5D-1:Fl. 4B. Originating in the era of Cauac ceramic production, it was replaced in TS. 15 by a structure assumed to be at least somewhat like its predecessor. It, too, dates from the era of Cauac ceramic production.

After a period of use (TS. 14), Str. 5D-15-5th was replaced in TS. 13 by a new structure, this one associated with an Early Classic plaza floor and cache. The latter suggests a ceremonial function for the new 5D-15-4th. If so, it may have continued the

TABLE 2.7
Structure 5D-15: Late Occupation Material

Study Category	Object	Lot Group			
		5b	5c	5d	5e
Pottery Artifacts	Figurines		1	5	1
	Censers	2	5	1	
	Centrally perforated sherds		5		1?
	Worked sherds		2		
	Pellet			1	
	Miscellaneous modeled object		1		
	Eccentric vessel		1		
Flaked Chert Artifacts	Flake cores		1		1
	Ovate bifaces		4[a]		
	Elongate biface				1
	Irregular bifaces		1		1
	Thin bifaces	3[b]	3		1
	Variably retouched flakes	2	5		2
	Prismatic blade		1		
	Used flakes	5	22[c]		5[e]
	Unused flakes	1[f]	6	1[d]	10
	Nodule	1			
Flaked Obsidian Artifacts	Thin biface		1		
	Prismatic blades	4	8		1
	Used flakes	1	1		
Ground, Pecked, and Polished Stone Artifacts	Manos		3[g]		2
	Metates		4		3
	Celt		1		
	Spindle whorl		1		
	Rubbing stones		2		
Bone	Splinters		3		
Other	Stucco fragments		2		

[a] 2 unfinished; [b] chalcedony; [c] 4 burned; [d] fire-spalled; [e] 1 burned; [f] unifacial; [g] 1 burned

function of preceding structures, both of which had red-painted stairways.

Time Span 12, while 15-4th was in use, seems to have been of long duration. Manik ceramics were replaced by Ik and, eventually, by Imix pottery. Then, in TS. 11, came a new beginning. The old 4th was demolished to make way for new 5D-15-3rd. This is the first structure for which we have reasonably complete information, and its basic form was to endure until Tikal was abandoned. Nevertheless, it did undergo revisions from time to time, most notably TS. 9, 7, and 5. All of this was in the era of Imix pottery production.

The last modification, a relatively minor one, defines TS. 3. Thereafter, in TS. 2, people were actually living in the building. Presumably, they are the ones who moved Col. Alt. 1 to its position (Fig. 50b) on the already dilapidated stairway (see Part

TABLE 2.8
Platform 5D-15: Time Spans

Time Span	Architectural Development	Unit	Special Deposit Cache	Lot Group	Other Data
1					Abandonment and continued ruin
2				5a–e	Last period of use as a residence by users of Eznab ceramics. Beginning breakdown of architecture, placement of Col. Alt. 1
3	5D-15-1st-A	15–17, 23			Creation of a small E room in the rear gallery; construction of steps in front of the central, E, and W doorways
4					Use of 1st-B
5	5D-15-1st-B	13		4 (part)	Final stairway built; Imix ceramics in use
6					Continued use of 2nd
7	5D-15-2nd-A	10, 12			Revision of front stairway
8					Use of 2nd
9	5D-15-2nd-B	9, 6?, 11			New lower stairway, revisions to upper stairway
10					Use of 3rd
11	5D-15-3rd	1–4, 6?, 7, 8, 14, 18–22			Demolition of earlier architecture and construction of new range-type structure; Imix ceramics in vogue
12					Use of 4th; Manik, Ik, and early Imix ceramics in vogue
13	5D-15-4th		167	2	Replacement of 5th; Manik ceramics in vogue; Muul Offertory Complex
14					Use of 5th
15	5D-15-5th			1	Replacement of 6th; Cauac ceramics in vogue
16					Use of 6th
17	5D-15-6th				Earliest architecture; Cauac ceramics in vogue

III). They may also be the ones responsible for the alterations inside and in front of the building, which seem shoddy compared to what went before. We do not, however, think that 5D-15 served as a house prior to this Terminal Classic occupation. Not only are there hints that preceding structures served ceremonial purposes, but the nine doorways and long undivided galleries seem to rule out residential use. These traits are shared with non-residential "palaces" of the twin pyramid groups (TR. 18), 5D-38 facing the East Plaza from the North Acropolis (TR. 14:664 and 667), and Str. 5D-72 on the front of the Central Acropolis (TR. 15; see also Harrison 2003:190). Also on the front of the Central Acropolis is non-residential Str. 5D-120, again with nine doorways, although in this case with seven rooms behind. Unlike these other structures, though, 5D-15 faces S. The nine doorways of these buildings are generally accepted as representing the nine lords of the Maya underworld (TR. 18). Moreover, the position of all but 5D-38 on the S sides of plazas places them as symbolically in the underworld. As for 5D-38, it is situated on the W edge of the East Plaza, the direction associated with death and descent into the underworld. This leaves 5D-15 as an "odd building out," the only one of its kind not tied to death and the underworld through its position and orientation.

There is one other S-facing structure with nine doorways: 5D-50-B on the Central Acropolis. But unlike 5D-15 and the other examples just mentioned, 5D-50-B has two stories. The nine doorways are on the first story but are not symmetrically arranged. Upstairs, there are but eight doorways. Moreover, the galleries of 5D-50, like those of 5D-120, are divided into several rooms (seven downstairs, and seven upstairs). As suggested by Loten, 5D-50-B seems suitable as a residence, perhaps for either an extended family or, as Harrison suggested, a boy's premarital house (see TR. 15).

Not only does 5D-15 resemble in most respects non-residential range-type structures, but it has little in common not just with Str. 5D-50-B, but with known residential "palaces" such as 5D-46 and 57 (TR. 15; see also Harrison 2003:178 and 186–189), or 7F-29 and 32 (TR. 22). We conclude that whoever was living in 5D-15-1st-A in TS. 2 was making opportunistic use of a building already falling into disrepair and originally built for other purposes.

Structure 5D-19

If Str. 5D-15 is the "alpha structure" of the West Plaza, 5D-19 is the "omega structure" (Str. 5D-144, though smaller, is not strictly speaking on the West Plaza, hidden as it is behind 5D-15). Tucked away behind North Acropolis Str. 5D-35, its small size (Fig. 50d) so intrigued a visitor to Tikal that special funding was secured for its excavation (TR. 12:35). Accordingly, in 1962, Harrison dug into its E-W axis as Op. 47B. At the same time, he cleared the SW quarter of its surface as Op. 47A (Fig. 28, 31, 51a).

The structure one sees today (Fig. 33) was built as a single architectural development. It consists of a series of five terraces, each one set back from the one below, with an axially placed stairway in front. Presumably, each terrace represents a separate construction stage, but the trench into its front (Fig. 28, 29) did not reveal any pause-lines in its core. Instead, what was seen was a continuous mixture of masonry blocks, smaller stones, earth, and trash. In short, there were no significant pauses as the architecture was built up. Facing applied to fill was of large, well-cut rectangular blocks installed as headers in the lower terrace (Fig. 28, 31). In upper terraces, blocks appear to be installed largely as headers (Fig. 28).

The stairway core is continuous with that of the structure proper, although its S end wall abuts the front of the terrace masonry (Fig. 32a,b). This stair-wall masonry is made up of stones of differing sizes, with smaller stones filling in spaces resulting from irregularities. The stairs themselves (Fig. 30) seem shoddy, in that tread depth is highly irregular. This varies from 0.45 m for the first tread to 0.83 m for the third. Most peculiar is the 0.14 m depth of the fifth tread. No finished plaster surfaces survive anywhere on the structure, so whether a building of perishable material stood on its summit is not known.

The floor of Plat. 5D-5, on which the structure was built, runs beneath it but continued in use in front. Thus, 5D-19 postdates the floor, but its connection with other plaza floors was not explored. Its elevation of 251.17 m compares with 251.13 m in front of Str. 5D-15 for the floor of Plat. 5D-5-1st. A reasonable assumption is that both surfaces are parts of the same pavement and date Str. 5D-19 to Late Classic times. Sherds from its core are a mix of Manik, Ik, and probable Imix. Given the apparently sloppy construction of its stairs, we suspect that it was built towards the end of Late Classic times.

EVIDENCE OF USE

Absence of special deposits suggests a secular, rather than ceremonial, use. A word of caution, however—the axial trench did not penetrate the structure sufficiently to rule out their presence deeper in or beneath it. Other than that, we cannot say. Material overlying the structure and plaza consists exclusively of domestic trash (see below), but probably relates to Terminal Classic activity.

LOT GROUPS

These are presented in Table 2.9. Core material obviously was drawn from a variety of sources, not necessarily all from Gp. 5D-10. Besides LG. 1, 2a probably is largely uprooted core material, though potentially with some occupation trash as well. In addition to the two objects listed in Table 2.10, a piece of charcoal was also found.

Lot Group 2b, though undoubtedly including some spilled-out core material, likely contains a good deal of occupation refuse. Artifacts (Table 2.10) all seem utilitarian, with the exception of the censer fragment. None would be out of place in a domestic context (TR. 20B:91–113). Lot Group 2c is of special note, consisting of closely packed sherds from several pots up to 0.50 m S of the stairwall, 0.70 m W of the structure facade, and 0.35 m above the plaza floor (Fig. 51b). Here, we have a deposit left on debris from an already collapsing structure by Terminal Classic occupants of (presumably) neighboring Str. 5D-15. Lot Group 2d seems to be a similar deposit, 0.20 to 0.40 m W of the stair, again on debris from the collapsing structure.

TIME SPANS

Three time spans are defined in Table 2.11. Time Span 3 saw construction without pauses between stages, probably late in Late Classic times (Fig. 33a,b). Use of the structure (TS. 2) continued into Terminal Classic times, with people leaving deposits of broken pottery on debris from the already deteriorating structure. Those responsible were likely the same people living in similarly deteriorating Str. 5D-15-1st-A. With their departure at the start of TS. 1, deterioration of 5D-19 continued uninterrupted until 1959.

Structure 5D-144

This small structure, unknown prior to excavation of neighboring 5D-15, took the form of a three-level platform, which may have been topped

TABLE 2.9
Structure 5D-19: Lot Groups

Lot Group	Object Lots	Provenience	Ceramic Evaluation
1	47B/1-3	Structure core	Manik, Ik, probable Imix
2a	47A/1	Surface over structure	Manik, Ik, possible Imix
2b	47A/2,5,6	Debris over plaza floor S and W of structure	Manik, Ik, Imix and/or Eznab
2c	47A/3	Concentration of sherds on the plaza floor in the corner between the S stair wall and W facade wall	Eznab
2d	47A/4	Deposit of sherds at foot of stairs, 0.15 to 0.20 m above plaza floor	?

TABLE 2.10
Structure 5D-19: Late Occupation Material

Study Category	Object	Lot Group		
		2a	2b	2d
Pottery Artifacts	Censer		1	
Flaked Chert Artifacts	Rectangular/oval biface		1	
	Used flakes	1	2	
	Unmodified cores (burned)	1	1	
	Nodules (burned)		3	
	Unidentified bifacial tool (edge fragment)			1
Ground, Pecked, and Polished Stone Artifacts	Mano		1	
	Metates		2	

TABLE 2.11
Structure 5D-19: Time Spans

Time Span	Architectural Development	Lot Group	Other Data
1			Abandonment and forest regrowth
2		Most of 2b, all of 2c,d	Use of structure, late Imix and Eznab pottery in vogue. Structure collapse begins before the end of occupation
3	5D-19	1, most of 2a	Construction; Imix pottery in use

by a building of pole and thatch. Located a mere meter behind 5D-15, this structure is known only from elements seen in an extension N of the section through 15 (Fig. 16).

A single architectural development is represented, seemingly built up in three stages (four, if one allows for a perishable building on top). As CS. 4, the lower level was built on the surface of existing U. 22 of Str. 5D-15, the supporting terrace (5D-15:U. 21) for 3rd. This establishes 5D-144 as later than 15-3rd. Turning up to U. 1, the front wall of the 144 lower level, is a resurfacing of U. 22, matching 5D-15:U. 6 between the two structures. Whether this resurfacing was related to CS. 4 of 5D-144 is not known; it could have been, or perhaps more likely it occurred at the end of CS. 2.

A small remnant of floor, U. 2, represents pavement that ran from the top of U. 1 to the base of U. 3, the remains of the front wall of the second platform level. A pause-line behind this wall marks the division between CS. 4 and 3. Topping the core material of CS. 3 is another plaster surface, U. 4. This meets the base of the wall, U. 5, fronting the upper platform level, built as CS. 2. Concurrent with these three stages, a back (S) wall (U. 7) was built. Of this, only the lowest course of masonry

TABLE 2.12
Structure 5D-144: Time Spans

Time Span	Architectural Development	Construction Stage	Unit	Lot Group	Other Data
1					Abandonment and disintegration of structure
2					Use of structure
3	5D-144	1		1	Assumed construction of pole-and-thatch building
		2	4-6,7(part) 5D-15:U.6		Construction of upper platform level
		3	2,3,7(part)		Construction of second platform level
		4	1,7(part)		Construction of lower platform level; Imix ceramics in vogue

remains in place (Fig. 47c). Topping the core material of CS. 2 was another pavement, of which U. 6 is a remnant.

EVIDENCE OF USE

In the absence of associated occupation trash (see below), we can only speculate about the use of this structure. All that can be said is that, architecturally, 5D-144 resembles other three-level platforms thought to have supported houses (TR. 20B:19), which at least raises the possibility that 5D-144 might have housed custodians of Str. 5D-15.

LOT GROUPS

A single lot group (LG. 1), represented by a single lot (42D/5), is all that can be reliably assigned to this structure. Consisting of partially sealed core material, it includes considerable Manik and some Preclassic sherds, along with at least one from an Imix pot. The latter is to be expected, given the stratigraphic relationship of 144 to 15-3rd. The earlier material is probably recycled from preceding versions of 5D-15.

Conceivably, occupation trash from 144 may be included in LG. 3a of 5D-15 (specifically, 42D/3). This, however, contains few sherds or other artifacts, and seems to consist of debris from collapse of the back wall of 15.

TIME SPANS

Only three time spans pertain to this structure (Table 2.12): TS. 3 for construction, TS. 2 for use, and TS. 1 for abandonment and subsequent deterioration. Time Span 3 dates to the Late Classic period, as does most, if not all, of TS. 2. Abandonment may have preceded that of 5D-15.

III

Stone Monuments and Associated Special Deposits

Introduction

Interest in the monuments of the West Plaza began in 1959, prompted by a program to record all sculpted surfaces at Tikal by the end of that year (TR. 14:675). This led to Haviland's clearing around St. 15, followed by the fitting of fragments found nearby. With excavations of all plain monuments on the Great Plaza underway at the same time, it was inevitable that those on the nearby West Plaza would also attract attention. Thus, Coe excavated around the plain monuments grouped together W of North Acropolis Str. 5D-35 in 1960. Two years later, as structure-oriented excavations were begun on the West Plaza, Dyson investigated the NW group of monuments.

In the following section, we have followed the format of TR. 14 (pp. 675–805) as an aid to comparison.

The East Group of Monuments

The eastern group of monuments consists of three plain stelae in an orderly row, stretching about 6 m N-S, with one plain altar positioned in front (W) of the most northerly stela. For reasons discussed below, the existence of this third monolith was not known until excavations uncovered its base. No altars accompanied the other two monuments.

Stela P30 and Cache 84

Illustrations

Fig. 35a,b.

Monument

LOCATION

West Plaza, 44 m W of North Acropolis Str. 5D-35, ca. 53 m S of Str. 5D-15-1st. Southernmost of three stelae, it stood 2 m S of St. P31. Op. 19B.

DESCRIPTION

Bedded limestone with parallel sides, flat front and back with rounded top, typical of the Tikal "Intermediate Set" of stelae (TR. 14:793). Reconstructed height: 1.78 m; thickness: 0.37 m; breadth not recorded.

DISTURBANCE

None evident, save damage from natural causes.

OFFERING

Ca. 84 (see below).

EXCAVATION DATA

The monument had fallen in place, its base overlying the pit in which it once stood. The pit penetrated three floors of Plat. 5D-5 (U. 1, 2, and 3) down to the surface of Preclassic U. 4. As noted elsewhere (Part II:Plat. 5D-5), these actually were westerly expanses of Plat. 5D-1 floors. The uppermost dates to about 9.11.0.0.0, a time of production of Ik ceramics, consistent with the type of stone and shape of the monument. These facts, and the depth of the pit, suggest original placement of the stela when floor U. 1 was laid. Dating of Ca. 84 is also consistent (see below).

DISCUSSION

Given the contemporaneity of Plat. 5D-5:U. 1 and the monument type, we presume that the stela is at its original setting. Still, its movement from some other place and intrusion through the uppermost floor cannot be ruled out. In keeping with this idea is the discrepancy between its cache and those beneath the other two monuments, as well as the paucity of the cahce's contents (see discussion of Ca. 84 below). Alternatively, its regular alignment with the other two stelae seems more in keeping with a primary setting than not. Given the usual pairing of stelae with altars (TR. 14:732, 795), however, the absence of the latter seems odd. Perhaps one once was placed here but later removed (as was the case for nearby St. P21, see below).

SEQUENTIAL POSITION

Intermediate Classic, Plat. 5D-5:TS. 7 (Table 2.2), ca. 9.11.0.0.0 (AD 652).

Cache

LOCATION

On and slightly below Plat. 5D-5:U. 3, in the bottom of the pit for St. P30. Op. 19B/2.

CONTENT AND ARRANGEMENT

Two Class 3(?) chert eccentrics, types EF 2 and X (TR. 27A:fig. 5f); 4 Class 1E obsidian eccentrics, types EO 1A and B (TR. 27A:fig. 24a,b) and 2 type EO 12C (TR. 27A:fig. 24a,b). Yikel Offertory Complex. No special arrangement was noted; undoubtedly it was disturbed when the monument fell.

DISCUSSION

Content of Yikel caches is described as "sparse," but this one seems particularly so (see TR. 27A:20). Yikel caches were made through Intermediate Classic times (TR. 27A:20), so it is not out of place with this monument. There is, though, a discrepancy between this cache and those beneath neighboring St. P31 and P21, also associated with Plat. 5D-5:U. 1. These latter two offerings are of the Bool B Offertory Complex, which generally are later than Yikel ones. An explanation of these differences might be that the monument and cache are in a secondary setting, some of the cache items having been "lost" in the course of movement from the original location.

Alternatively, the style of St. P30, which matches that of the two other monuments, and the regularity of their in-line spacing, suggest all were set up at the same time.

SEQUENTIAL POSITION

Intermediate Classic, Plat. 5D-5:TS. 7 (Table 2.2), in conjunction with the setting of St. P30.

Stela P31 and Cache 95

Illustrations

Fig. 35a, 36a,b.

Monument

LOCATION

West Plaza, middle of eastern set of stelae, in line with and 2 m N of St. P30, 2 m S of St. P21. Op. 19B.

DESCRIPTION

Bedded limestone with flat surfaces, parallel sides and rounded (side to side) top and bottom. Typical of the Tikal "Intermediate Set" of stelae. Reconstructed height: 2.65 m; thickness: 0.46 m; breadth: 0.80 m.

DISTURBANCE

None evident other than from natural causes.

OFFERING

Ca. 95 (see below).

EXCAVATION DATA

As found, the monument lay in pieces, with several fragments lying on the broken surface of Plat.

5D-5:U. 1. Its base, however, was still in place in the stela pit. This pit penetrated plaza floors down to U. 4. Because the situation here duplicates (with the exception of the stela base still in situ) that of St. P30, the association of the monument with Intermediate Classic Plat. 5D-5:U. 1 is assured.

DISCUSSION

The shape of the monument and stone suggest placement sometime in Intermediate Classic times, between ca. 9.6.0.0.0 and 9.13.0.0.0. The floor of Plat. 5D-1-1st-E, of which Plat. 5D-5:U. 1 is thought to be a part, dates to about 9.11.0.0.0. Though doubtful, we cannot rule out a later date, that is to say, secondary placement of a monument older than the floor through which it was intruded.

SEQUENTIAL POSITION

Plat. 5D-5:TS. 7 (Table 2.2), no earlier than 9.11.0.0.0.

Cache

LOCATION

Beneath the base of St. P31. Below sharply rounded butt, primarily on the N side. Op. 19B/6.

CONTENT AND ARRANGEMENT

Nine Class 1 chert eccentrics, types EF-1 through 7, 2 EF 9 (TR. 27A:fig 2e); 9 Class 2 incised obsidians, types IO-1A through 9 (ibid., fig. 44b), along with most of a child's skeleton. Bool B Offertory Complex. Arrangement was not specified, and presumably was "scrambled."

DISCUSSION

Although Class EF-1 eccentrics are said in TR. 27A (p. 21) to date between 9.13.0.0.0 and 10.2.0.0.0 (AD 692–869), Moholy-Nagy (pers. comm., 2015) now says that they were in use by 9.8.0.0.0. Incised obsidians appear around 9.6.0.0.0 (AD 554) and were used until at least 10.2.0.0.0 (TR. 27A:26), with possible use a bit before and after both dates. In Bool caches, human bones are sometimes present, as here (ibid., 18). In his discussion of Ca. 94 (another Bool B offering, beneath neighboring St. P21), Coe (TR. 14:711) sees no conflict with the dating of U. 1 (i.e., part of the floor of Plat. 5D-1-1st-E).

SEQUENTIAL POSITION

Late Intermediate Classic, Plat. 5D-5:TS. 7 (Table 2.2).

Miscellaneous Stone 38 (Stela P21, Fragment 2), Altar P26, and Cache 94

Illustrations

Fig. 35a, 36c.

Monument

LOCATION

Northernmost of the eastern set of West Plaza monuments, the stela stood 2 m N of St. P31, in line with it and St. P30. The altar was 0.50 m W. Op. 19B.

DESCRIPTION

Stela: as given in TR. 14:710. The type of stone and formal attributes are those of a late Intermediate Classic stela (TR. 14:732). The altar was of similar stone, with a thickness of 0.37 m and a diameter of ca. 1.32 m.

DISTURBANCE

As described in TR. 14:711, the Maya deliberately broke off the top two-thirds of the stela (Frag. 1), which was transported to the Great Plaza and erected there (TR. 14:732, 802). The base (Frag. 2), however, was left in place.

OFFERING

Cache 94 (see below).

EXCAVATION DATA

The pit in which St. P21 stood originally, like those of the two neighboring ones, penetrated U. 1, 2, and 3 of Plat. 5D-5, with U. 4 as its floor. After the pit was dug, the cache was deposited, stony material dumped over it, and the stela then put in place. Its base sat a full 0.18 m above U. 4. To stabilize the stone, more of the stony deposit was placed around its base up to the level of U. 1. Whether this floor or a later one was laid up to it is an open question. We think it was, in spite of the accompanying

Alt. P26 resting on a level almost 0.20 m above U. 1. This suggests a floor, of which no trace remains, once was laid at this elevation. In TR. 14:711, Coe sees St. P21 originating in late Intermediate Classic times, which matches the time Plat. 5D-5:U. 1 came into being.

Just when the Maya broke off Frag. 1 for placement in Gp. 5D-2 is not known (TR. 14:711). If U. 1 was the pavement in use at the time, the top of Frag. 2 would have projected about 0.23 m above that surface. On the other hand, if the underside of Alt. P26 rested on a later surface, as is suspected (see discussion of Plat. 5D-5-1st in Part II), then at most 6 or 7 cm would have projected above that surface. Allowing for several hundred years of post-abandonment disturbance, it is believed that the late floor covered the butt. A consideration is that it would have been much easier for the Maya to break off the top of the monument before that later pavement was laid. One might posit, then, that the removal of Frag. 1 for placement elsewhere was carried out at the time of this last repaving. If so, this raises the question: why would an altar be placed in front of where a stela no longer stood?

SEQUENTIAL POSITION

Primary setting in TS. 7 of Plat. 5D-5 (Table 2.2), around 9.11.0.0.0 in Intermediate Classic times. The date of removal of the upper section is unknown. Placement of the altar occurred after 9.13.0.0.0, on the floor of Plat. 5D-5-1st (TS. 3 or 2, Table 2.2).

Cache

LOCATION

Beneath the butt (Frag. 2) of St. P21 (TR. 14:710). Op. 19B/5.

CONTENT AND ARRANGEMENT

Eight Class 1 chert eccentrics, types EF-1A, 3A1, 4A1, 5A, 6A2, 7A1, 2 EF-9A (TR. 27A:fig. 2d); 9 Class 2 incised obsidians, types IO-1B, 2A, 3A2, 4B, 5D, 6B, 7B, 8A2, 9A2 (ibid., fig. 44a); a few scraps of bone, probably human. Decidedly a Bool Offertory Assemblage (TR. 14:710), specifically Bool B. Objects were concentrated on the S side of the stela butt. No special arrangement was evident.

DISCUSSION

The absence of the expected ninth chert eccentric is a bit of a surprise. At the time of recovery of the cache, all backdirt was searched to make sure the missing item had not been lost at the time, but without result. Was the omission of the eccentric an oversight on the part of the Maya? Or was the cache moved from somewhere else, and the piece lost (or "pocketed") by the Maya? We do not know, but suspect the former.

Coe (TR. 14:711) sees this cache as contemporary with the stela and the pavement of Plat. 5D-1-1st-E (our Plat. 5D-5:U. 1). Therefore, the stela and cache likely date from this time.

SEQUENTIAL POSITION

Ca. 9.11.0.0.0, Plat. 5D-5:TS. 7 (Table 2.2).

General Discussion of East Group Monuments

As noted in their discussions, the in-line placement of the monuments at regular 2 m intervals suggests all were set as a single act. On the other hand, the absence of altars in front of two stelae, and the position of an altar higher than expected in front of a third stela, raises questions. So, too, does the paucity of chert and obsidian eccentrics in the Yikel cache with St. P30.

To speculate, and in spite of these peculiarities, we think the three stelae were set up with Plat. 5D-5:U. 1, in the era of Ik ceramic production. Altars probably accompanied them but were later removed. Later yet, one was retrieved and set before the remnant of St. P21, perhaps at the time its top was removed for placement on the Great Plaza. Precisely when this happened remains unknown (TR. 14:711).

The Northwest Group of Monuments

These three stelae and three altars, in contrast with the eastern group of monuments, show a helter-skelter distribution (see TR. 11). All appear to have been set up later than those of the Eastern Group. This includes Early Classic St. 15, which clearly had been brought here from an earlier location.

If one ignores (for the moment) the altars, it looks as if the stelae might once have formed a N-S row, spaced, more or less, at regular intervals, like their eastern counterparts. Perhaps the altars were abandoned, in the course of movement either to or from the stelae.

Stela 15 and Cache 122

Illustrations

Fig. 37a–c, 51c; TR. 33A:fig. 21a–c, fig. 92b9.

Monument

LOCATION

The northernmost of the NW group of West Plaza stelae, 20 m S of Str. 5D-13, 15 m E of Plat. 5D-5:U. 29, the West Plaza wall between Str. 5D-11 and 12. The circumstances of discovery are described in TR. 33A:36. Op. 19A.

DESCRIPTION

See TR. 33A:36.

DISTURBANCE

Reset through an Intermediate Classic floor; absence of a paired altar is consistent with resetting. No more recent disturbance noted.

OFFERING

Cache 122 (see below).

EXCAVATION DATA

Opening Op. 19A in 1959, Haviland cleared around the stela, but not until 1962 was the pit in which it stood, with Ca. 122, discovered (by Dyson). The pit penetrated a floor (Plat. 5D-5:U. 5) 0.42 m below ground surface to a depth of 0.20 m, much too shallow to afford adequate support for the standing stone (Fig. 51c). However, 44 cm S, a later floor was identified (Plat. 5D-5:U. 19), some 0.50 m above the bottom of the pit. If set up with this floor, the monument would have been well supported, without obscuring any of the carving on the front or sides (see TR. 33A:fig. 21).

DISCUSSION

Given the stela dedicatory date of 9.3.0.0.0 (AD 495), and the clear presence of sherds from Ik and probable Imix ceramics below Plat. 5D-5:U. 19, it is certain that the monument was reset here, having been moved from its original location. Just when this happened is an open question; it could have been when U. 19 was laid, or it could have been at some later date.

SEQUENTIAL POSITION

Plat. 5D-5:TS. 5 (Table 2.2), some time after the appearance of Imix ceramics, ca. 9.13.0.0.0 (AD 692), probably several years later.

Cache

LOCATION

Pit in which St. 15 was set. From the surface of Plat. 5D-5:U. 5 to its floor, the pit was lined with stones. Op. 19A/6.

CONTENT AND ARRANGEMENT

Class 3 chert eccentrics, types EF-1, 2, 7, 10 (2), 13, 15, 16, 17, X (TR. 27A:fig. 5i,j); Class 1 obsidian eccentrics EO-2, 12 (TR. 27A:fig. 19b); 2 shaped nacreous shells could have been from mosaic elements or other inlays. Three flakes may be part of the offering. The objects were on the floor of the pit, seemingly "scrambled" together.

DISCUSSION

This is assigned to the Yikel Offertory Complex, dating around the time of Manik IIIB ceramics (9.2.5.0.0–9.6.0.0.0; see TR. 22:table 1.2); its content is fully consistent with the date on St. 15. Given that the monument was removed from its original location and reset here, the original cache seems to have been as well. Perhaps this accounts for the presence of only two eccentric obsidians. In any case, this seems to refute Coe's statement (TR. 14:926) about "a total lack of evidence for placement of caches, either reused or newly assembled, with secondarily installed stelae."

SEQUENTIAL POSITION

Yikel Offertory Complex, dating to Manik IIIB times, reset with stela sometime after 9.13.0.0.0 in Plat. 5D-5:TS. 5 (Table 2.2).

Stela P32

Illustrations

Fig. 5b, 8a, 38a–c, and 51d.

Monument

LOCATION

Southernmost of the NW group of West Plaza stelae, 16 m E of Str. 5D-11, about 5 m S of St. P33. Op. 19H.

DESCRIPTION

Reconstructed as a late-set monument, it was made of bedded limestone, and its sides clearly contracted towards its base. Height is unknown; maximum breadth: 1.35 m; thickness: 0.24 m.

DISTURBANCE

As found, the stela was lying broken into three large fragments (Fig. 51d), undoubtedly from natural causes. No other disturbance was evident.

OFFERING

Unknown.

EXCAVATION DATA

Investigated in the course of excavation of the Op. 19N West Plaza test trench, the stela lay where the stratigraphy has been severely disturbed. Some 0.20 m to its N, however, a sequence of three floors were noted: U. 19, 0.14 m below current ground surface; U. 5, 0.18 m below that; and U. 6, 0.20 m below U. 5. Of these, the deepest is well preserved, U. 5 somewhat less so, with U. 19 being barely detectable. Sherd samples down to the level of U. 6 are a mixture of Preclassic, Early Classic, Intermediate Classic, and Late Classic ceramics, with Ik and/or Imix the most abundant. Our interpretation is that the uppermost floor, U. 19, is a Late Classic pavement, and the monument fragments lay on its surface. The shape and stone of the monument are consistent with this.

No sign of a stela pit was seen, but there was no excavation beneath the monument. Based on investigation of other West Plaza monuments, this is where one would expect the pit to be, probably with U. 6 as its floor. All that can be said, however, is that the monument probably stood here with U. 19 the associated pavement, but there is no proof.

DISCUSSION

As noted, the assumption is that the monument has fallen from its placement, but the possibility cannot be ruled out that the Maya left it lying here, abandoned in transport.

SEQUENTIAL POSITION

Unknown, but probably when neighboring monuments were set. Plat. 5D-5:TS. 5 (Table 2.2), after 9.13.0.0.0.

Stela P33

Illustrations

Fig. 7, 39a–c, and 52a.

Monument

LOCATION

Northwest group of West Plaza monuments, 5 m S of St. 15, about the same distance N of St. P32 and 14 m E of Plat. 5D-5:U. 29, which runs between Str. 5D-11 and 12. As found, it was lying shattered on what appears to have been a floor about 0.10 to 0.20 m below the ground surface. Op. 19N.

DESCRIPTION

Bedded limestone, reconstructed as being ca. 2.16 m tall, 0.85 m wide near the top, 0.72 m near the base, and 0.50 m thick. Sides were not parallel, expanding towards the top. Typical of the Tikal Late Monument Set (TR. 14:793), postdating 9.13.0.0.0 (AD 692).

DISTURBANCE

None detectable, other than its having fallen, but see discussion.

OFFERING

Unknown.

EXCAVATION DATA

In the Op. 19N West Plaza test trench (Fig. 7), which encompassed the monument, the only floor seen is some 0.16 m beneath the stela, but a change in the color and texture of material 0.20 m below the surface corresponds to the underside of the stone. Believed is that this change marks the one-time presence of the Late Classic floor with which the other monuments are associated. Its elevation is close to other exposures, and Imix sherds are abundant in the vicinity. Of midden quality, they are present even at the deepest level excavated. Most likely, a midden was "raided" to use as fill beneath the uppermost floor, and over the centuries, with pavement disintegration, the deposit was disturbed by tree roots.

DISCUSSION

No stela pit was found nearby, but failure to find one may be the result of insufficiently deep excavation beneath the monument. Otherwise, it may have been dragged here and never erected. But if set up, it would have served with Plat. 5D-5:U. 19.

SEQUENTIAL POSITION

Plat. 5D-5:TS. 5 (Table 2.2), sometime after 9.13.0.0.0.

Altar P27

Illustrations

Fig. 7, 40a,b, and 52b.

Monument

LOCATION

West Plaza NW group of monuments, 4.16 m W of St. P33, about midway between it and the W edge of the plaza. Op. 19N.

DESCRIPTION

Bedded limestone with a flat top and underside, but slightly bulging sides. Maximum diameter is 0.95 m, small compared to other altars of similar stone (TR. 14:table 152); thickness 0.70 m.

DISTURBANCE

No disturbance is evident, but see general discussion of NW monuments.

EXCAVATION DATA

The altar rested on a compact layer of limestone fragments 0.20 to 0.30 m below the present ground surface, the same elevation at which St. P33 lay (see its excavation data).

DISCUSSION

The compact layer of limestone on which the altar rested falls close to the elevation of Plat. 5D-5:U. 19, and is undoubtedly the badly ruined remains of the same Late Classic floor. The type of stone of this altar was not used prior to 9.6.0.0.0, but the minimally bulging sides suggest a later date (TR. 14:794). There is, then, no reason to doubt its association with the Late Classic pavement. The absence of a paired stela seems odd; no search was made for a nearby stela pit.

SEQUENTIAL POSITION

Plat. 5D-5:TS. 3 (Table 2.2), sometime after 9.15.0.0.0.

Altar P28

Illustrations

Fig. 37a, 41a–c, 52c.

LOCATION

West Plaza, NW group of monuments, 2.30 m E of St. 15. Op. 19A.

DESCRIPTION

A typical round altar of bedded limestone, with flat surfaces top and bottom and generally parallel sides. Thickness: 0.44 m; maximum diameter: 1.10 m.

DISTURBANCE

No disturbance was evident other than from natural causes. Absence of a paired stela, however, raises questions (see general discussion of NW monuments).

EXCAVATION DATA

As found (Fig. 52c), the altar was tilted with its N side up, S side down, penetrating Plat. 5D-5:U. 19. Two slab-like pieces had broken from the underside.

DISCUSSION

Although badly ruined, traces of Plat. 5D-5:U. 19 were seen beneath the altar, close enough to the same elevation as at St. P33 and Alt. P27. Although its S side was later depressed through this Late Classic floor, it surely rested upon it. Whether this was its original intended location, however, remains an enigma (see discussion of Alt. P29).

SEQUENTIAL POSITION

Stone type and presence of Imix sherds beneath Plat. 5D-5:U. 19 clearly date placement of Alt. P28 sometime after 9.15.0.0.0, in Plat. 5D-5:TS. 3 (Table 2.2).

Altar P29

Illustrations

Fig. 42a,b.

Monument

LOCATION

West Plaza, NW group of monuments, about 2.5 m E of Alt. P28. Op. 19A.

DESCRIPTION

Bedded limestone, with flat surfaces and slightly bowed sides. Thickness: 0.60 m; maximum diameter: 1.05 m.

DISTURBANCE

As found (Fig. 50b), the altar was badly disturbed by a fallen tree, with one end depressed into an old floor and a large piece broken off. Any trace of earlier disturbance is long gone. Absence of a paired stela raises questions, however, which are discussed below.

EXCAVATION DATA

The floor referred to above was badly ruined, but detectable nonetheless. Its elevation, close to that of Plat. 5D-5:U. 19 as seen around the other monuments of this group, identifies it as the same surface. Confirmation comes from the presence of an earlier floor below, close to the elevation of Plat. 5D-5:U. 5. Hence, the sequence accords at the two exposures. The position of the altar relative to the uppermost floor is consistent with a position on that floor prior to its upset by the tree fall.

DISCUSSION

As discussed in the cases of Alt. P27 and P28, stone type and sherds beneath Plat. 5D-5:U. 19 are consistent in dating placement of all three altars on that floor sometime after 9.13.0.0.0. But as noted in the cases of those other monuments, the absence of associated stelae raises questions about possible secondary placement.

SEQUENTIAL POSITION

Plat. 5D-5:TS. 3, in Late Classic times, sometime after 9.15.0.0.0.

General Discussion of Northwest Monument Group

At Tikal, it was not uncommon for both stelae and altars to be removed from their original settings, moved about, and set up in new locations (cf. TR. 14:731, 795–798). Given the norm, at least in later Classic times, of stela/altar couplings (TR. 14:732, 795), the presence on the West Plaza of altars without stelae, and stelae without altars, not to mention haphazard arrangement of the altars, raises questions: have they been removed from their original settings, and what were their intended destinations? In the case of St. 15, we know that the answer to the first question is "yes," and we know its final destination (here on the West Plaza). As for its apparent lack of associated altar, it may be that one of the three nearby either was destined for placement with it, or had been so-placed, but later removed.

As for the other stelae and altars, unknown is whether St. P32 or P33 were ever properly set up. In neither case were excavations sufficiently extensive to say that pits for their erection were present. In fact, a pit seen 0.74 m SW of St. 15 (Fig. 37a) could have been for a monument either intended or removed from it. On the other hand, the way the stelae came to rest suggests that the three were set in line, like their eastern counterparts, in this case at about 5 m intervals. It would not require much digging to confirm or refute this suggestion.

As for the altars, the presence of three and the same number of stelae, all clustered here, indicates that they were intended as pairs, even given the mismatch between the stone used for the altars and that of St. 15. Such mismatches are not unknown elsewhere at Tikal (cf. TR. 14:802). But whether stelae and altars were ever reset as pairs, were reset but (unlike St. 15) later moved, or were abandoned in efforts to place them elsewhere, we cannot say.

Column Altar 1

Illustrations

Fig. 16, 50b; TR. 33A:fig. 62b, 110a.

Monument

LOCATION

On the axis and near the base of the front stairway of Str. 5D-15-1st.

DESCRIPTION

See TR. 33A:83–84.

DISTURBANCE

None noticeable following its placement here.

OFFERING

None.

EXCAVATION DATA

As found, the altar lay horizontally with its carved surface right side up, facing a viewer in the plaza. There, it was lying on the debris of ruined stairs of 15-1st that overlay stairs of 2nd (see Fig. 16). Sherd samples from debris overlying the stairs, as well as elsewhere over the structure, included large numbers from Eznab vessels.

DISCUSSION

The tapered base of the altar and its similarity to two other such stones led Jones and Satterthwaite (TR. 33A:83–84) to propose that this was one of a set of two, if not three, ballcourt markers, this one in a secondary setting based on its findspot. The excavation data confirm this last suggestion. Although the monument bears a calendar round date apparently placing it in the Long Count at 9.15.17.10.4 (TR. 33A:84), it clearly was placed where found sometime after 10.2.0.0.0, when Eznab ceramics made their appearance.

SEQUENTIAL POSITION

Str. 5D-15:TS. 2 (Table 2.6), after 10.2.0.0.0.

IV

Chultuns

In 1963, Dennis Puleston excavated the two chultuns, 5D-2 and 3, located W of Str. 5D-2 and E of the Tozzer Causeway intersection with the West Plaza (see TR. 11 for their location). As part of his investigations of all chultuns at Tikal (TR. 12:29), his interest in these two was piqued by their presence in the Tikal epicenter, where such features were a rarity (Puleston 1965:26; 1971:327). Otherwise, they were a common feature in residential areas (ibid., 1965:26, 29; 1971:327). With other investigations of West Plaza structures under way, it seemed that light might be shed on the reason for their presence here.

Chultun 5D-2

Excavation Data

Excavated as Op. 66T, this chultun was found to consist of three chambers in a common "dumbbell" arrangement (Fig. 43a,b). A typical manhole-like orifice gave access to an antechamber (Chm. 1) with a floor only slightly higher than those of the two lateral chambers. The shaft beneath the orifice becomes slightly constricted about 0.36 m below the bedrock surface, suggesting that it may have had a shelf-like configuration to hold a stone cover. If so, one wonders how such a lid so deep in the shaft could have been accessed. In the fill of Chm. 3 is what appears to be a badly battered stone lid (Fig. 43a and 43b:4, which brings to mind a similar situation in Ch. 2G-11 (TR. 20A:45).

Chamber 1 has a round shape at floor level, with walls that flare outward widely from the shaft above. Chamber 2 was entered from the antechamber through an opening restricted on both sides and above; a high sill (Fig. 43b:1) once prevented any water flowing into Chm. 1 from entering Chm. 2, but this had been worn down by human use. The cavity itself had a dome-like shape, although its back wall was reasonably straight. The floor was relatively level.

The entrance to Chm. 3, opposite that of Chm. 2, was restricted on the sides, but not above. Nor was a sill present; any water entering Chm. 1 would easily have flowed into Chm. 3. This raises the possibility that the chultun was originally constructed as the common two-chamber type (see Appendix III), with Chm. 2 added to correct for a water problem. Chamber 3 itself was round in plan, but with relatively straight walls, and level floor.

Contents

As found, the chultun was full of a mix of earth and discarded rubbish. Color ranged from dark brown at the top to a lighter gray at the bottom. The top of the deposit was 0.20 to 0.30 m below the bedrock surface and was uniform through all three chambers. It did not, however, completely fill Chm. 2 and 3. Experience from excavating other chultuns suggests that the Maya deliberately filled this one, but as it reached the top of the entrances to the two lateral chambers, it left empty spaces in them beneath the ceilings. Over the years since, as the fill continued to settle, more of it would have slumped to the sides.

Lot Groups

Four lot groups are defined in Table 4.1, with artifacts listed in Table 4.2; ceramic sherds (largely Chuen) are discussed in TR. 25B. Although fill was clearly a single deposit (see above), objects on or near the floor have been separated (LG. 2) from those above (LG. 1). This was done on the off chance that at least some of LG. 2, such as a quantity of sherds on the floor of Chm. 1, may have been left by those who used the chultun. That said, there is no significant difference in the content of the two lot groups. Indeed, human bones were scattered in object lots both on the floor and above.

The material used to fill the chultun is typical of domestic refuse (TR. 20B:91, 112); even human bones are sometimes found in such trash (TR. 27B:63, 66). Those found here, however, could have come from one or more disturbed burials. Of note, too, is a tapir skeleton, parts of which were found in both Chm. 1 and 3. It appears that the Maya drew from a fill source originating sometime between 600 and 1 BC, when Tzec and/or Chuen ceramics were in vogue. The possible Manik sherds in LG. 1 came from high in the fill of Chm. 3, were few in number and too weathered for certain identification. If they were from Manik pots, they likely fell into the chamber as the fill slumped over the years.

Lot Group 3, from the surface around the orifice, probably consists of material eroded out of West Plaza contexts and is of little relevance here. Lot Group 4, on the other hand, is a midden containing features of both Chuen and Tzec ceramics. Unfortunately, its provenience is not known (cockroaches ate the tag on the bag).

Time Spans

The sequence here is summed up in three time spans (Table 4.3). Time Span 1 is the most recent, and absence of overlying plaza floors precludes certainty as to when the chultun was filled. It is likely that this happened when those in Gp. 5D-2 were abandoned, and for the same reason (TR. 14:669, 671)—they were in the way of formal civic-ceremonial construction at the heart of Tikal. The lack of sherds later than Chuen in the fill is consistent with Late Preclassic dating.

In view of this, TS. 3 must date earlier in Preclassic times. Given the usual presence of chultuns in domestic groups, there must have been one or more houses nearby. It may have been trash originating in them that was used to fill the chultun chambers. We think construction took place as a single operation, although in three stages, one for each chamber. This in spite of the possibility noted above, that this could have originated as a two-chambered chultun, with the third chamber added later.

Certainly, some chultuns of this "dumbbell" configuration did originate in this way, one being Ch. 6E-6-1st (TR. 20A:310), another Ch. 6C-11

TABLE 4.1
Chultun 5D-2: Lot Groups

Lot Group	Lot	Provenience	Ceramic Evaluation
1	66T/2–6, 8, 9, 11, 12	Fill	Largely Chuen and/or Tzec, possible Manik
2	66T/7, 10, 13	On floor	Chuen and/or Tzec
3	66T/1	Surface	Ik and/or Imix, Manik, much Preclassic
4	66T/14	Unknown (lost)	Chuen or Tzec

TABLE 4.2
Chultun 5D-2: Artifacts

Study Category	Object	Lot Group			
		1	2	3	4
Pottery Artifacts	Censer			1	
	Figurines	1?	1		
	Centrally perforated sherd disk		1		
	Stamp?				1
	Miscellaneous modeled object		1		
Flaked Chert Artifacts	Core		1		
	Ovate bifaces	2			
	Unmodified flakes	9	9	16	
	Nodules	2			
Flaked Obsidian Artifacts	Prismatic blade		1		
Ground, Pecked, and Polished Stone Artifacts	Manos	1		1	
	Metate	1			
	Rubbing stones	1			1
Objects of Shell and Bone	Unmodified shell (*Pomacea*)	1			
	Unworked human bone	27	c.40		
	Unworked animal bone	10*	1		
Other objects	Wood	4	4		

TABLE 4.3
Chultun 5D-2: Time Spans

Time Span	Architectural Development	Construction Stage	Lot Group	Other Data
1			1, 2 (most)	Chultun deliberately filled; Late Preclassic, Chuen or Cauac ceramics in vogue
2			Part of 2?	Inferred use
3	Ch. 5D-2	1		Construction of third Chm. 2 or 3
		2		Construction of second Chm. 2 or 3
		3		Construction of antechamber, Tzec or Chuen ceramics in vogue

(ibid., pp. 269–270). The lack of a sill in 5D-2 for Chm. 3, but the presence of one in the entrance to Chm. 2, in particular, seems similar to the case of 6C-11. On the other hand, three of the four apparently contemporary chultuns of Gp. 5D-2 (TR. 14:668–674) fit the same "dumbbell" shaped category as Ch. 5D-2, and these three seem to have been provided with all three chambers from the start.

Of the "dumbbell"-shaped chultuns listed in Appendix III, the three just mentioned in Gp. 5D-2 date from Preclassic times. So, too, does Ch. 6E-6, as may 5G-15. The latter could, however, date to the Early Classic period, as do Ch. 3G-5, 5C-5, 6C-6-2nd, and 6C-11-1st. Chultun 6E-7-1st-A and B are the only ones known to be later. Thus, this type of chultun seems to have been popular only in the early history of Tikal. Consistent, then, is a Preclassic date for Ch. 5D-2.

Chultun 5D-3

Excavation Data

We are handicapped in this case in that Puleston's field drawing cannot be found. What we know is that this is another three-chambered chultun, but his field notes do not specify the arrangement. We suspect a "dumbbell" shape, but only because all but one other chultun here and in Gp. 5D-2 took this form. A ragged opening 0.23 m in diameter penetrated the ceiling of Chm. 1 (not the antechamber). A mixture of earth and trash entered though this opening, filling it to a depth of ca. 0.80 m. The origin of this opening is not known.

Contents

The antechamber itself (Chm. 2) was left unfilled, save for about 0.20 m of brownish-gray soil on the floor. Chamber 3 was likewise left empty except for a similar 0.23 or 0.24 m accumulation on its floor. It is not known how the chultun was sealed, as it must have been, or how the contents of Chm. 1 were kept from spilling into Chm. 2.

Lot Groups

Lot Group 1 (Table 4.4) includes the few objects found in Chm. 1 (Table 4.5). Lot Group 2a and 2b are of the most interest, these on the floors of Chm. 2 and 3, respectively. Their contents (Table 4.5) consist of detritus that accumulated during use of the chultun and was left behind when it was abandoned. The sole object in LG. 2b consisted of a rich, reddish material that looked like pulverized wood. It was submitted to A. E. Parkinson for analysis, who (in 1964) reported:

The specimen is heterogeneous but analysis of several samples provided the following results: Organic matter, not more than 3.6%; moisture, 24.5%; calcium compounds, as calcium carbon-

TABLE 4.4
Chultun 5D-3: Lot Groups

Lot Group	Lot	Provenience	Ceramic Evaluation
1	72B/2-5	Deposit in Chm. 1	All Preclassic, perhaps Chuen; 1 possible Ik
2a	72B/6	0.20 m accumulation on floor of Chm. 2	Few sherds; nothing identifiable
2b	72B/7,8	0.23 or 0.24 m accumulation on floor of Chm. 3	No sherds
3	72B/1,9	Surface to bedrock	Ik and/or Imix but more Preclassic, including Tzec and Chuen

TABLE 4.5
Chultun 5D-3: Artifacts

Study Category	Object	Lot Group 1	2a	2b	3
Flaked Chert Artifacts	Ovate biface Point-retouched flake	1			1
Flaked Obsidian Artifacts	Prismatic blades		2		1
Ground, Pecked, and Polished Stone Artifacts	Carved altar fragment (MS. 70)				1
Bone	Human long-bone fragment	1			
Other	Charcoal samples Unknown object (see text)	6	5	1	

TABLE 4.6
Chultun 5D-3: Time Spans

Time Span	Architectural Development	Construction Stage	Lot Group	Other Data
1			3	Chultun sealed and abandoned; Late Preclassic, Chuen or Cauac ceramics in vogue
2			2a,b	Use
3	Ch. 5D-3	1		Construction of Chm. 1 or 3
		2		Construction of Chm. 1 or 3
		3		Construction of antechamber (Chm. 2)

ate, iron compounds and a trace of copper, 66.1%; silica, 4.9%. The brown color is probably due to the presence of iron oxides, not to organic matter, which is present in only very small amounts.

Surface material in LG. 3 is equivalent to LG. 3 of Ch. 5D-2 (Table 4.2).

Time Spans

Three time spans apply: TS. 3 for construction, TS. 2 for use, and TS. 1 for abandonment (Table 4.6). Sherds in LG. 1 were not plentiful, but all seem to be from vessels that are Preclassic, perhaps Chuen. There is one exception: a probable Ik sherd in the top 0.20 m, but this undoubtedly fell in from the surface (see LG. 3). In the absence of any evidence to the contrary, this chultun is contemporary with Ch. 5D-2, that is, built, used, and abandoned in Preclassic times. Why this one was left empty and the other was not remains a mystery.

V

Summary and Conclusions

Mindful of the fact that five structures (5D-12, 13, 16, 17, and 18), arranged around the edges of Plat. 5D-5, have not been investigated, we turn now to a reconstruction of the history of Gp. 5D-10, the West Plaza. The only basis for this consists of the previous discussions of two chultuns, four structures, various monuments, and plaza trenches (for references to artifacts from 5D-10 illustrated in TR. 27A and B, see Appendix IV).

That said, what is known about the West Plaza is summarized in the twelve time spans of Table 5.1. This begins with TS. 12, which covers the construction and use of the two chultuns, with whatever structures existed in the vicinity. What is documented (and it is very little) suggests a domestic situation, beginning in a time of Tzec pottery production, between 600 and 350 BC (TR. 25A:table 1), continuing through the era of Chuen pottery production (to 0 BC/AD). Sometime between then and AD 250, this domestic occupation came to an end in TS. 11, as the early civic-ceremonial center of Tikal expanded into the area. This marks the start of Gp. 5D-2:TS. 11 (TR. 14:821). Concurrent with this was construction of the earliest version (6th) of non-residential Str. 5D-15.

Group TS. 10 saw the use of this early architecture, with periodic refurbishing of the plaza in front of 15-6th. This came to an end with the replacement of 15-6th with 5th in TS. 9. Cauac ceramics, which had been in vogue since TS. 11, continued in use, as they did in subsequent TS. 8. This relatively long period saw two major repavings of the plaza in front of 15-5th, but no other construction is known.

Towards the end of TS. 8, Manik pottery made its appearance, ca. AD 250.

Time Span 7 witnessed yet another renewal of Str. 5D-15 with demolition of 5th and construction of 4th. This was accompanied by an extensive repaving of the plaza in front. There followed another extended period of use (Gp. TS. 6), during which local repaving of the plaza was undertaken, and Ca. 167 was installed in front of 15-4th. By the end of this time span, Ik ceramics had made their appearance.

Although Str. 5D-15-4th continued in use, major changes came to the West Plaza in Gp. TS. 5. This is when Str. 5D-2-2nd was built, causing a partial separation between the Great and West Plazas. A new floor was laid over both and, on the latter, a new structure (5D-11-2nd) was built on its W edge. On the plaza itself, three plain stelae were set up near its center, more-or-less midway between the new Str. 5D-2-2nd and 5D-11-2nd (a bit closer to the former rather than the latter). All of this was part of a massive remodeling operation in the ritual center of Tikal, prompted, it is believed, by the accession of the 25th ruler around 9.11.0.0.0 (AD 652), and before his disastrous military defeat on 9.11.4.5.14 (AD 657; see discussion in Part II of Plat. 5D-5:TS. 7).

Group TS. 4 covers another period of use, perhaps 40 years, during which construction of Str. 5D-2-1st and extension of the S terrace of the North Acropolis completed the effective separation of the West and Great Plazas (besides the alleyway between the structure and terrace, access from the latter was possible via stairs from its W end; see TR. 14:fig. 6l). Later, ca. 9.15.0.0.0 (AD 731), the West Plaza was

TABLE 5.1
Group 5D-10: Time Spans

Group Time Spans	Plat. 5D-5 (Table 2.2)	Str. 5D-11 (Table 2.5)	Str. 5D-15 (Table 2.8)	Str. 5D-19 (Table 2.11)	Str. 5D-144 (Table 2.12)	Ch. 5D-2 (Table 4.1)	Ch. 5D-3 (Table 4.6)	Date
1	1	1	1	1				-950 AD
			2	2				
			3	3?	1			
			4					
			5					
			6					
			7					
			8		2			
			9		3			
2	2		10					
3	3		11					
	4	2						
	5	3						-731? AD
4	6	4						
5	7	5						-652 AD
	8							-554 AD
	9							
6	10		12					
7	11		13					
	12							-250 AD
	13							
	14							
8	15							
			14					
9			15					
10	16		16					
11	17		17			1	1	
						2	2	-350 BC
12						3	3	-600 BC?

given what was to be its last repaving, and three new monuments were set up in its NW quarter. One of these was actually an Early Classic carved stela which, with its cache, was moved here from a location elsewhere. We suspect that it was at this time that one of the original West Plaza monuments was broken off, its top being moved for resetting on the Great Plaza. Structure 5D-11-1st, with Bu. 77, probably originated as part of this renewal, although we cannot be certain that it was not later, in Gp. TS. 3.

Another major project, replacement of long-used Str. 5D-15-4th by 3rd, is the basis for Gp. TS. 3. Taking place late in the Late Classic period (after AD 731), this was accompanied by new pavement of the plaza immediately in front of the new structure, and new pavements W of the plaza S of Str. 5D-11. The two events are equated here, although alteration off the W edge of the plaza could have been accomplished late in TS. 4 or any time in TS. 2. The large number of censer fragments in trash associated with 5D-11 is seen as reflecting its importance as a place for ritual activity.

Another lengthy interval is TS. 2, lasting until after AD 869, perhaps as late as AD 950. Two major and two minor alterations of 5D-15 were carried out during this period, and two new structures were added, 5D-19 and 144. For reasons given in its discussion, 5D-19 is thought to be a very late addition to the group, although this is far from certain. It could have been contemporary with TS. 5, or even TS. 7 of 5D-15, though we doubt any earlier. Although its dating is far from precisely known, Str. 5D-35 of the North Acropolis must have preceded 5D-19 (TR. 14:462–463). Surely, the westward extension of the S terrace of the North Acropolis must have anticipated 5D-35 construction, and this dates not far from the time the final floor of the West Plaza was laid, in Gp. TS. 4.

Construction of 5D-144 is known to be later than TS. 11 of 5D-15. The equation of TS. 3 of 5D-144 with TS. 9 of 15 seems reasonable, but it could equate with TS. 7 of 15. The structure appears to have been abandoned before 5D-15, as there is no trash postdating AD 869 in its vicinity. We suspect 5D-144 served an adjunct function to 5D-15.

Late in Gp. TS. 2, there was a change in function in Gp. 5D-10. Structures long used for non-residential purposes now became "home" to people living in 5D-15, strewing their trash over and around neighboring structures. Precisely when this change occurred has not been established, but these late occupants probably are responsible for the crude partition in the back room of 5D-15 (see its TS. 3). They are also thought to have stripped the veneer masonry off the back of 5D-11, perhaps using some of it for the wall in 5D-15. In any event, they kept living here as the structures continued to disintegrate around them. They cooked their food over the hearth in front of the central doorway of 15, and for reasons known only to them, planted the column altar in detritus overlying the 5D-15 stairway. Speculatively, this act may have to do with a relationship between 15-3rd, the South Acropolis, and Str. 5C-54 (the "Lost World" Pyramid). The South Acropolis and Str. 5D-15 happen to face each other across the Temple Reservoir (see TR. 11). If one draws a line through the center doorway of 5D-15 from the center of Str. 5D-104, the central temple of the South Acropolis, and another line from here to the center of 5C-54, one has a right angle. A line from the center of 5C-54 back to the center doorway of 5D-15 completes a nearly perfect 3-4-5 triangle. If Harrison (1999:190) is correct about the importance of integral right triangles to the planned growth of Tikal, we doubt that this is coincidental, especially given the central position of Str. 5D-104 in relation to several such triangles (ibid., p. 172). Column Altar 1 was placed directly on the axis from 5D-15 to 5D-104. Furthermore, the altar commemorates a victory over the ruler of Holmul (Martin, pers. comm., 2016) by Yik'in Chan K'awiil, the 27th ruler of Tikal, in 748 AD (Harrison 1999:157–158). It seems likely that this is the very same ruler in whose reign 5D-15-3rd was built. In other words, it is likely that the altar was deliberately selected and set on an important alignment of a building associated with the king whose victory was referenced on the monument. It was not just any old monument, convenient to pick up and move, but one carefully chosen for placement here.

Column Altar 1 was not the only one moved by these late residents of 5D-15. They also moved altars on the plaza in front. Finally, by AD 950, these people departed their crumbling abode, leaving the West Plaza to be reclaimed by the forest.

Appendix I: Test Pits North of the West Plaza: Locations and Contents

Although assigned to TR. 17 (TR. 12:appendix A), these test pits appear to have little to do with Gp. 5D-10 and, in any case, seem to provide little relevant information.

Location	Operation/Lot	Provenience	Content
	10F	Str. 5D-12 off SW corner	No data
Between Causeway Reservoir and Str.5D-18, ca. 70 m N of 5D-18	22I/1	First test strip; surface to 0.25 m	Sherds: no evaluation
			Chert artifacts: 3 cores 2 elongate bifaces 1 prismatic blade 2 variably retouched flakes 1 point-retouched flake 1 used flake
			Obsidian artifacts: 2 green prismatic blades
			human bone fragment, burned
	22I/2	0.25 to 0.60 m	Sherds: no evaluation
			Chert artifacts: 1 flake
			Obsidian artifacts: 1 thin biface (green) 2 prismatic blades
			4 human skull fragments

Location	Operation/Lot	Provenience	Content
	22I/3	0.60 to 0.90 m	Sherds: no evaluation
			1 pottery censer
			1 red-painted stone
			1 green obsidian prismatic blade
			human bone fragments
	22I/4	0.90 to 1.10 m	Sherds: no evaluation
	22I/5,10	1.10 to 1.15 m	Sherds: no evaluation
	22I/6	2nd test strip surface to 0.50 m, beside Lots 1, 2	Sherds: no evaluation
	22I/7	Below Lot 6 to 0.75 m	Sherds: no evaluation
	22I/8	Below Lot 7 to 1.10 m	Sherds: no evaluation
	22I/9	Below Lot 8 to 1.20 m	Sherds: no evaluation
	22I/10	Below Lot 9 to bedrock	Sherds: no evaluation
	22I/11	3rd test strip surface to 0.50 m	Sherds: no evaluation
	22I/12	Below Lot 11 to 0.75 m	Sherds: no evaluation
			1 pottery censer fragment
			1 reworked sherd (square)
			1 obsidian prismatic blade
			1 hammer stone
			human skull fragments (with Lot 2 parts of 5 skulls)
	22I/13	Below Lot 12 to 0.90 m	Sherds: no evaluation
			2 censer fragments
			1 chert hammer stone

APPENDIX I

Location	Operation/Lot	Provenience	Content
	22I/14	4th test strip surface to 0.25 m	Sherds: no evaluation
	22I/15	Below Lot 14 to 0.50 m	Sherds: no evaluation
	22I/16	Below Lot 15 to 0.80 m	Sherds: no evaluation
	22I/17	Below Lot 16 to bedrock	Sherds: no evaluation
	22I/18	5th test strip surface to 0.25 m	Sherds: no evaluation
	22I/19	Below Lot 18 to 0.50 m	Sherds: no evaluation 1 piece orange-painted stucco
	22I/20	Below Lot 19 to sterile soil	Sherds: no evaluation
	22I/21	6th test strip surface to 0.25 m	Sherds: no evaluation
	22I/22	Below Lot 21 to 0.45 m	Sherds: no evaluation 1 pottery figurine fragment 1 chert elongate biface
	22I/23	Below Lot 21 to sterile soil	Sherds: no evaluation
About 1.02 m N of Str. 5D-18	22Q/1,2	Surface to bedrock at 0.30 m	Sherds: Imix, possible Ik
About 88 m N of Str. 5D-15	22R/1	Surface to 0.25 m	Sherds: Manik, Ik, Imix 1 chert "chopping tool" (ovate biface?)
	22R/2	Below Lot 1 to 0.50 m	Sherds: mostly Manik, some Ik and/or Imix 1 chert "celt" (ovate biface?) 1 obsidian "projectile" (thin biface?)

Location	Operation/Lot	Provenience	Content
	22R/3	Below Lot 2 to 0.78 m (to floor remains)	Sherds: predominantly Manik, some Ik and/or Imix
			1 chert "chopping tool" (ovate biface?)
	22R/4	Below Lot 3 to 1 m (below floor)	Sherds: probably all Manik
			1 reworked sherd
	22R/5	Below Lot 4 to 1.20 m	Sherds: Manik, seems late
	22R/6,7	Below Lot 5 to bedrock	Sherds: Late Manik
About 48 m N of Str. 5D-14, in line with its long axis	22S/1	Surface to 0.20 m	Sherds: Ik and/or Imix
	22S/2	Below Lot 1 to 0.50 m	Sherds: Ik and/or Imix
			1 metate
	22S/3	Below Lot 2 to 0.75 m	Sherds: Ik and/or Imix
			1 human skull fragment
	22S/4	Below Lot 3 to 1 m	Sherds: "cylinders"
	22S/5	Below Lot 4 to 1.30 m	Sherds: "some polychrome"
			mano fragment used as a pounder
			1 stucco fragment painted red
	22S/6	Below Lot 5 to bedrock	Sherds: no evaluation
2 m E of 22/R 4D:424S, 230E	22T/1	Surface to bedrock at 0.20–0.40 m	Sherds: Ik and/or Imix
About 116 m NE of Str. 5D-18	22U/1	Surface to 0.25 m	No sherds or artifacts found
About 74 m N of Str. 5D-20 and 28 m E of Op. 22J	22V/1	Surface to 0.25 m	Sherds: Ik and/or Imix

Location	Operation/Lot	Provenience	Content
	22V/2	Below Lot 1 to 0.50 m	Sherds: Ik and/or Imix
	22V/3	Below Lot 2 to 0.75 m	Sherds: Ik and/or Imix, some Manik
	22V/4	Below Lot 3 to 0.83 m (bedrock pit)	Sherds: Cimi
			1 clam shell
About 0.60 m N of Str. 5D-20 and 40 m E of Op. 22I	22W/1	Surface collection (bedrock at 0.25 m)	Sherds: no evaluation
4D:454S, 226E, just N of terrace, N of West Plaza, on the slope down to the Causeway Reservoir. Trench 1.50 by 2 m	23G/1	Surface to ? (no information, presumably 0.25 m levels)	Sherds: a few weathered Manik, Ik, and/or Imix
	23G/2		Sherds: weathered Manik, Ik, and/or Imix
	23G/3		Sherds: Preclassic through Late Classic
			1 censer fragment: polychrome, basal flange, cloth impressed
	23G/4 (to floor)		Sherds: few, weathered, all Classic
	23G/5 (to lower floor)		Sherds: Manik
			1 miniature vessel
	23G/6		Sherds: Manik
	23G/7		Sherds: Manik
			1 chert core
			4 used obsidian prismatic blades

Location	Operation/Lot	Provenience	Content
			5 unused obsidian prismatic blades
			1 mano
			1 metate
			1 worked bone
			1 unmodified bone
	23G/8		Sherds: Cimi and earlier
			1 unmodified obsidian prismatic blade
			1 animal tooth pendant
			1 deer phalanx
			1 bird bone
	23G/9		Sherds: Preclassic including Cimi
	23G/10		Sherds: Preclassic, including Cimi
			1 carbon sample
5D:6 m S, 220 m E; N of Str. 5D-15 and E of S end of Str.5D-14	23H/1,2	Surface to 0.50 m	Sherds: few, Classic and Preclassic
			1 chert ovate biface
	23H/3	0.50 to 0.90 m	Sherds: few, Preclassic?
	23H/4	0.90 to 1.25 m	Sherds: few, weathered, Preclassic including Tzec
	23H/5	1.25 to 1.70 m	Sherds: few, weathered, Preclassic, including Tzec
			1 miniature vessel
			1 reworked chert ovate biface

APPENDIX I

Location	Operation/Lot	Provenience	Content
	23H/6	1.70 to 2.10 m	Sherds: few, Preclassic, including Tzec
			1 pottery figurine
			1 chert ovate biface
	23H/7	2.10 to 2.35 m	Sherds: few, Preclassic?
			1 unmodified chert flake
	23H/8	2.35 to 2.60 m	Sherds: few, Preclassic
			1 unmodified obsidian prismatic blade
			1 human skull fragment
	23H/9	2.60 to 2.90 m	Sherds: few, Preclassic
			1 chert ovate biface
			1 used chert flake
			2 unmodified obsidian prismatic blades
	23H/10,11	2.90 to 3.65/ 3.85 m	Sherds: few, Preclassic
			1 unmodified chert flake
			1 limestone rubbing stone
W of Str.5D-14, 4D: 495S, 190E Trench 1.5 by 2 m	23I/1	Surface to 0.25 m	Sherds: Ik and/or Imix, some Manik
			1 stemmed jade earplug fragment
	23I/2	0.25 to 0.50 m	Sherds: Ik and/or Imix, Manik
			5 chert flake cores
			1 chert "celt" (ovate biface?)
			19 unmodified chert flakes

Location	Operation/Lot	Provenience	Content
			4 used obsidian prismatic blades
			4 unmodified obsidian prismatic blades
			2 green obsidian prismatic blades
			4 unmodified animal bone fragments
	23I/3	0.50 to 0.75 m	Sherds: Middle Manik (see TR. 25B)
			worked and incised pottery sherd
			1 miniature jar
			1 miniature vessel
			1 discoid chert core
			1 cut *Oliva* shell tinkler
			30 unworked animal bone fragments
			stucco fragment
	23I/4	0.75 to 1.00 m	Sherds: Middle Manik (see TR. 25B)
			2 miniature vessels
			1 eccentric vessel
			1 chert "scraper"
			1 metate fragment
			31 animal bone fragments
	23I/5	1.00 to 1.25/1.50 m	Sherds: Middle Manik (see TR. 25B)
			5 unworked animal bones
	23I/6	1.25/1.50 m to 1.50/1.78 m (floor)	Sherds: Early Manik (see TR. 25B)
			1 miniature vessel

APPENDIX I

Location	Operation/Lot	Provenience	Content
			1 chert prismatic blade
			1 unmodified chert flake
			1 unidentified, unworked skull fragment
			5 pieces red-painted stucco
	23I/7	1.50/1.78 to 1.75/2.00 m	Sherds: Early Manik (see TR. 25B)
			1 miniature vessel
			2 chert core fragments (1 charred)
			1 chert "celt" (ovate biface?)
			5 used, 3 unmodified obsidian prismatic blades
			1 bone pin tip
			6 fragments unidentified, unworked bone
			4 stucco red-painted fragments
	23I/8	1.75/2.00 to 2.00/ 2.25 m.	Sherds: Early Manik (see TR. 25B)
			1 unperforated sherd disk
			2 unmodified chert cores
			1 unmodified thick chert flake
			1 used chalcedony flake
			4 red-painted stucco fragments
	23I/9	2.00/2.25 to 2.25/2.50 m	Sherds: Early Manik (see TR. 25B)
			7 unmodified core and nodule fragments (4 charred and fire-spalled)
			1 animal tooth
			1 animal scapula
			1 small unworked animal bone fragment
			4 red-painted stucco fragments

Location	Operation/Lot	Provenience	Content
	23I/10	2.25/2.50 to 2.60/2.85 m	Sherds: Early Manik (see TR. 25B)
			1 miniature jar
			1 oblong, unperforated worked sherd
			3 chert unmodified cores
			1 chert "celt" (ovate biface?)
			1 chert "side scraper"
			chert prismatic blades (number unspecified)
			3 used chert flakes
			8 unmodified chert flakes
			3 used obsidian prismatic blades
			12 unmodified obsidian prismatic blades
			4 modeled red-painted stucco fragments
			5 modeled plain stucco fragments
	23I/11	2.60/2.85 to 2.80/3.10 m	Sherds: scanty Late Preclassic
			5 unmodified chert cores
			1 small chert flake core
			1 chert "chopper" (ovate biface?) edge
			1 used chert flake
			3 unmodified obsidian prismatic blades
			3 plain stucco fragments
			2 modeled red-painted stucco fragments
	23I/12	2.80/3.10 to 3.00/3.35 m	Sherds: scanty Late Preclassic
			10 unmodified chert cores
			2 small chert "celt" (ovate biface?) edge pieces
			1 chert "side scraper"

Location	Operation/Lot	Provenience	Content
			1 chert "double-side scraper"
			1 unmodified chert prismatic blade
			3 unmodified chert flakes
			3 obsidian prismatic blades
			2 unmodified obsidian flakes
			3 unmodified limestone pebbles (2 charred)
			4 modeled red-painted stucco fragments
			3 plain stucco fragments
	23I/13	3.00/3.35 to 3.30/3.60 m	Sherds: scanty Late Preclassic
			1 chert core
			3 unmodified chert flakes
			1 plain stucco fragment
	23I/14	3.30/3.60 to 3.60/3.70 m	Sherds: scanty Late Preclassic
			2 unmodified chert cores
			1 chert "celt" (ovate biface?)
			2 chert elongate bifaces
			1 chert point-retouched flake
			5 unmodified chert flakes (2 charred)
			1 obsidian used blade core
			4 used obsidian prismatic blades
			1 retouched obsidian flake

Appendix II: Report by Robert H. Dyson Jr. and Peter D. Harrison on the West Plaza Resistivity Survey

During the 1961 season at Tikal, Richard Linnington of the Museum Applied Science Center for Archaeology (MASCA) at the Penn Museum in Philadelphia, made extensive tests at the site of Tikal using various geophysical methods. One of the areas chosen was the West Plaza that lies immediately W of the North Acropolis and main center of the site. This area was chosen as it was relatively flat and had produced Preclassic sherds from deep in the fill. It was hoped that buried structures dating to the Preclassic period might be located first without digging and, then, later excavated.

Drawing upon a memorandum submitted to the Tikal Project by Linnington in August of 1961 that outlined the work carried out from March 29th to May 17th, 1961, the following may be stated. Readings totaling 2,872 were made with a Geohm resistivity instrument. A strip 12 m wide by 110 m long with a projection 12 by 20 m to the W was surveyed. Two lines of survey pegs were laid out at 5 m intervals running N-S and 8 m apart E-W. North-south lines of readings were taken over the whole area. East-west readings were taken over all but the northern 30 m.

Results of this work were plotted on a map in the form of a contour diagram showing the resistance values. On the resulting diagram, it was assumed that the low resistance features were most significant. The most striking was an anomaly lying in the I50 general area of the map. This anomaly showed "clustering" of lines as if in a stepped-down structure. Although Linnington was unable to ascertain whether the measurement reflected a rise in bedrock or a hole in the ground, he nevertheless concluded that a "Large scale survey shows very interesting patterns of resistance features, with a reasonable chance of correlation with archaeological features."

During February and early March of 1962, the Tikal Project undertook to include the resistivity problem in its excavation program aimed at a general study of the West Plaza area. The approach to the problem was made in two stages: first, direct trenching across the major anomaly; second, selection of specific resistance contours over known depths of deposit in the trenches and testing these lines at other points to see whether the contours could be converted to a depth scale.

For the trenching, two trenches were laid out across the anomaly in an E-W direction running from I50.5 W 7 m to P50.5 and from A50.5 7 m W to H50.5. The trenches formed a line E and W lying between N-S lines 51 and 52, being a meter wide. These trenches were part of a wider system of study and consequently are designated Op. 19D and 19E (see Fig. 2). Trench 19E was carried to bedrock throughout its length: trench 19D was only carried to bedrock in one section, although most of the trench has at present been carried down to the heavily compacted materials for much of its length. The resulting sections, drawn along the N side of the trench, are shown in Fig. 3 and 8b.

The trenches excavated show several important features. First, there is a prominent slope in bedrock, which is a compact soft limestone, from the E to the W. It is immediately apparent by comparing the resistivity graph that there is no correlation between the resistance contours and the profile of the bedrock. We, therefore, necessarily conclude that the reading does not reflect the bedrock surface. Secondly, it is equally clear from the stratigraphy involved in these two sections, as well as in a third trench farther W (Op. 19C and L), that the West Plaza area in this location has grown from E to W through the accumulation of successive, roughly built retaining walls of limestone blocks holding a fill of dense, dark gray clayey earth and stones and pebbles (see Fig. 9, 10a,b). These fills are exceedingly compact and require heavy pickwork to disengage. The general profile of this compact mass indicates some relationship to the resistivity graph. This relationship is particularly clear in the section of Op. 19D (Fig. 8b) where the general fall in the graph from E to W follows a similar fall in the compaction surface of clayey earth and stone fill. At the time of writing, this fill had not been excavated to bedrock, but given the overall section of both trenches there is little doubt of its essential nature. An examination of the section of Op. 19E, on the other hand, shows no such clear-cut parallel. The compact materials rise slightly in the center of the section and drop slightly at either end. The drop at the E end of the graph may perhaps be accounted for in part by the presence of a pit in the bedrock that occurs in the trench, but not in the section (where it is represented dotted in). It must be noted, however, that this pit and the shallow stratum immediately overlying it are composed of a compacted dark gray, clayey soil and stones similar to that already seen in the compact surface of Op. 19D. It is, however, a separate deposit which, while appearing similar to the naked eye, may well have distinct qualities in terms of moisture, density, and so forth. In summary, then, the comparison of the section of Op. 19E and the expected contouring as represented by the resistivity contours were less satisfactory, with the crest of the resistance graph being displaced somewhat to the W of the crest of the denser materials in the section. An evaluation of this circumstance in relation to the readings and calculations of the resistance equipment is beyond our abilities at present in Tikal.

In both sections, the upper strata consist of soft gray soils with small pebbles and occasional patches of lime plaster floors. This upper zone, perhaps an average of a meter below the present surface, is normally subject to much disturbance through root action, falling trees, and other intrusions. It is distinctly less compact than the compacted masses underlying it as described above. There seems little reason, therefore, to conclude that these strata, taken individually, have much effect on the resistivity readings. The significant differences, both in the field physically, and apparently on the resistance graphs, would seem to fall between the upper, less dense zone and the lower compact material (with bedrock forming a third distinct division that in the present instance did not enter into the final result in any significantly visible way).

In order to ascertain whether the main conclusion indicated by the preceding data was valid, namely, that the resistance contours measured a significant difference in compaction at varying depths below the surface, two additional test blocks were made. These were laid out along the I line to the E and each measured 1 by 1.5 m. Operation 19Q was located from I46 to I47.50, and Op. 19R from I45 to I43.50, between lines H and I (see Fig.2 for location). Resistivity lines i-m passed through Op. 19Q and e-g through Op. 19R.

In Op. 19Q, the upper soft gray and pebbly fill rested upon a stratum of beige-colored, relatively compact crushed rocky material. The stratum is a northward extension of that seen in the section of Op. 19E (Fig. 3, right), where it appears below 250 m elevation. The upper surface of this fill is encountered in Op. 19Q at an average depth below surface of about 0.90 m. At a deeper level, averaging about 1.10 m below surface, large blocks of stone begin to appear mixed with the fill. The compaction level along the W section of the operation that marks the top of this fill is relatively even. It is crossed by five resistance contours that give the effect of a slope on the map. By looking at the section of Op. 19D, it appears that these same lines also cross the section along a relatively level compaction surface there. This compaction surface is approximately 1 m below actual surface, which measurement compares well with the similar situation in Op. 19Q. It is immediately suggested that the surface of this more compact material underlying the upper softer levels is the level being indicated by the resistivity readings. It is further suggested that given a resistivity contour map such as this one, and a major test to identify the depths of the material being measured, that such a map may then be used as a rough guide to the relative depth below actual surface of more compact deposits. There is no indication that there is any way further to differentiate the composition of these various deposits.

Operation 19R (Fig. 2), however, presents a problem. Again, the change in material from soft gray fill to the deeper beige-colored fill occurs essentially at a depth of 0.90–1.00 m. The beige fill in this instance is not so homogeneous as in 19Q, having some lenses of gray soil in it. The occurrence of stones begins at a depth of 1.10–1.30 m, or somewhat lower than 19Q. Three resistance lines cross the operation. These same lines occur in section 19D lying over a relatively level compaction surface, but at a depth of 1.60 m. Thus, the same resistance lines give a reading for a compaction surface 1.60 m deep, in the case of 19D, while only 1.30 m or less in 19R. Remembering the displacement visible in the readings of 19E, one wonders whether a similar effect is present here. Excavation has not proceeded far enough to determine this. In any case, it is apparent that 19R lies somewhat deeper than 19Q in terms of distance below surface of the more compact materials and there is therefore a greater depth value for lines e, f, and g than for lines i-m as seen in these two operations. This differential is borne out in Op. 19D, where lines e-g reflect a deeper compaction surface than do lines i-m. It seems probable, then, with adequate additional trenching, that an approximate value in depth could be established for groups of these resistance lines that would allow the contoured map to be used as a guide to deeper superficial deposits.

Appendix III: A Preliminary Classification of Tikal Chultuns

(For those interested in comparing the Chultun 5D-2 and 5D-3 with other Tikal chultuns, the following preliminary classification is provided.)

Type	Chultun	Location	Tikal volume (see TR. 12:57–61)
One chamber "bottle-shape"	2G-11	Gp. 2G-1	TR. 20
	4F-4	Gp. 4F-5	TR. 20
	5G-2	Gp. 5G-2	TR. 21
	5G-3	Gp. 5G-2	TR. 21
	5G-20	Gp. 5G-1	TR. 21
	6B-2-2nd	Gp. 6B-1	TR. 21
"Cylindrical"	3F-4	3F: S215 E266	TR. 20
	3F-5	3F: S220 E265	TR. 20
Other	4F-3	Gp. 4F-1	TR. 19
	7F-8	Gp. 7F-1	TR. 22
One or two chamber	6C-11-2nd	Gp. 6C-5	TR. 20
Two chamber "shoe-shape"	2B-15	Gp. 2B-1	TR. 20
	2G-2-1st	Str. 2G-61	TR. 20
	2G-5	Gp. 2G-1	TR. 20
	3F-6	Gp. 3F-1	TR. 20
	4F-1	Gp. 4F-2	TR. 19
	4F-2-A and B	Gp. 4F-7	TR. 20
	4G-2	4G: S286 E200	TR. 20

Type	Chultun	Location	Tikal volume (see TR. 12:57–61)
	4H-9	Gp. 4H-1	TR. 21
	4H-10	Gp. 4H-1	TR. 21
	5B-11	Gp. 5B-3	TR. 20
	5C-6	5C: S330 E90	TR. 20
	5F-5-2nd	Gp. 5F-1	TR. 20
	5G-18-2nd	Gp. 5G-1	TR. 21
	5G-19-2nd	Gp. 5G-1	TR. 21
	5G-21	Gp. 5G-2	TR. 21
	6C-7	Gp. 6C-5	TR. 20
	6C-9	Str. 6C-60	TR. 20
	6C-10	Str. 6C-60	TR. 20
	6E-6-2nd	Gp. 6E-1	TR. 20
	6F-3-5th	Str. 6F-62	TR. 20
	7C-3	Gp. 7C-1	TR. 20
	7F-9	Gp. 7F-2	TR. 20
Two or three chamber "linear"	2G-2-2nd	Str. 2G-61	TR. 20
Three chamber "linear"	2F-5-2nd	2F: S320 E440	TR. 20
	4H-5[1]	Gp. 4H-4	TR. 21
	6C-6-1st	Gp. 6C-5	TR. 20
	6F-3-1st-A, B[2]	Str. 6F-62	TR. 20
	6F-3-4th-A, B[2]	Str. 6F-62	TR. 20
"Dumbbell shape"	3G-5	Gp. 3G-1	TR. 20
	5C-5	Str. 5C-56	TR. 20
	5D-1	Gp. 5D-2	TR. 14
	5D-2	Gp. 5D-10	TR. 17
	5D-4?	Gp. 5D-2	TR. 14
	5D-5[3]	Gp. 5D-2	TR. 14
	5G-15[4]	Gp. 5G-1	TR. 21
	6C-6-2nd	Gp. 6C-5	TR. 20
	6C-11-1st	Gp. 6C-5	TR. 20
	6E-6-1st-A, B	Gp. 6E-1	TR. 20
	6E-7-1st-A, B	Gp. 6E-1	TR. 20
Three chamber unknown	5D-3	Gp. 5D-10	TR. 17
Three or four chamber "linear"	6E-7-2nd	Gp. 6E-1	TR. 20

APPENDIX III

Type	Chultun	Location	Tikal volume (see TR. 12:57–61)
Four chamber	5D-6[5]	Gp. 5D-2	TR. 14
	5F-5-1st	Gp. 5F-1	TR. 20
	5G-18-1st	Gp. 5G-1	TR. 21
	6B-2-1st	Gp. 6B-1	TR. 21
	6F-3-1st-B	Str. 6F-62	TR. 20
	6F-3-2nd[6]	Str. 6F-62	TR. 20
	6F-3-3rd	Str. 6F-62	TR. 20
Five chamber	2F-5-1st-A, B	2F:S320 E440	TR. 20
	2G-1-1st	Str. 2G-61	TR. 20
	2G-1-2nd	Str. 2G-61	TR. 20
Problematical	2G-10[7]	Gp. 2G-2	TR. 20
Nine chamber	5C-8-1st[8]	Str. 5C-56	TR. 20
Problematical	5G-19-1st[9]	Gp. 5G-1	TR. 21

Notes:

[1] Rooms stepped down: two below one, three below two

[2] Rooms curve around

[3] Rooms arranged in an arc

[4] Might be classified as one room, but pedestal beneath orifice divides chamber (reminiscent of Ch. 6E-6-1st)

[5] Three-lobed arrangement of inner chambers off antechamber

[6] Chm. 2 and 3 functioned as a single chamber

[7] Five chambers may not have functioned together; may have originated as one- or two-chambered chultuns

[8] Possibly six chambers original (2nd), three added (1st)

[9] Could be one bottle-shaped chamber, or two chambers with two orifices

Appendix IV: Artifacts from General Excavations in Group 5D-10 Illustrated in Tikal Report 27A and 27B

Artifact	Lot Group	Illustration
Centrally perforated worked sherds	Ch. 5D-2:LG.2	TR. 27B:fig. 131d-d'
	Str. 5D-15:LG. 5c	TR. 27B:fig. 132f (with entoptic design)
	Str. 5D-15:LG. 5c	TR. 27B:fig. 132i
Pottery stamp	Ch. 5D-2:LG. 4	TR. 27A:fig. 219q
Chert ovate bifaces	Str. 5D-15:LG. 5c	TR. 27B:fig. 6c
	Plat. 5D-5:LG. 3	TR. 27B:fig. 8d
	Ch. 5D-2:LG. 1	TR. 27B:fig. 12c
Chert thin bifaces	Str. 5D-11:LG. 3b	TR. 27B:fig. 22m
	Plat. 5D-5:LG. 7a	TR. 27B:fig. 35o
	Plat. 5D-5:LG. 4	TR. 27B:fig. 43g
Obsidian thin biface	Str. 5D-15:LG. 5c	TR. 27B:fig. 66x
Ground stone mano	Str. 5D-15:LG. 5e	TR. 27B:fig. 79b
Ground stone celt	Str. 5D-15:LG. 5c	TR. 27B:fig. 100a
Jade ear ornament	Str. 5D-15:LG. 3a	TR. 27A:fig. 130i (erroneously labeled from "temple cache")
Perforated carved and inscribed tube	Str. 5D-11:LG. 3b	TR. 27A:fig. 213o
Inscribed bone	Plat. 5D-5:LG. 5c	TR. 27A:fig. 215f (MT. 356)
	Str. 5D-11:LG. 3b	TR. 27A:fig. 215s (mat motif)

References

Chase, Arlen F., and Diane Z. Chase
    2014   Peter D'Arcy Harrison, 1937–2013. *The SAA Archaeological Record* Nov. 2014:40.

Coggins, Clemency C.
    1975   Painting and Drawing Styles at Tikal: An Historical and Iconographic Reconstruction. Ph.D. dissertation, Harvard University. Ann Arbor: University Microfilms.

Culbert, T. Patrick
    1973   The Maya Downfall at Tikal. In *The Classic Maya Collapse,* edited by T. Patrick Culbert, pp. 63–92. Albuquerque: University of New Mexico Press.

Harrison, Peter D.
    1963   A Jade Pendant from Tikal. *Expedition* 5(2):12–13.

———.
    1999   *The Lords of Tikal: Rulers of an Ancient Maya City*. London: Thames and Hudson.

———.
    2003   The Central Acropolis of Tikal. In *Tikal: Dynasties, Foreigners, and Affairs of State*, edited by Jeremy A. Sabloff, pp. 171–206. Santa Fe, NM: School of American Research.

———.
    2012   A Marvel of Maya Engineering: Water Management at Tikal. *Expedition* 54(2):19–26.

Haviland, William A.
    1997   The Rise and Fall of Sexual Inequality: Sex and Gender at Tikal, Guatemala. *Ancient Mesoamerica* 8:1–12.

Jones, Christopher
    2003   The Tikal Renaissance and the East Plaza Ball Court. In *Tikal: Dynasties, Foreigners, and Affairs of State*, edited by Jeremy A. Sabloff, pp. 207–225. Santa Fe, NM: School of American Research.

Martin, Simon
    2003   In the Line of the Founder: A View of Dynastic Politics at Tikal. In *Tikal: Dynasties, Foreigners, and Affairs of State*, edited by Jeremy A. Sabloff, pp. 3–45. Santa Fe, NM: School of American Research.

Puleston, Dennis E.
   1965   The Chultuns of Tikal. *Expedition* 7(3):24–29.

———.
   1971   An Experimental Approach to the Function of Classic Maya Chultuns. *American Antiquity* 36:122–335.

Tikal Reports (see TR. 12):

TR. 11:
Carr, Robert F., and James E. Hazard
   1986   Map of the Ruins of Tikal, El Peten, Guatemala. In *Tikal Reports 1–11*. Facsimile Reissue of Original Reports Published 1958–1961, pp. iii–26. Philadelphia: University of Pennsylvania Museum of Archaeology and Anthropology.

TR. 12:
Coe, William R., and William A. Haviland
   1982   *Introduction to the Archaeology of Tikal, Guatemala*. Philadelphia: University of Pennsylvania Museum of Archaeology and Anthropology.

TR. 14:
Coe, William R.
   1990   *Excavations in the Great Plaza, North Terrace and North Acropolis of Tikal*, Vols. 1–4. Philadelphia: University of Pennsylvania Museum of Archaeology and Anthropology.

TR. 15:
Loten, H. Stanley, for Peter D. Harrison
   n.d.   *Excavations in the Central Acropolis of Tikal*.

TR. 18:
Becker, Marshall J., for Christopher Jones
   n.d.   *Excavations in the Twin Pyramid Groups of Tikal*.

TR. 19:
Haviland, William A., with Marshall J. Becker, Ann Chowning, Keith A. Dixon, and Karl Heider
   1985   *Excavations in Small Residential Groups of Tikal: Groups 4F-1 and 4F-2*. Philadelphia: University of Pennsylvania Museum of Archaeology and Anthropology.

TR. 20A:
Haviland, William A.
   2014   *Excavations in Residential Areas of Tikal: Non-elite Groups without Shrines: The Excavations*. Philadelphia: University of Pennsylvania Museum of Archaeology and Anthropology.

TR. 20B:
Haviland, William A.
   2014   *Excavations in Residential Areas of Tikal: Non-elite Groups without Shrines: Analysis and Conclusions*. Philadelphia: University of Pennsylvania Museum of Archaeology and Anthropology.

TR. 22:
Haviland, William A.
    2015   *Excavations in Residential Areas of Tikal: Group 7F-1*. Philadelphia: University of Pennsylvania Museum of Archaeology and Anthropology.

TR. 25A:
Culbert, T. Patrick
    1993   *The Ceramics of Tikal: Vessels from the Burials, Caches and Problematical Deposits*. Philadelphia: University of Pennsylvania Museum of Archaeology and Anthropology.

TR. 25B:
Culbert, T. Patrick, and Laura J. Kosakowsky (with content editing by Hattula Moholy-Nagy)
    n.d.   *The Ceramic Sequence of Tikal*. Philadelphia: University of Pennsylvania Museum of Archaeology and Anthropology.

TR. 27A:
Moholy-Nagy, Hattula, with William R. Coe
    2008   *The Artifacts of Tikal: Ornamental and Ceremonial Artifacts and Unworked Material. Part A*. Philadelphia: University of Pennsylvania Museum of Archaeology and Anthropology.

TR. 27B:
Moholy-Nagy, Hattula
    2003   *The Artifacts of Tikal: Utilitarian Artifacts and Unworked Material. Part B*. Philadelphia: University of Pennsylvania Museum of Archaeology and Anthropology.

TR. 30:
Monge, Janet, and William A. Haviland
    n.d.   *The Skeletal Series of Tikal*.

TR. 33A:
Jones, Christopher, and Linton Satterthwaite, Jr.
    1982   *The Monuments and Inscriptions of Tikal: The Carved Monuments*. Philadelphia: University of Pennsylvania Museum of Archaeology and Anthropology.

Illustrations

Gp. 5D-10: Plan as drafted by Peter Harrison, based on the figures that follow.

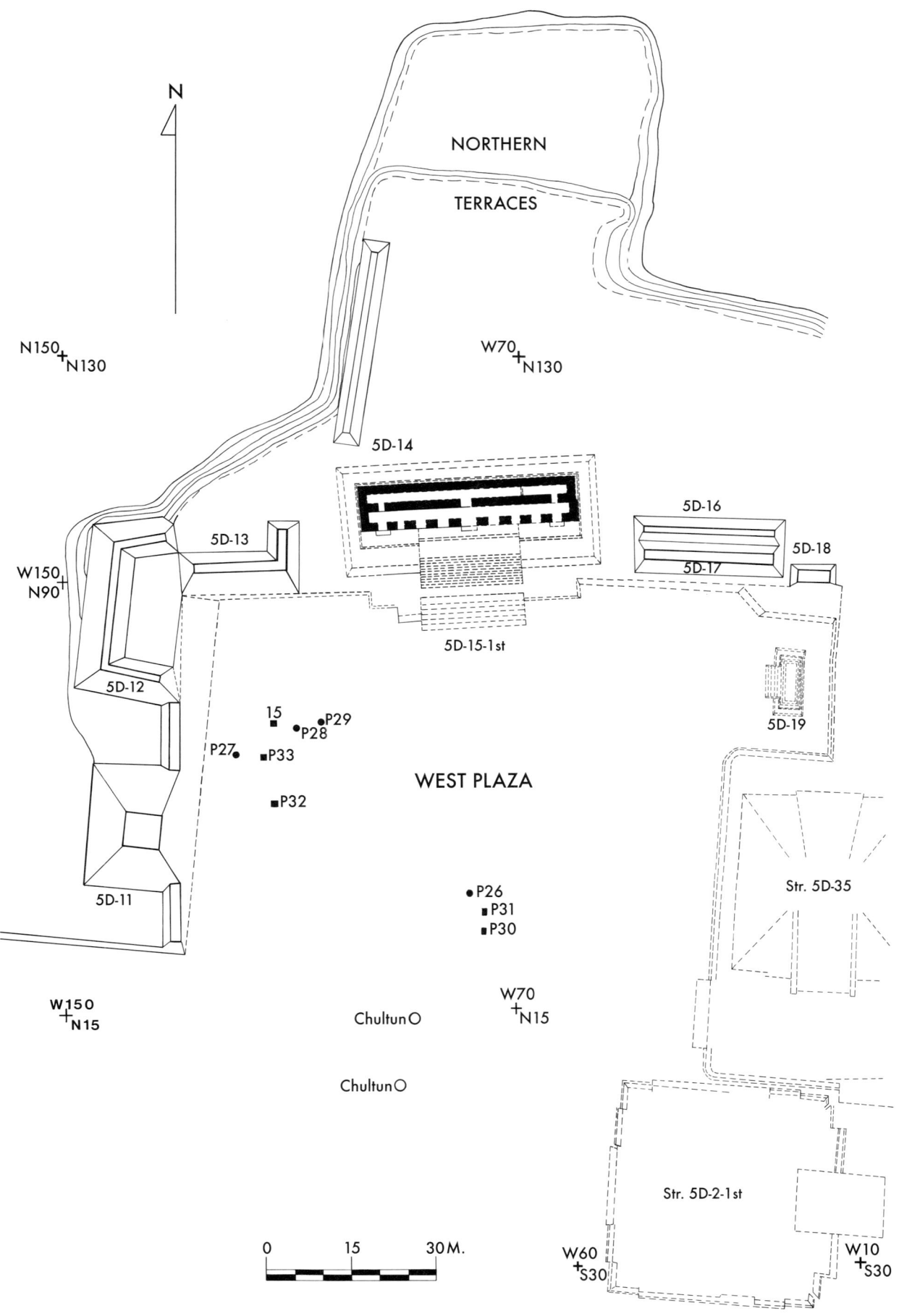

FIGURE 1

FIGURE 2

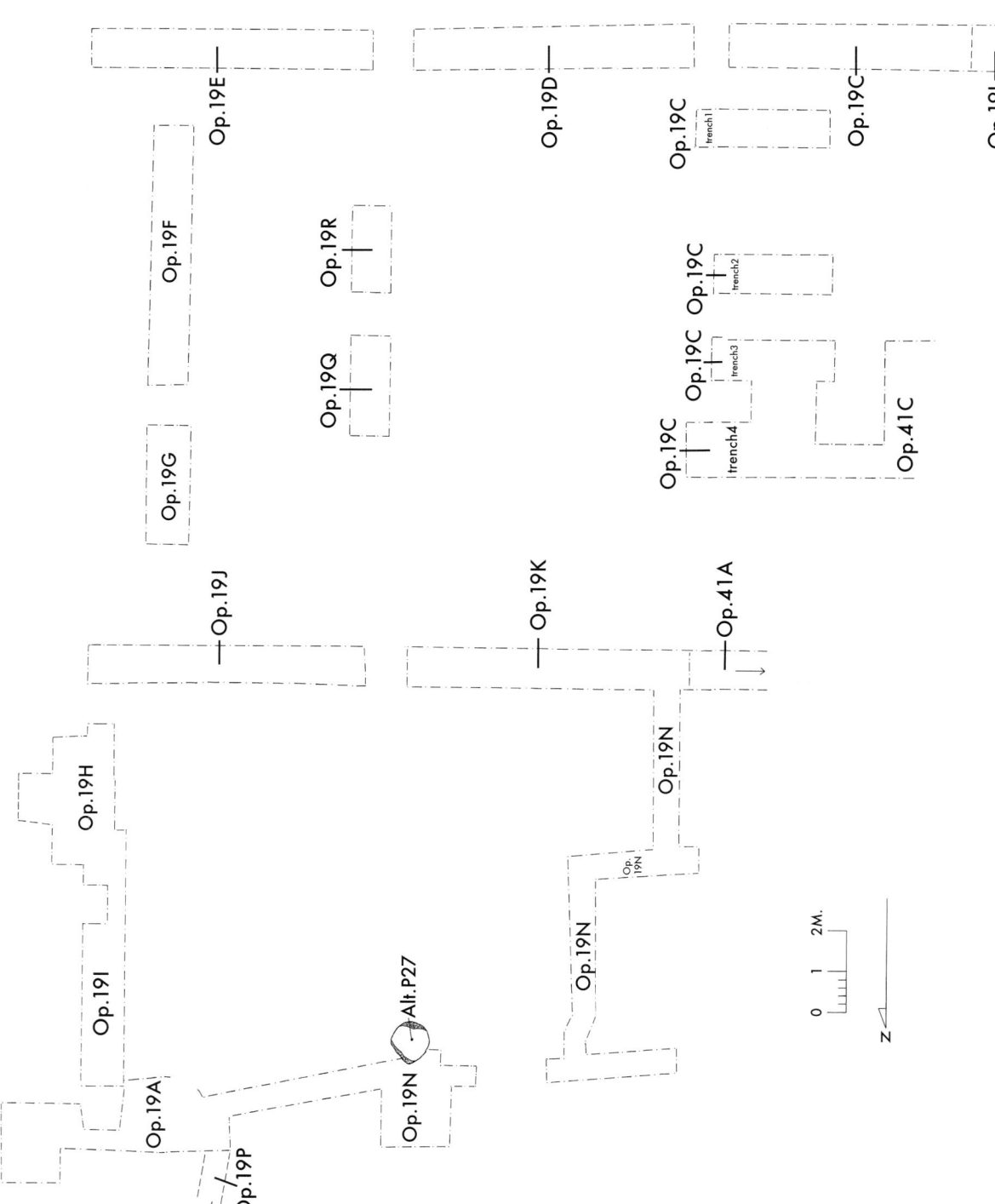

Overall plan showing test trenches in the West Plaza excavations (Plat. 5D-5), reconstructed from four partial drawings at different scales by Peter Harrison.

FIGURE 3

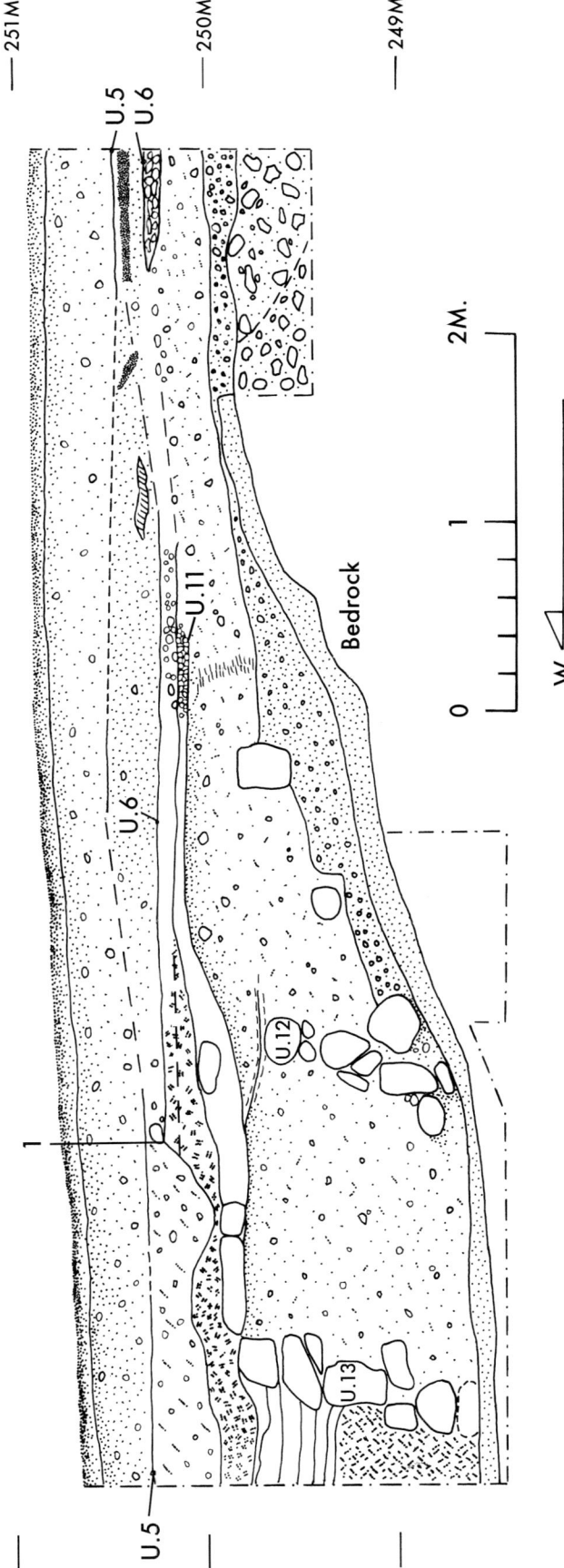

Op. 19E: Section. For location, see Fig. 2. Pertinent to Plat. 5D-5: *1*, The point at which U. 6 was torn out for Intermediate Classic construction. U. 5, Floor for 2nd. U. 6, Floor for 3rd. U. 11, Floor for 4th. U. 12, 13, Construction walls in core of 4th.

FIGURE 4

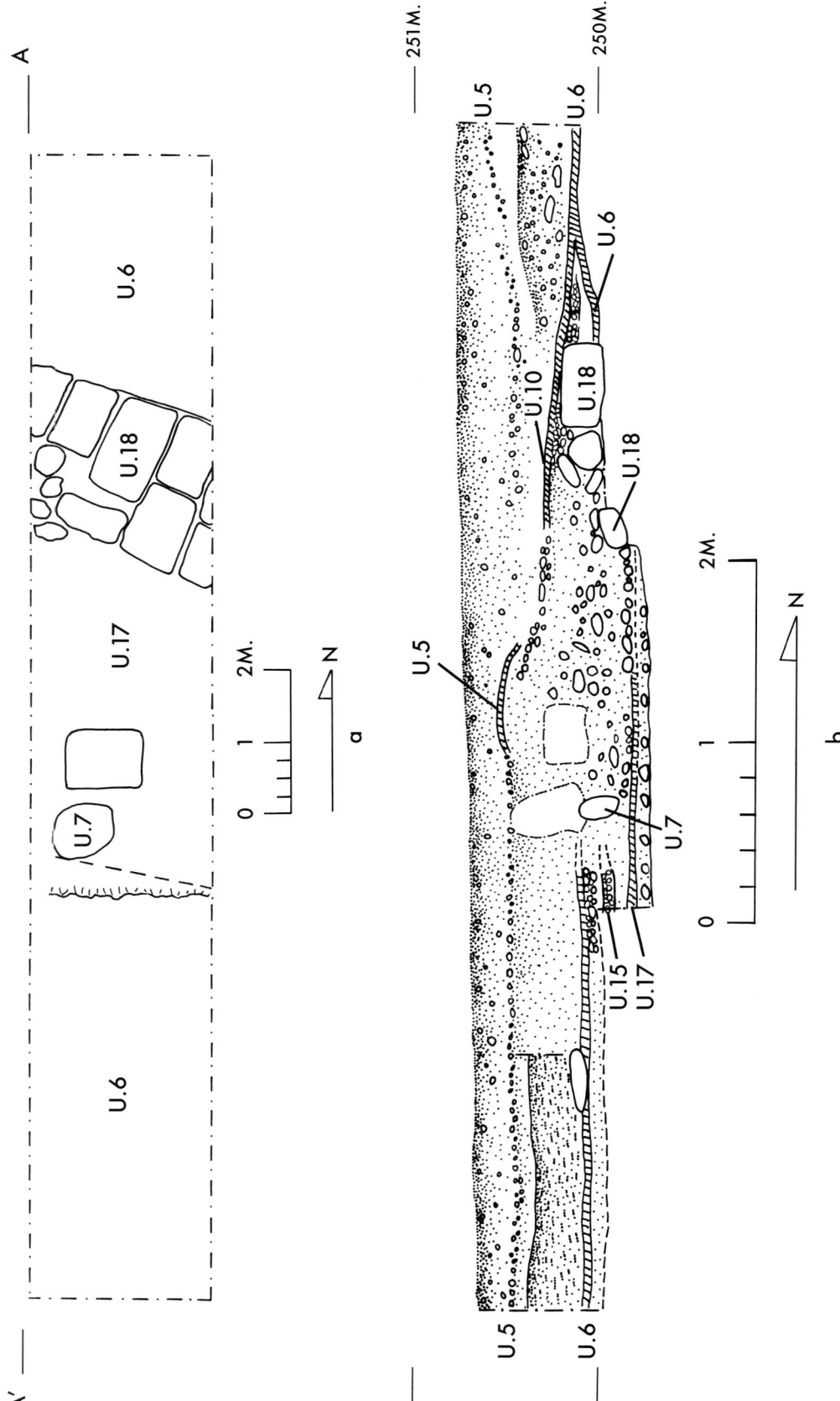

Op. 19F: Plan (*a*) and Section (*b*). For location, see Fig. 2.
Pertinent to Plat 5D-5: U. 5, Floor for 2nd. U. 6, Floor for 3rd. U. 7, Remains of wall expanding U. 18 to S. U. 10, Patch on floor (U. 6) of 3rd. U. 15, Floor for 4th. U. 17, Floor for 5th. U. 18, Wall to which U. 17 turns up.

FIGURE 5

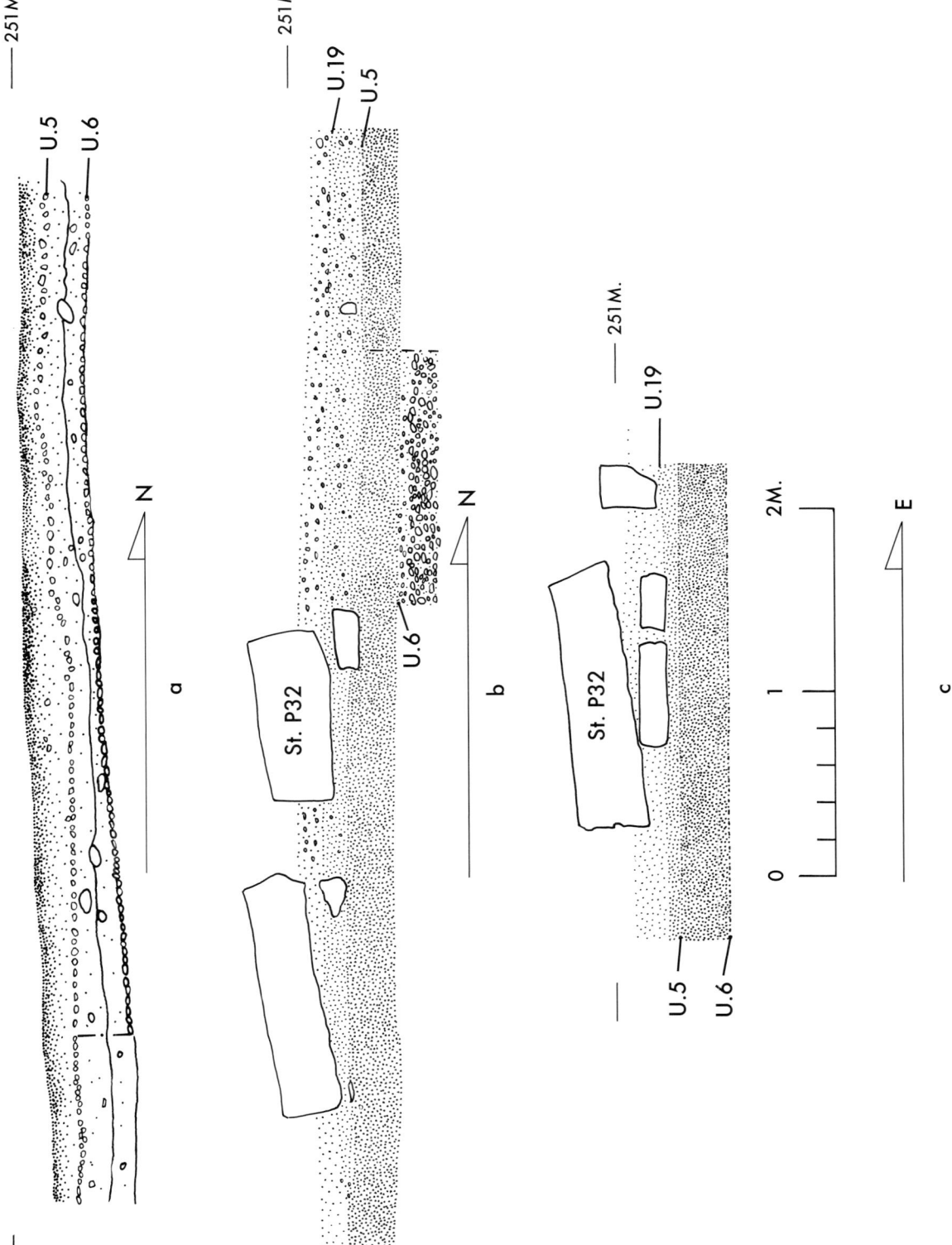

Op. 19G: Section (a); 19H and St. P32 N-S (b) and E-W (c) Sections. For location, see Fig. 2. *Pertinent to Plat. 5D-5*: U. 5, Floor for 2nd, badly broken up. U. 6, Floor for 3rd. U. 19, Remains of body for floor of 1st; becomes indistinct below St. P32.

FIGURE 6

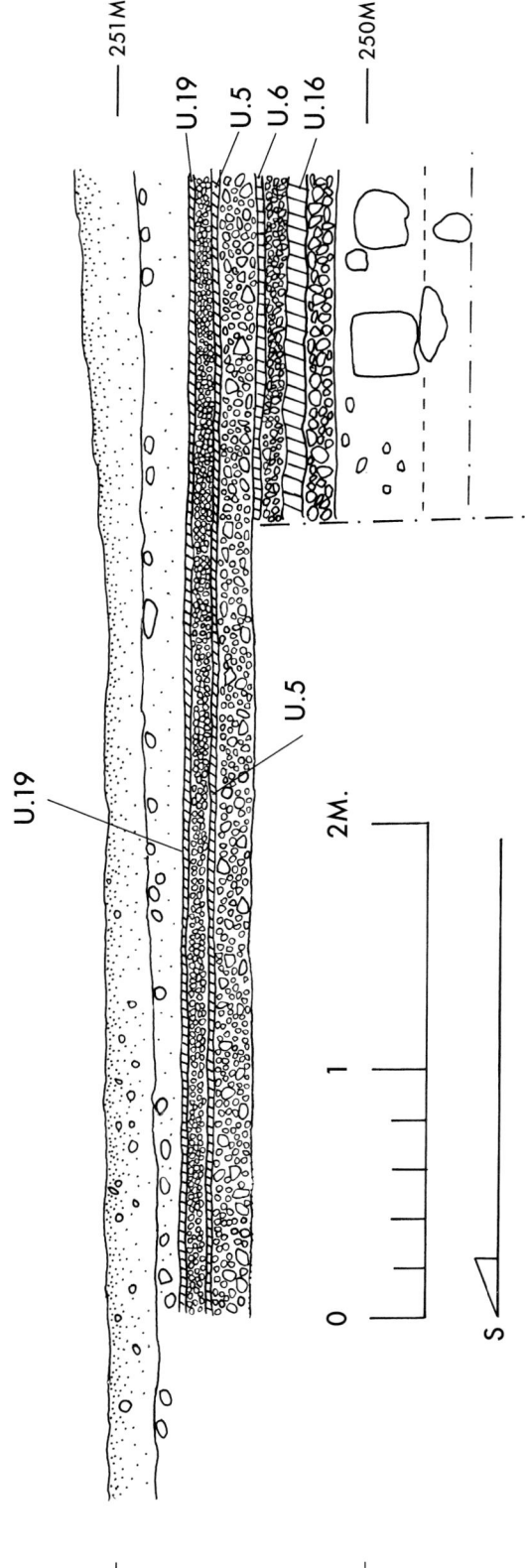

Op. 19I: Section. For location, see Fig. 2. Pertinent to Plat. 5D-5: U. 5, Floor for 2nd. U. 6, Floor for 3rd. U. 16, Probable part of floor for 4th. U. 19, Floor for 1st.

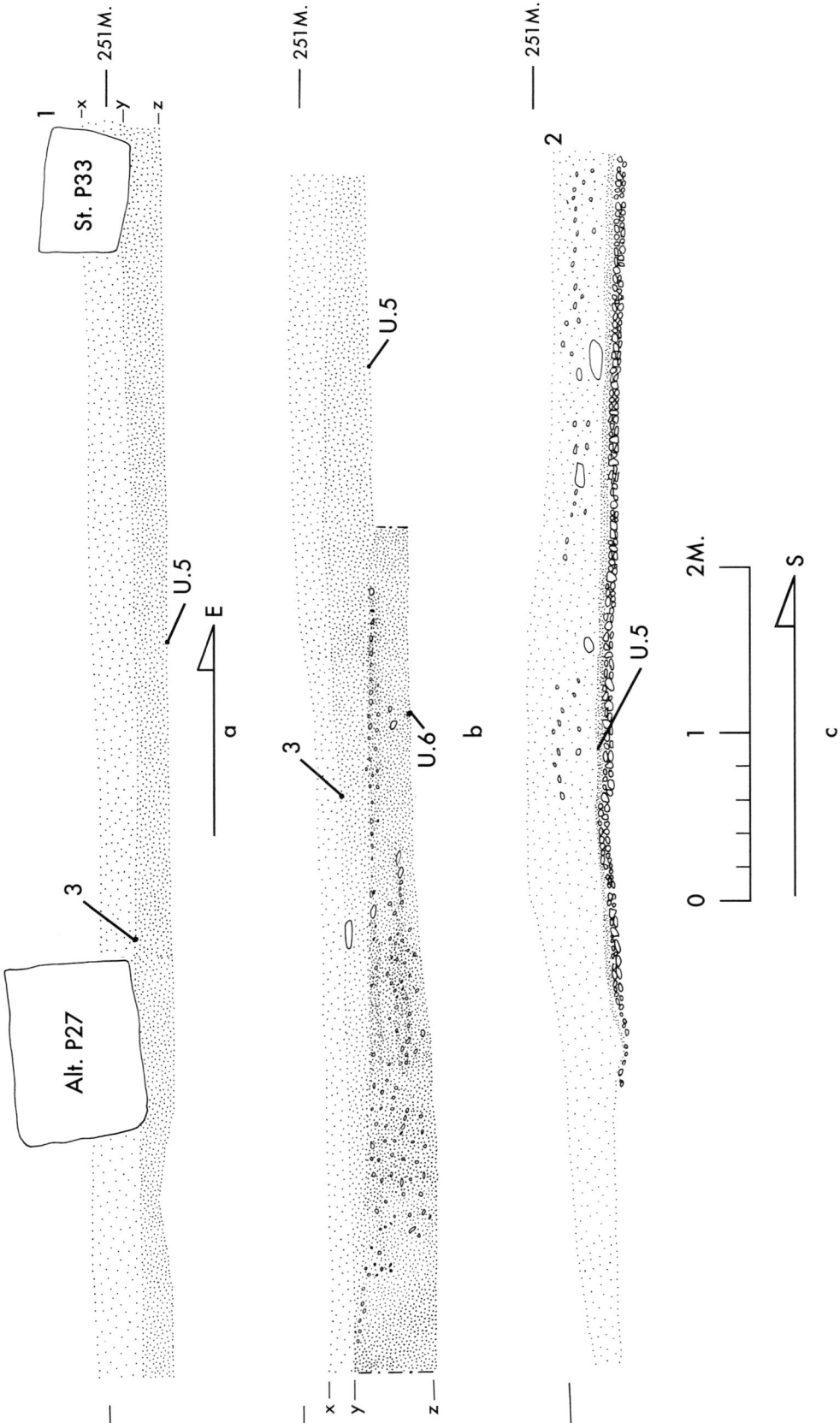

FIGURE 7

Op. 19N, St. P33, and Alt. P27: Section. Trench begins at Op. 19A (Fig. 2), runs W, then S, again W, and finally S to Op. 19K (c).
Pertinent to Plat. 5D-5: 1, End of trench near Op. 19A. *2*, Intersection with Op. 19K trench. *3*, Soil change from humus to stony fill, marks the position of floor for 1st. U. 5, Floor for 2nd. U. 6, Floor for 3rd.

FIGURE 8

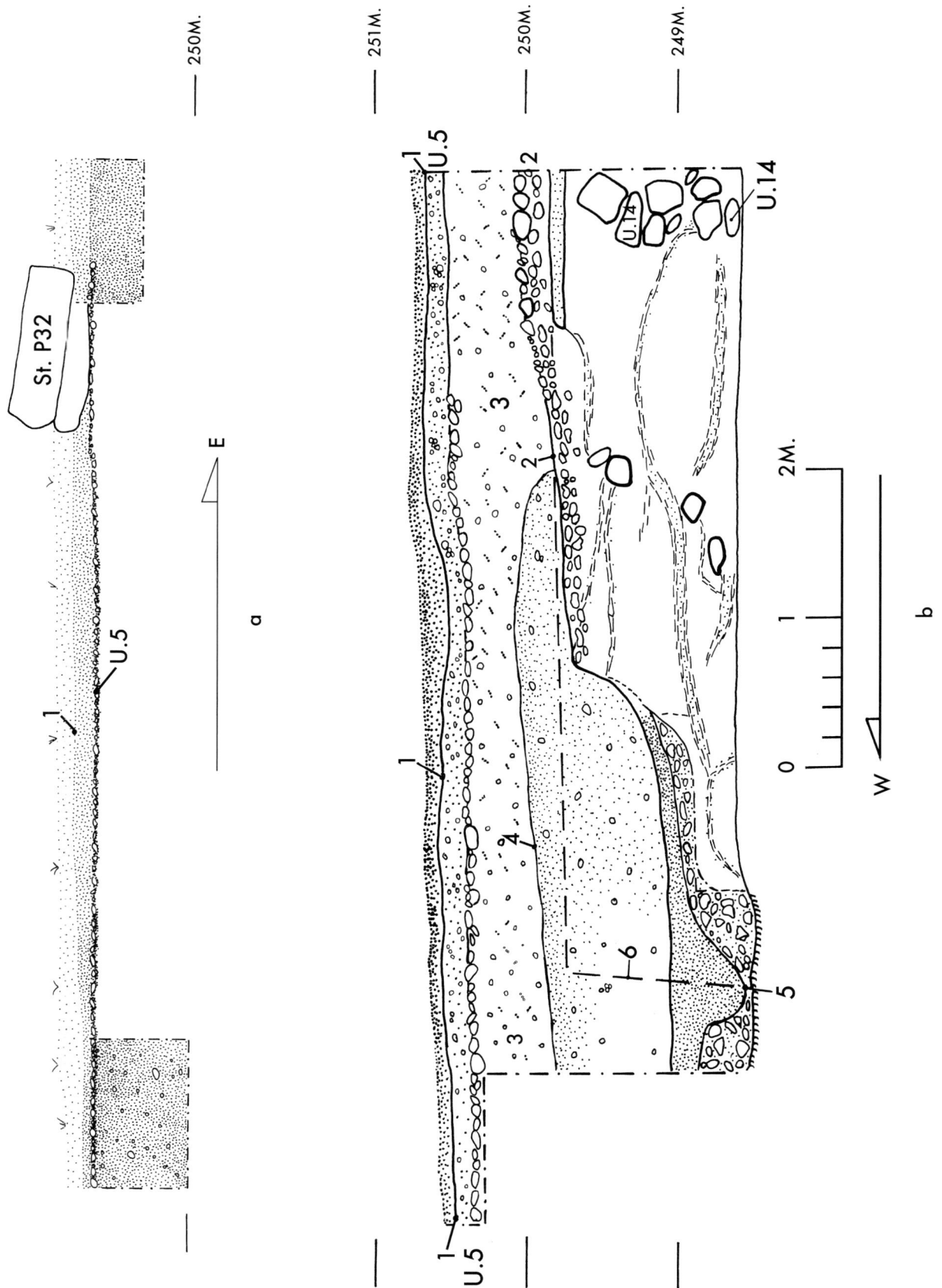

Op. 19J with St. P32 Section (*a*) and Op. 19D Section (*b*). For location, see Fig. 2. *Pertinent to Plat. 5D-5: 1*, Soil change at approximate position of floor for 1st. *2*, Top of remaining material beneath U. 6 (floor of 3rd). *3*, Gray material below U. 5; contains a mixture of ceramics from Preclassic to Late Classic. *4*, Top of loose brown soil with pebbles; latest ceramics are Ik Complex. *5*, Compact black earth with Tzec, Chuen, Manik, and possible Ik sherds; possible location of retaining wall (*6*) for U. 11 (the floor of 4th; see text). U. 5, Floor for 2nd. U. 14, Construction wall in fill of 4th.

FIGURE 9

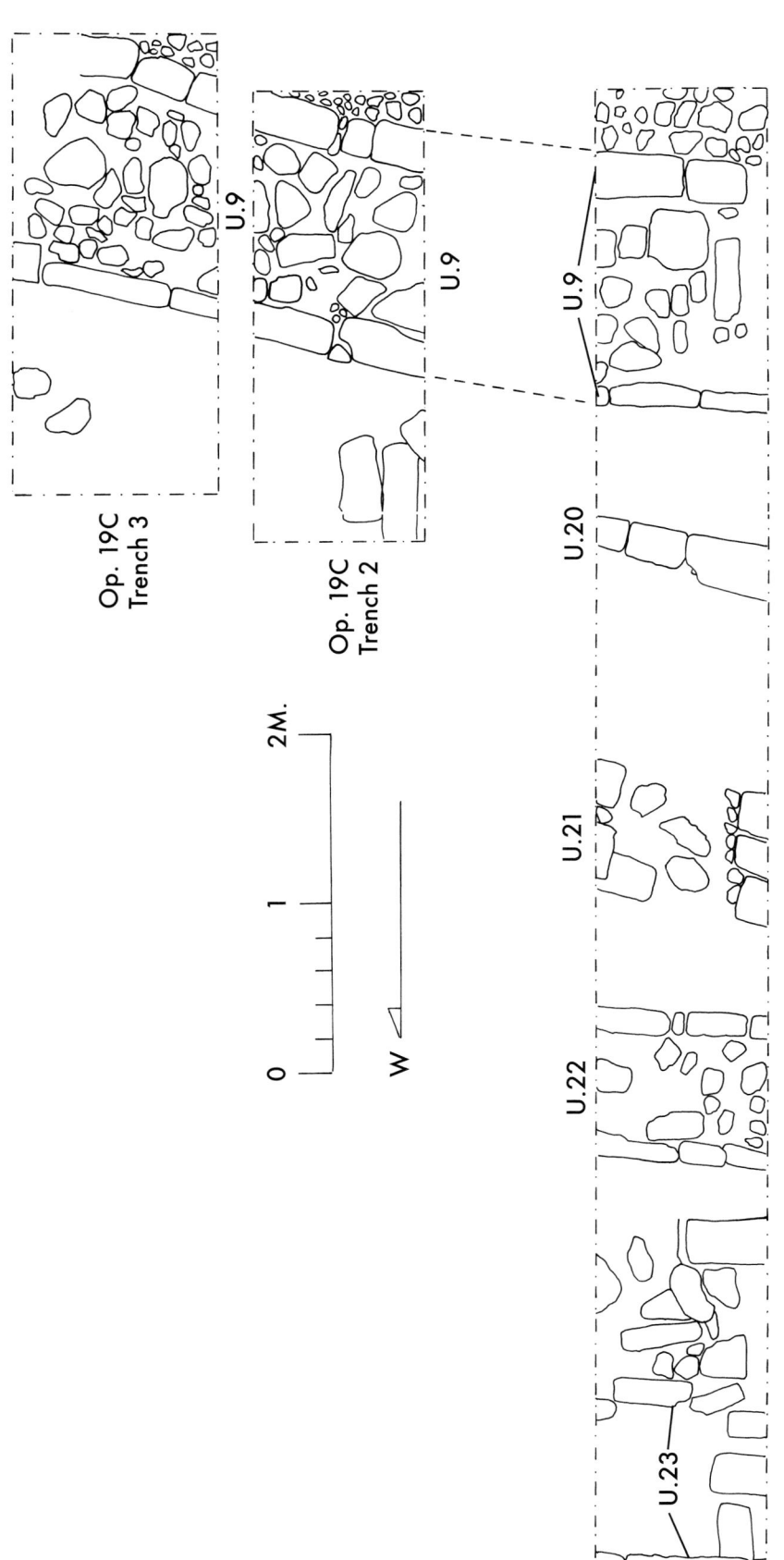

Op. 19C and L: Plans. For location, see Fig. 2.
Pertinent to Plat. 5D-5: U. 9, Probable W wall of 3rd, underlies floor of 2nd. U. 20, Probable W wall of 2nd. U. 21, Rough wall in core material for 1st. U. 22, W wall of 1st-B. U. 23, W wall of lower terrace of 1st-B (see also Fig. 12b).

FIGURE 10

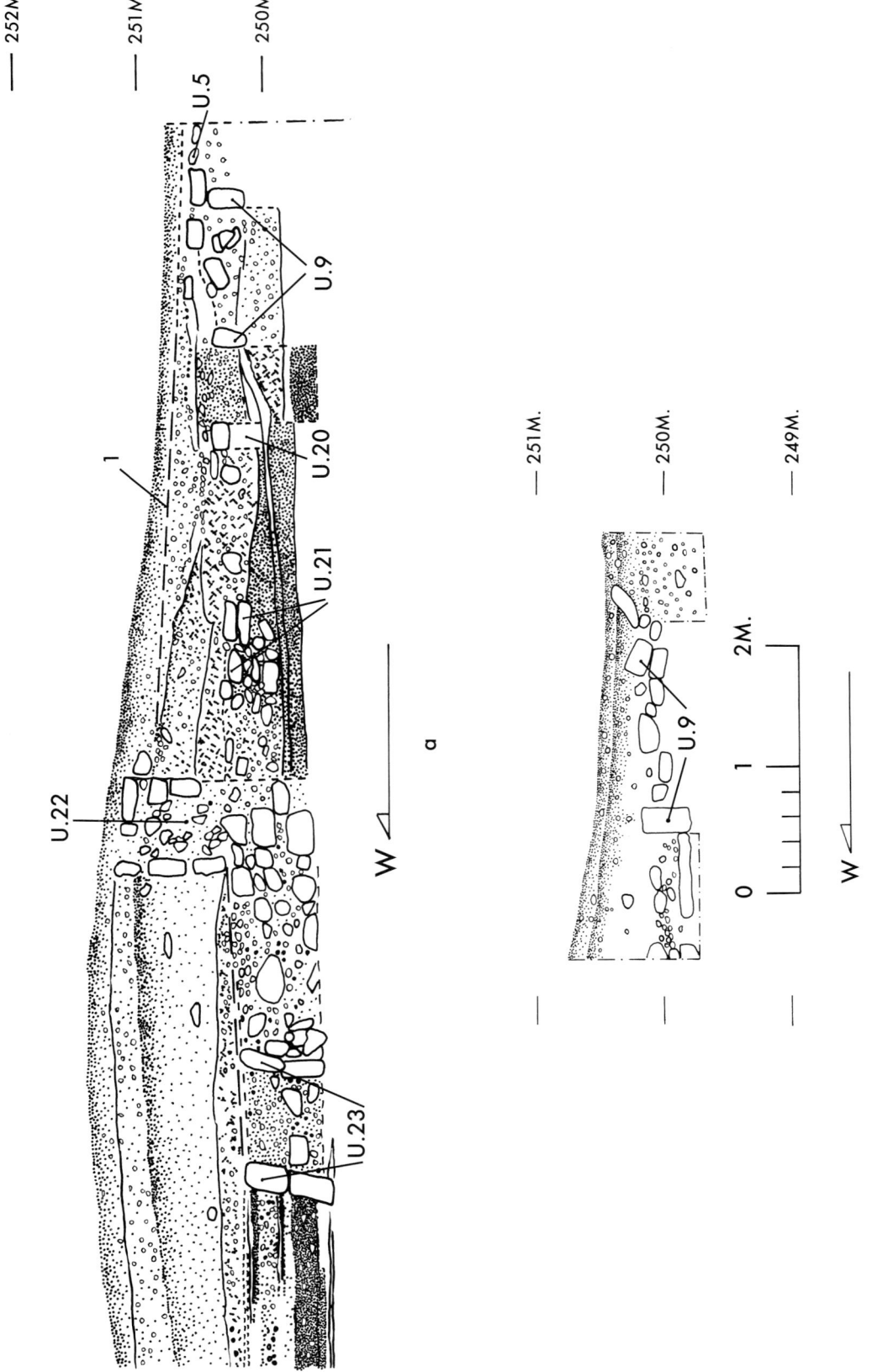

Op. 19C and L: Section in Main Trench (a) and 19C: Trench 1 (b). For location, see Fig. 2; for plan, Fig. 9. *Pertinent to Plat. 5D-5: 1*, Floor level of 1st. U. 5, Floor for 2nd. U. 9, Probable W wall for 3rd; compact layer of lime abuts its W face. U. 20, Probable W wall of 2nd, based on the layer of compact lime noted above. West of the wall, this layer served as an informal occupation surface. U. 21, Construction wall in core material of 1st. U. 22, W wall of 1st-B. U. 23, Lower terrace wall of 1st-B. U. 24–26, Floors abutting U. 23.

FIGURE 11

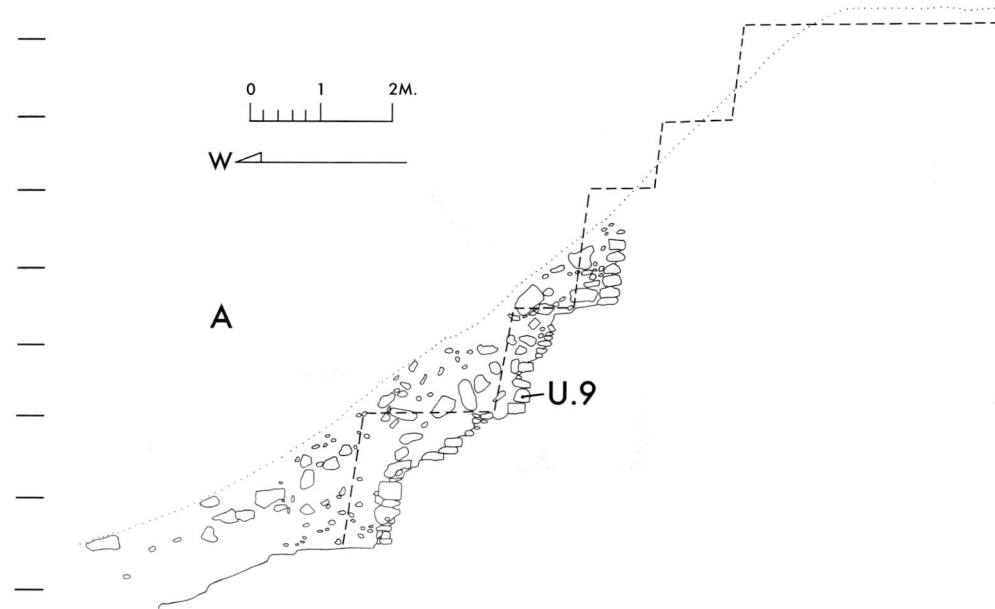

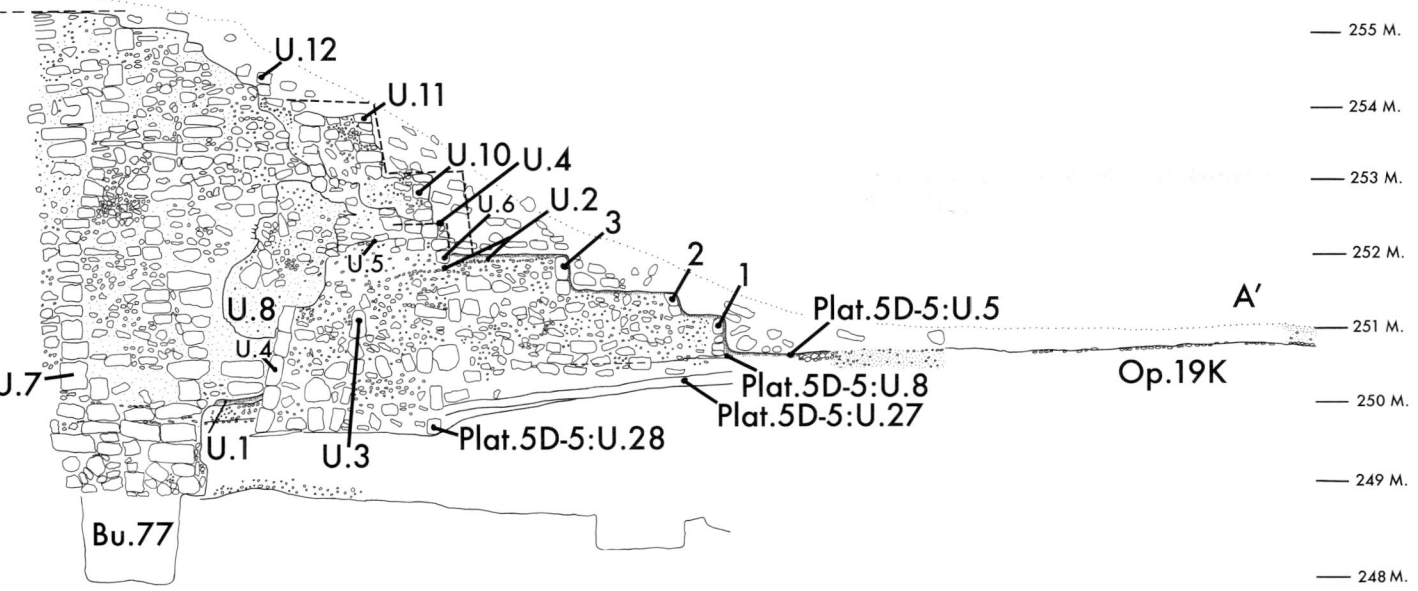

Str. 5D-11: Section A-A'; includes Op. 19K trench. For location, see Fig. 2 and 12.

Pertinent to Str. 5D-11: *1*, Lowest step of 2nd and 1st. *2*, Second step of 2nd and 1st. *3*, Third step of 2nd and 1st. *4*, Broken line reconstruction of tread for U. 6 (see below). U. 1, Floor abutting back wall of 2nd; may be surface of lower terrace (see Fig. 15). U. 2, Limestone pebbles that cap material of CS. 3 of 2nd. U. 3, Construction wall retaining fill of CS. 4 and 3 of 2nd. U. 4, Rear wall of 2nd. U. 5, Marks the top of the remaining core of 2nd as construction of 1st began. U. 6, Remnant of fourth stair riser or terrace wall (see Fig. 12) for 2nd. U. 7, Construction wall of 1st: CS. 4. U. 8, Enigmatic pocket of loose material in core of 1st. U. 9, Rear wall of 1st. U. 10, 11, 12, Reconstructed terrace levels on E face of 1st. *Pertinent to Plat. 5D-5*: U. 5, Floor of 2nd, turns up to Str. 5D-11-2nd. U. 8, Construction surface for Str. 5D-11-2nd; in S side of trench it runs 1.70 m farther W. U. 27, Occupation surface W of 3rd, abuts U. 28. U. 28, Retaining wall for material beneath U. 27.

Str. 5D-11: Plan, as revealed by surface clearing.
Pertinent to Str. 5D-11: *2, 3*, Second and third steps of 2nd and 1st; see Fig. 11. U. 6, Remains of riser for 4th step of 2nd and 1st (see Fig. 11). U. 9, Rear wall of 1st. U. 10, 11, 12, see Fig. 11. U. 13, Jumble of masonry, thought to be ruins of a stairway. U. 14, Remains of 7th stair riser of 1st. U. 15, N side wall of inset stairs of 1st. *Pertinent to Plat. 5D-5*: U. 5, Floor of 2nd S of Str. 5D-11-1st. U. 29, Parapet abutting 5D-11-1st and running N to Str. 5D-12. U. 40, Floor that runs beneath U. 29. Masonry extending W from SW corner of 5D-11 may be remains of a wall of Plat. 5D-5.

FIGURE 12

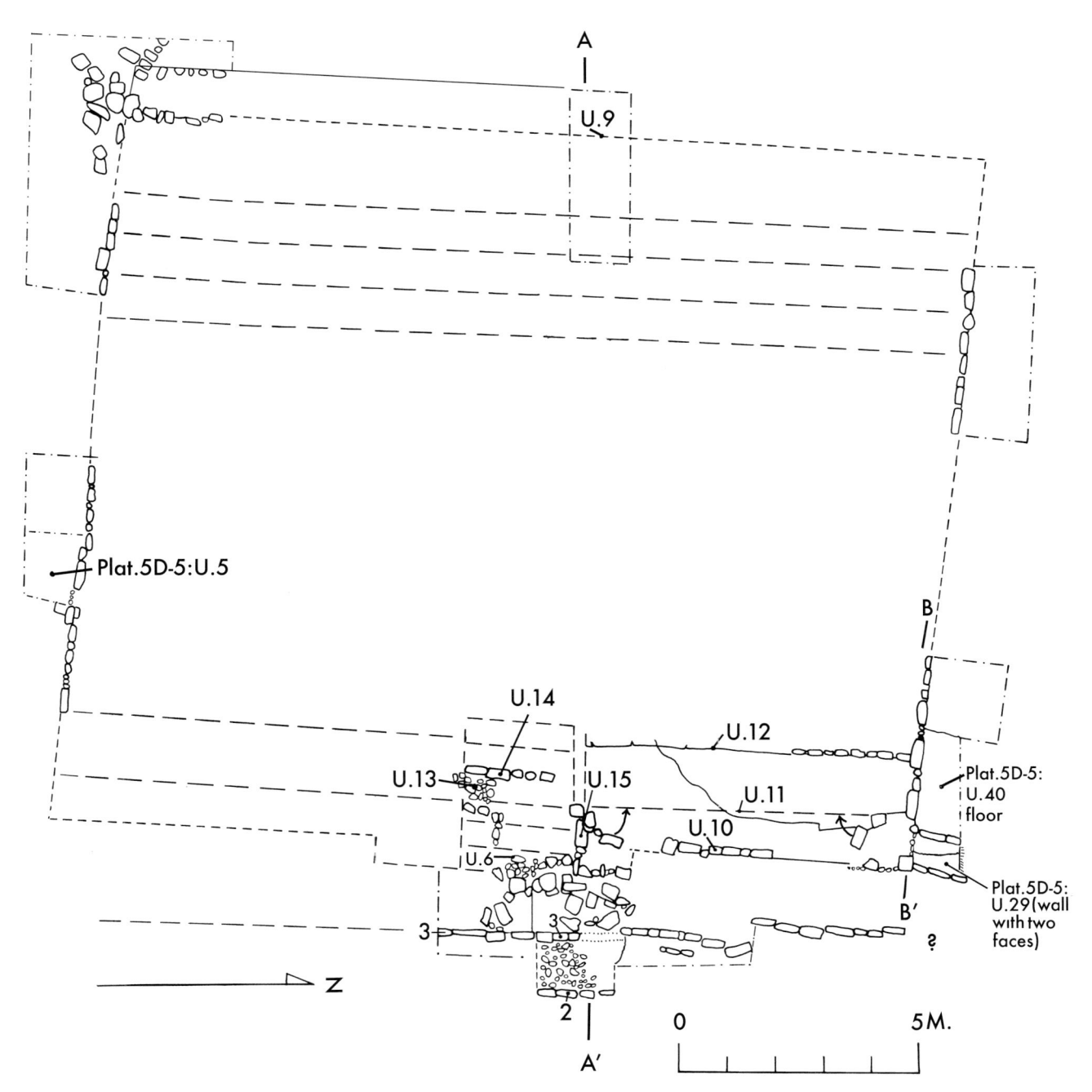

Plat. 5D-5 and Str. 5D-11: Section B-B' (*a*). For location, see Fig. 12. Schematic drawing (*b*) shows position of plaza walls in relation to Str. 5D-11-1st.

(*a*) *Pertinent to Str. 5D-11*: N wall masonry. *Pertinent to Plat. 5D-5*: U. 29, Where it abuts wall of Str. 5D-11-1st. U. 40, Occupation surface beneath the U. 29 wall. (*b*) *Pertinent to Plat. 5D-5*: U. 9, The two faces of the W wall of 3rd, positioned E of later location of Str. 5D-11 (for vertical position, see Fig. 10). U. 22, Parapet on W edge of 1st-B. U. 23, W face of wall marking edge of 1st-A. U. 24, Floor W of the plaza.

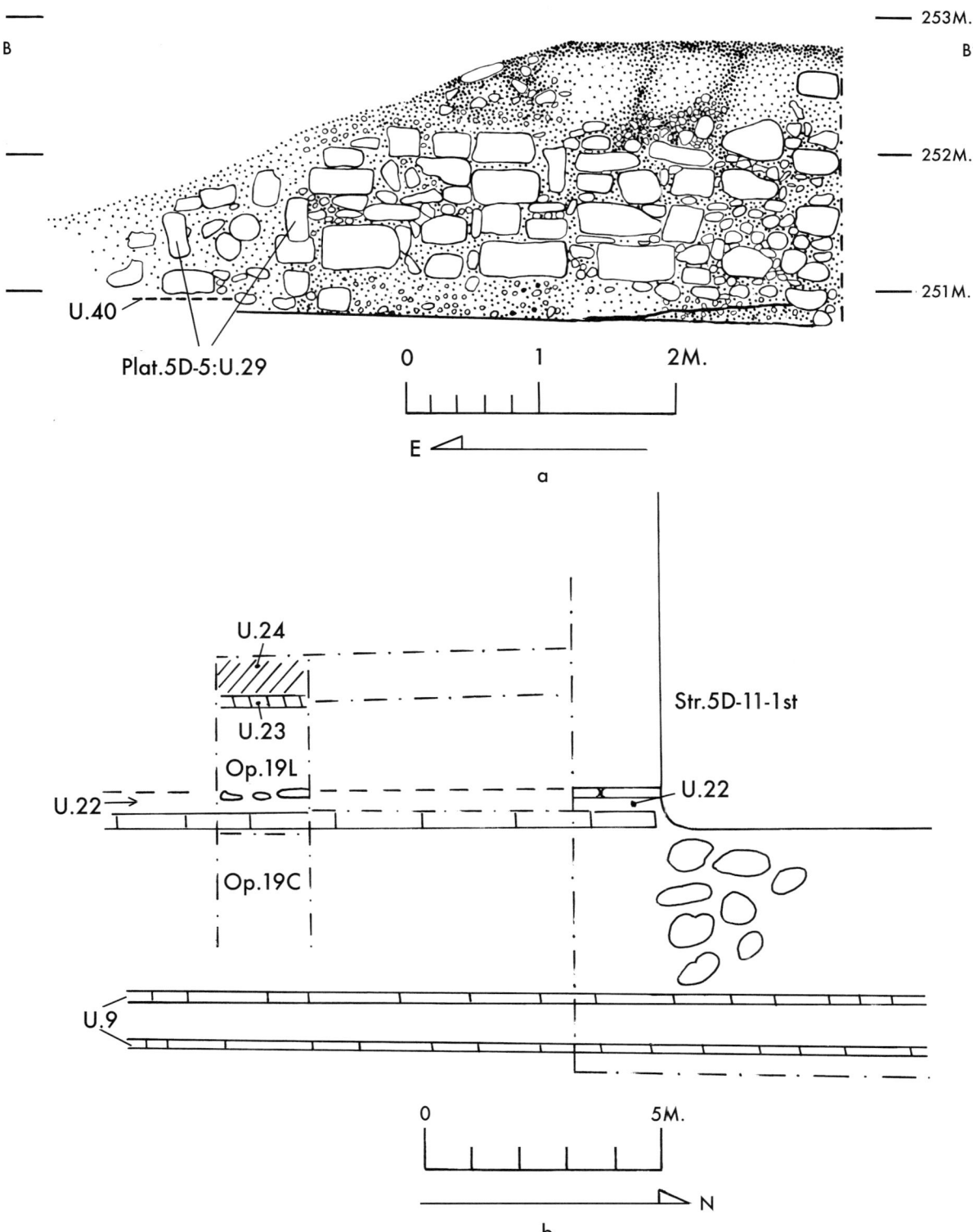

FIGURE 13

FIGURE 14

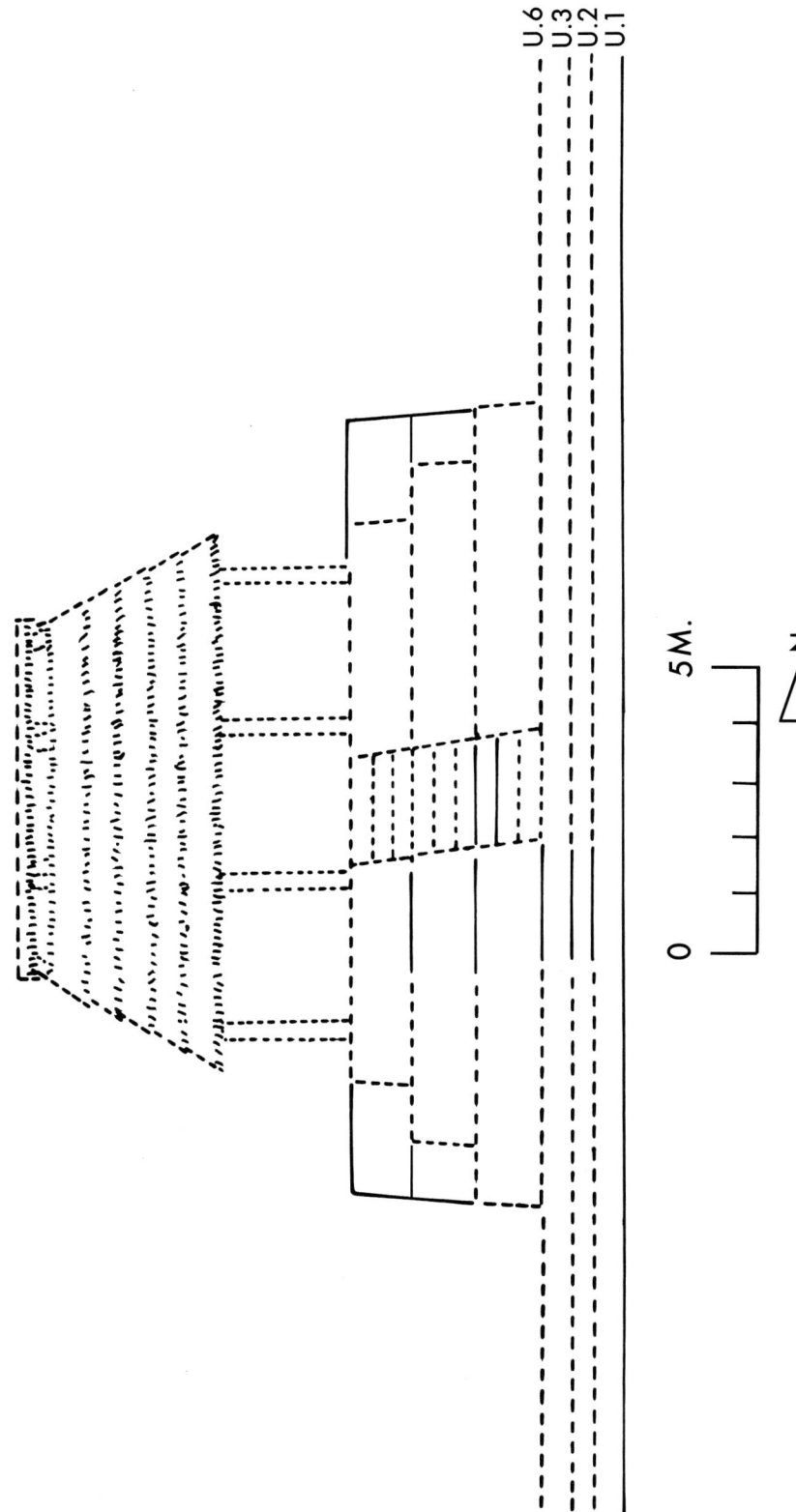

Peter Harrison's reconstruction of Str. 5D-11-1st, viewed from the front. Given the condition of the ruin, the reconstruction is highly speculative. Solid lines on either side reflect the reality of surface features shown in Fig. 12.

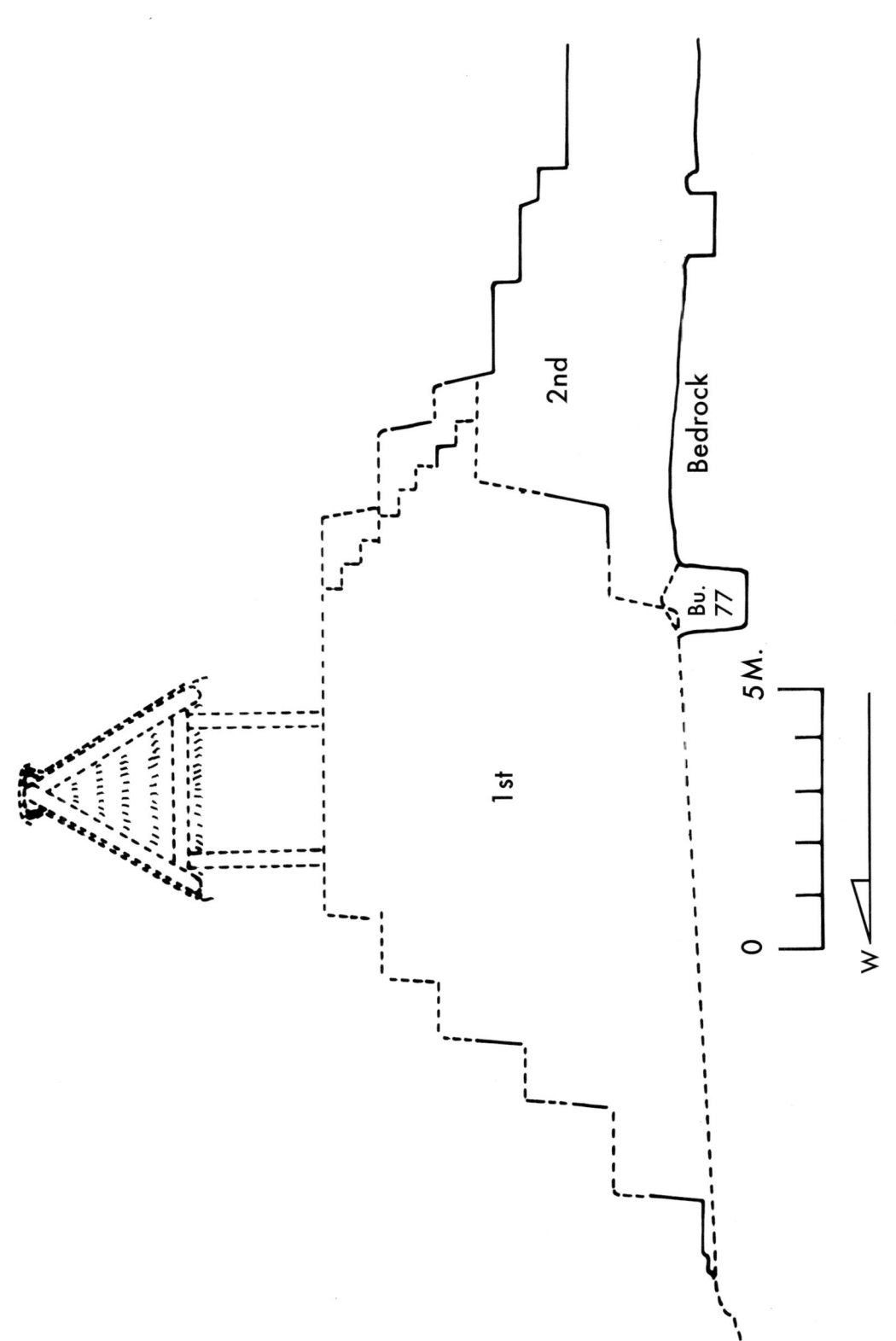

Schematic representation of Str. 5D-11-1st and its relation to 2nd. See also Fig. 15. Note reconstruction of 1st stairway as inset.

FIGURE 16

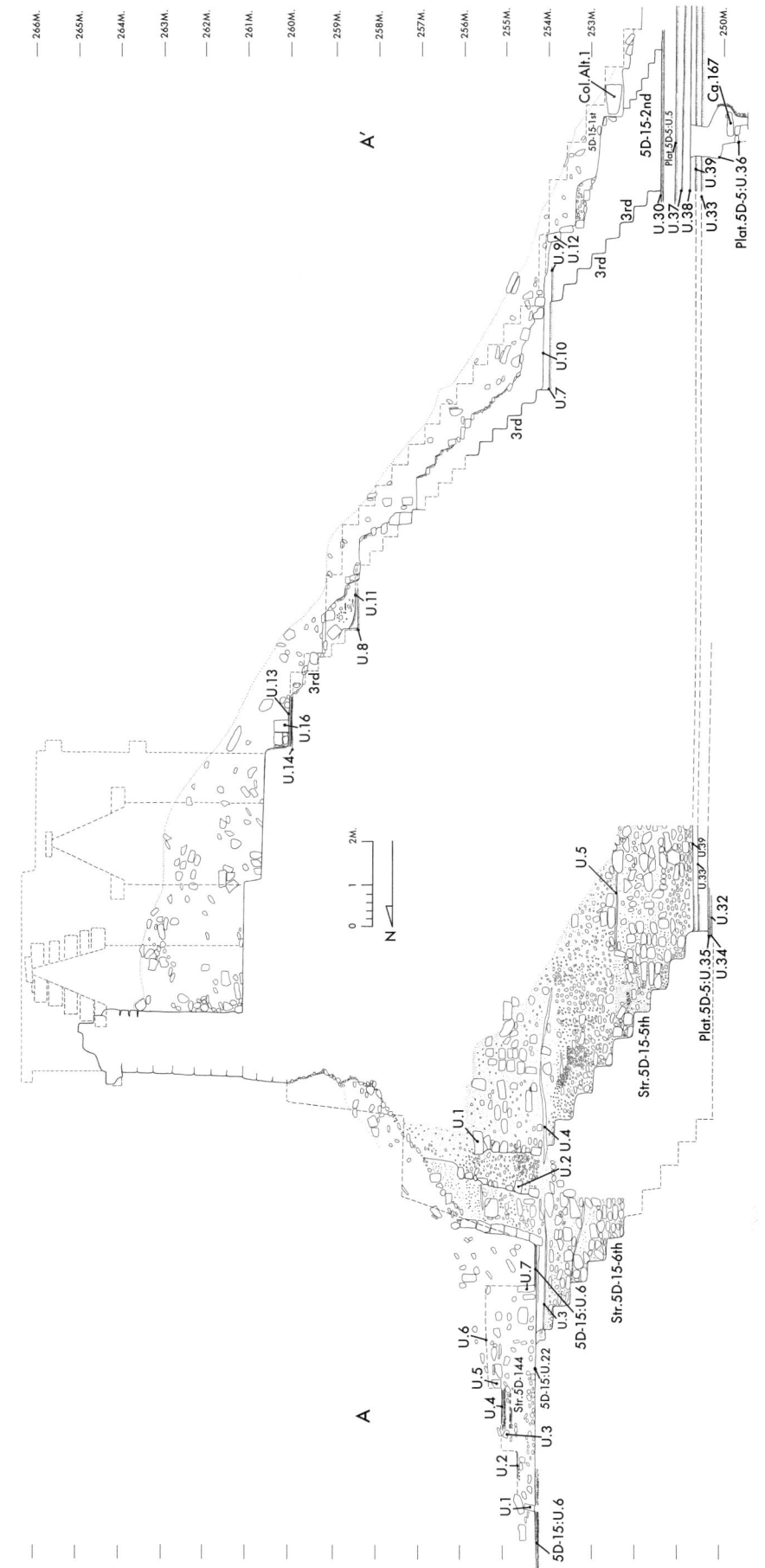

Figure 16 Full (*see next page for detail enlargement*)

Str. 5D-15 and 5D-144: Axial Section A-A'. For location, see Fig. 17.
Pertinent to Str. 5D-15: U. 1, 2, Construction walls in substructure of 3rd. U. 3, 4, Pause-lines, marking top of 5th and 4th cores prior to construction of 3rd. U. 5, Pause-line in core of 3rd. U. 6, Resurfacing of original floor of basal terrace (U. 21) of 15-3rd, turns up to its rear wall and base of Str. 5D-144 back wall (see Fig. 47c). U. 7, Surface of lower stair landing of 15-3rd. U. 8, Surface of second stair landing of 3rd. U. 9, Extension of lower stair landing for 2nd-B. U. 10, Surface of lower stair landing for 2nd-A. U. 11, Resurfacing of second stair landing for 2nd. U. 12, Stair riser to lower landing of 2nd. U. 13, Resurfacing of U. 14 (see below). U. 14, Original floor on substructure summit of 3rd, on which the building platform stands. U. 16, Masonry step in front of central doorway, part of 1st-A. U. 22, Floor of basal terrace (U. 21) of 3rd, turns up to back wall of 3rd but runs under Str. 5D-144. *Pertinent to Str. 5D-144:* U. 1, Front wall, lower level. U. 2, Floor runs from base of U. 3 to top of U. 1. U. 3, Front wall of 2nd platform level. U. 4, Floor runs from top of U. 3 to base of U. 5. U. 5, Front wall of upper (3rd) platform level. U. 6, Reconstructed summit of 3rd platform level. U. 7, Basal masonry of rear wall. *Pertinent to Plat. 5D-5:* U. 5, Floor of 2nd. U. 30, Floor of 1st, runs under Str. 5D-15-3rd. U. 32, Floor of 6th. U. 33, Thought to be floor of 5th. U. 34, 35, Resurfacings of floor of 6th. U. 36, Wall encountered by the Maya when preparing receptacle for Ca. 167. Its top is at the same elevation as U. 32. U. 37, Floor of 3rd-A that seals Ca. 167. U. 38, Floor of 3rd-B through which pit for Ca. 167 was dug. U. 39, Thought to be floor of 4th.

FIGURE 16 Detail

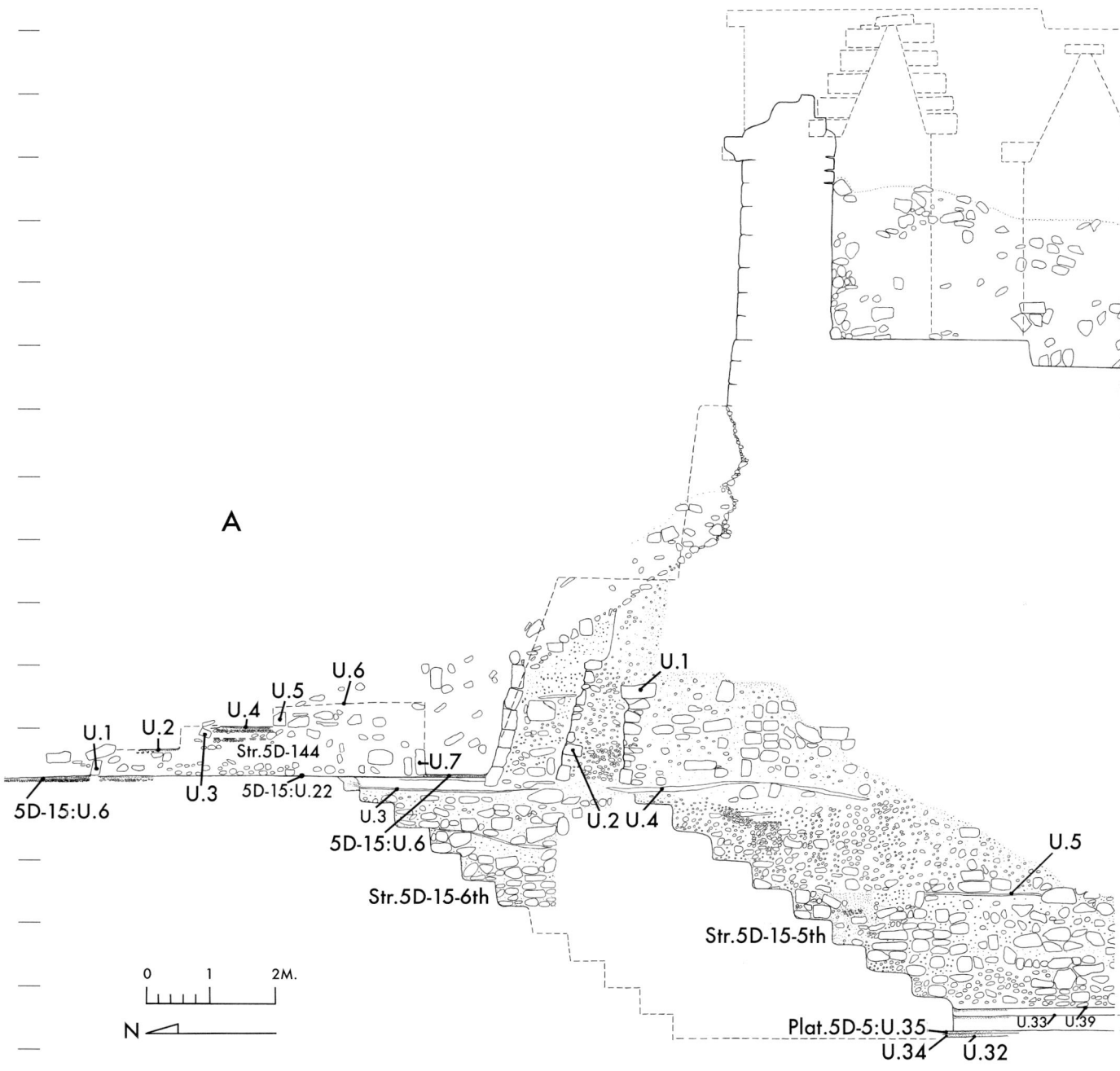

Figure 16 Detail (*caption repeated*)

Str. 5D-15 and 5D-144: Axial Section A-A′. For location, see Fig. 17.
Pertinent to Str. 5D-15: U. 1, 2, Construction walls in substructure of 3rd. U. 3, 4, Pause-lines, marking top of 5th and 4th cores prior to construction of 3rd. U. 5, Pause-line in core of 3rd. U. 6, Resurfacing of original floor of basal terrace (U. 21) of 15-3rd, turns up to its rear wall and base of Str. 5D-144 back wall (see Fig. 47c). U. 7, Surface of lower stair landing of 15-3rd. U. 8, Surface of second stair landing of 3rd. U. 9, Extension of lower stair landing for 2nd-B. U. 10, Surface of lower stair landing for 2nd-A. U. 11, Resurfacing of second stair landing for 2nd. U. 12, Stair riser to lower landing of 2nd. U. 13, Resurfacing of U. 14 (see below). U. 14, Original floor on substructure summit of 3rd, on which the building platform stands. U. 16, Masonry step in front of central doorway, part of 1st-A. U. 22, Floor of basal terrace (U. 21) of

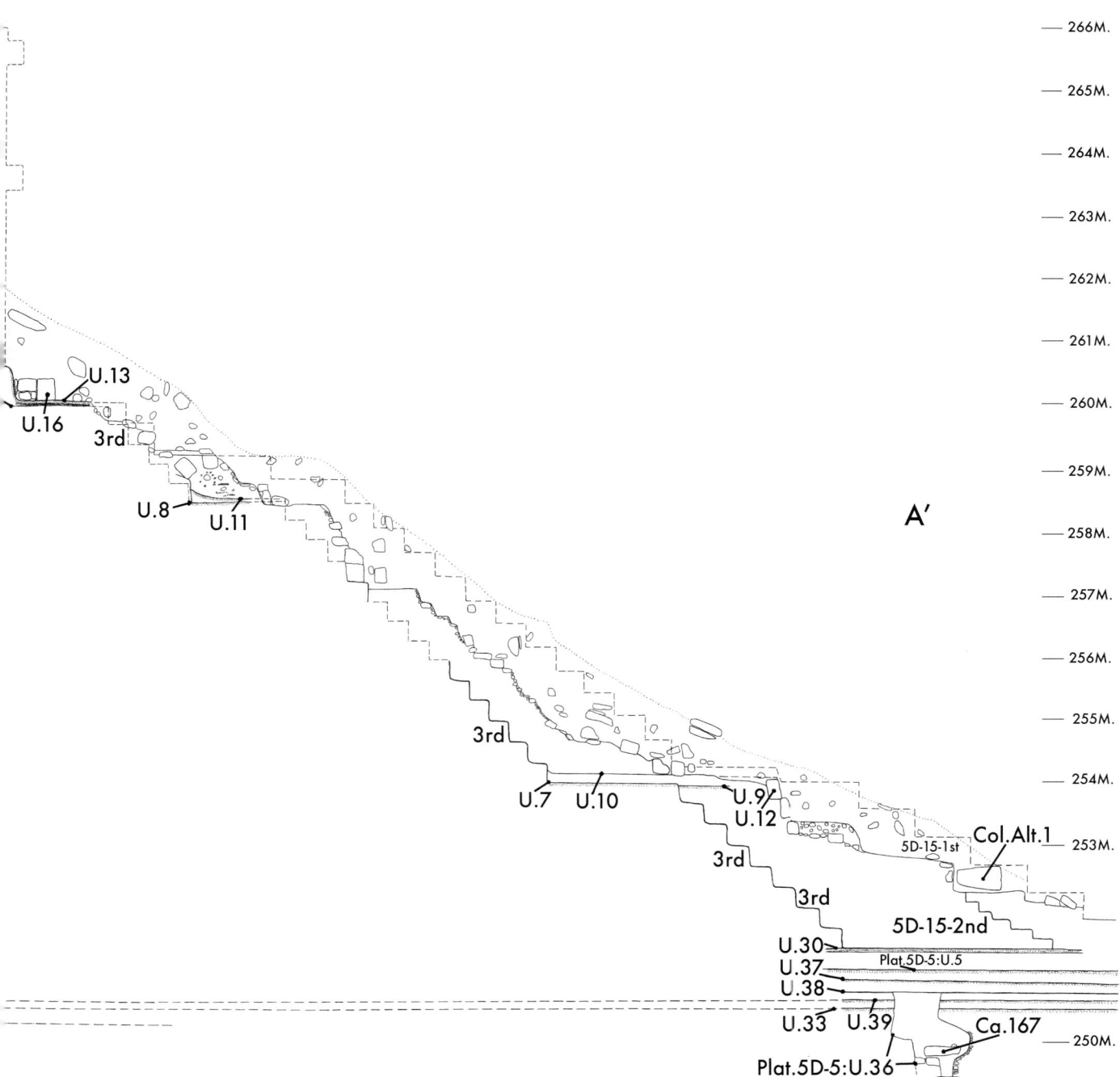

3rd, turns up to back wall of 3rd but runs under Str. 5D-144. *Pertinent to Str. 5D-144*: U. 1, Front wall, lower level. U. 2, Floor runs from base of U. 3 to top of U. 1. U. 3, Front wall of 2nd platform level. U. 4, Floor runs from top of U. 3 to base of U. 5. U. 5, Front wall of upper (3rd) platform level. U. 6, Reconstructed summit of 3rd platform level. U. 7, Basal masonry of rear wall. *Pertinent to Plat. 5D-5*: U. 5, Floor of 2nd. U. 30, Floor of 1st, runs under Str. 5D-15-3rd. U. 32, Floor of 6th. U. 33, Thought to be floor of 5th. U. 34, 35, Resurfacings of floor of 6th. U. 36, Wall encountered by the Maya when preparing receptacle for Ca. 167. Its top is at the same elevation as U. 32. U. 37, Floor of 3rd-A that seals Ca. 167. U. 38, Floor of 3rd-B through which pit for Ca. 167 was dug. U. 39, Thought to be floor of 4th.

FIGURE 17

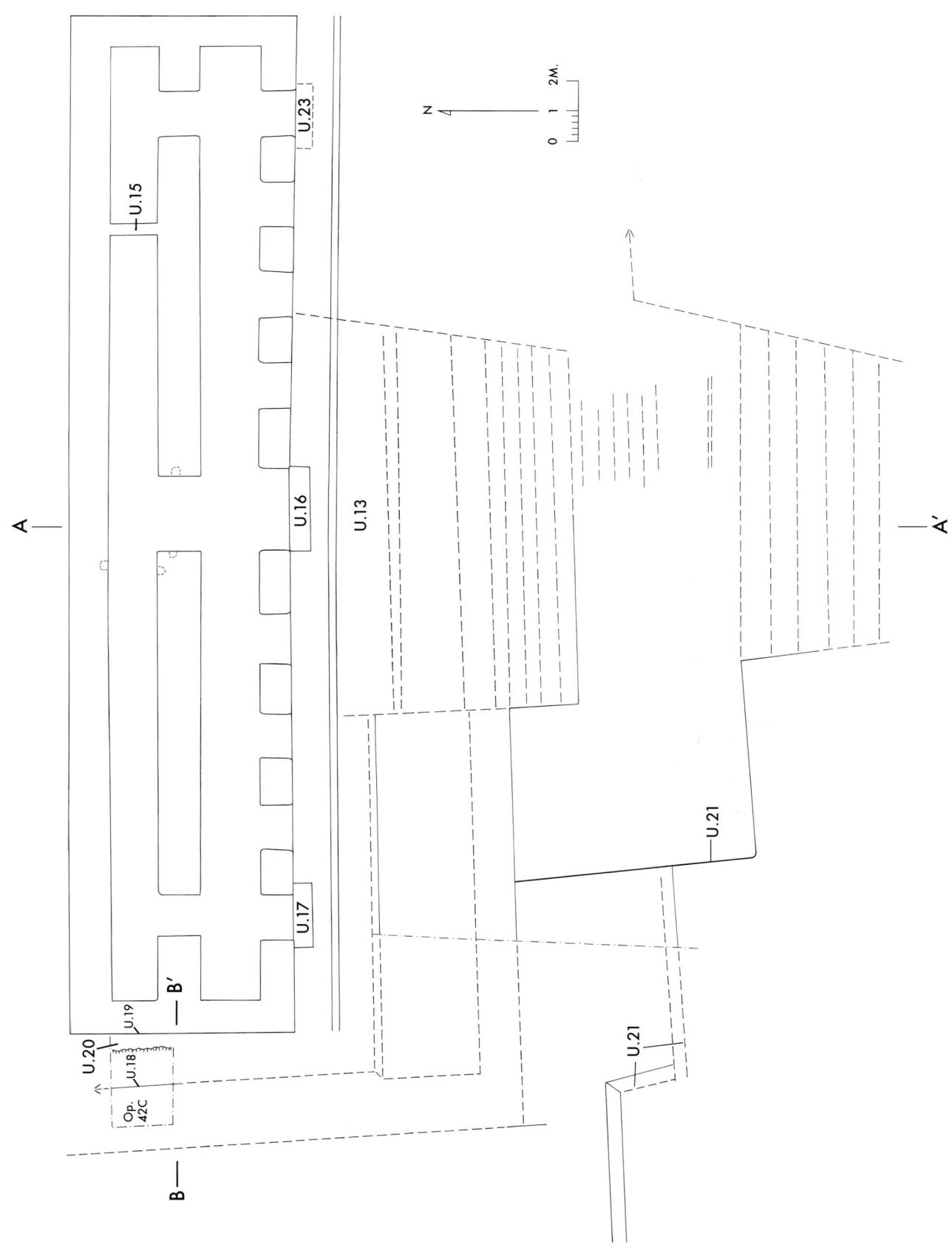

Str. 5D-15-1st: Plan.

At the time of Harrison's death, he was rethinking his plan of this structure in order to reconcile inconsistencies between existing drawings as well as the section (Fig. 16). The plan shown here is a reconstruction based on the conviction that Fig. 16 is accurate, using three different plans of the structure, a front elevation (Fig. 22a,b), and measurements recorded in his field notes (see TR. 15 for discussion of inconsistencies in measurements of "palaces"). Minor inconsistencies may remain; most problematical is the stairway, as it lay entirely in ruins (see Fig. 47a). *Pertinent to Str. 5D-15*: U. 13, Floor in front of building platform (see Fig. 16). U. 15, Late wall added to rear gallery, creating a separate room; defines 1st-A. U. 16, 17, 23, Late steps added in front of central, W, and E doorways (see Fig. 16). U. 18, 19, 20, Walls of two substructure terraces and floor capping the lowermost (see Fig. 20). U. 21, Large platform surrounding 5D-15, the summit at the same elevation as U. 6 behind, and also the base of U. 18.

FIGURE 18

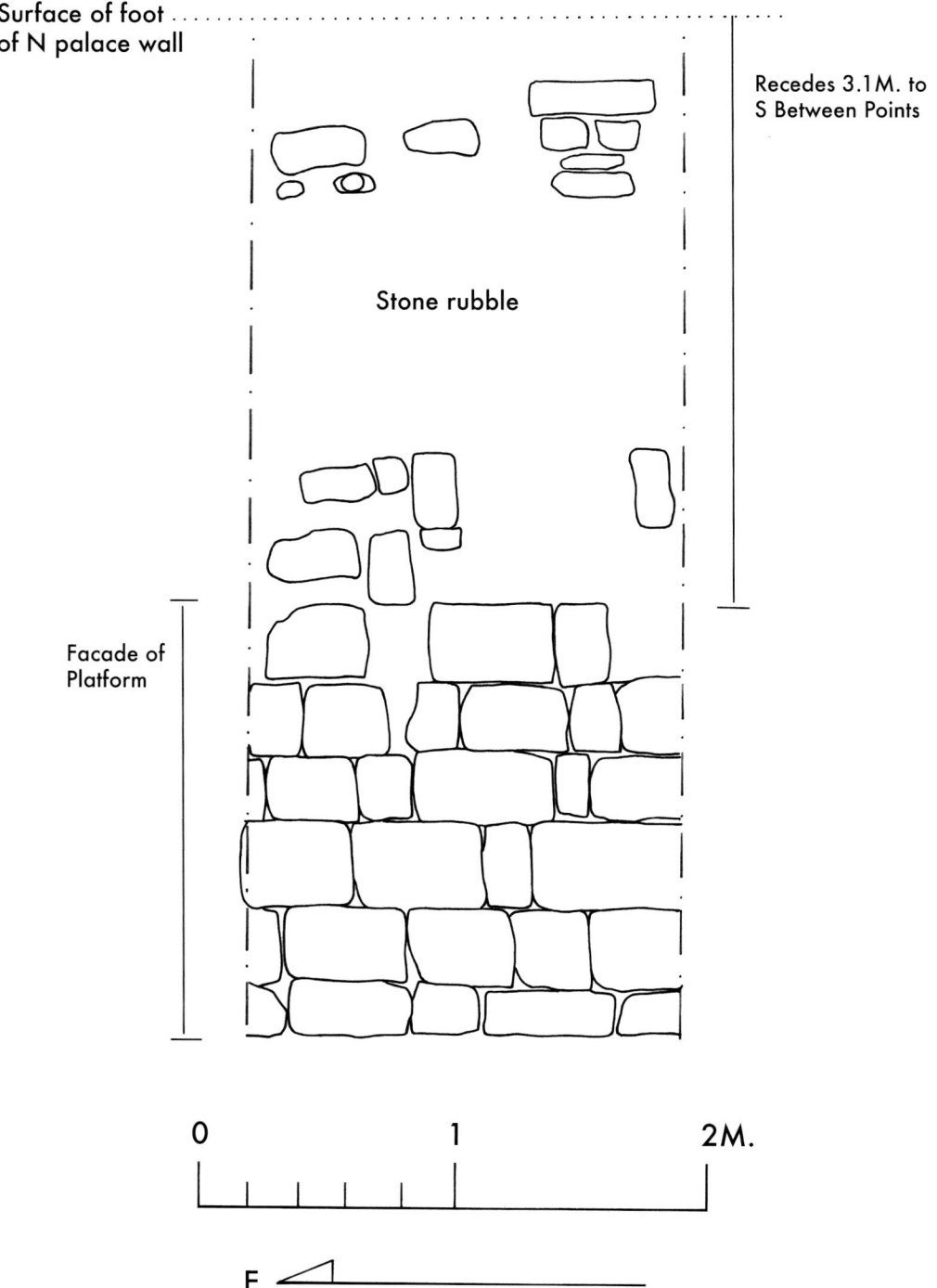

Str. 5D-15: Elevation showing rear wall masonry of 3rd exposed in axial trench. (Fig. 16, 47b). Note combination of headers and stretchers.

FIGURE 19

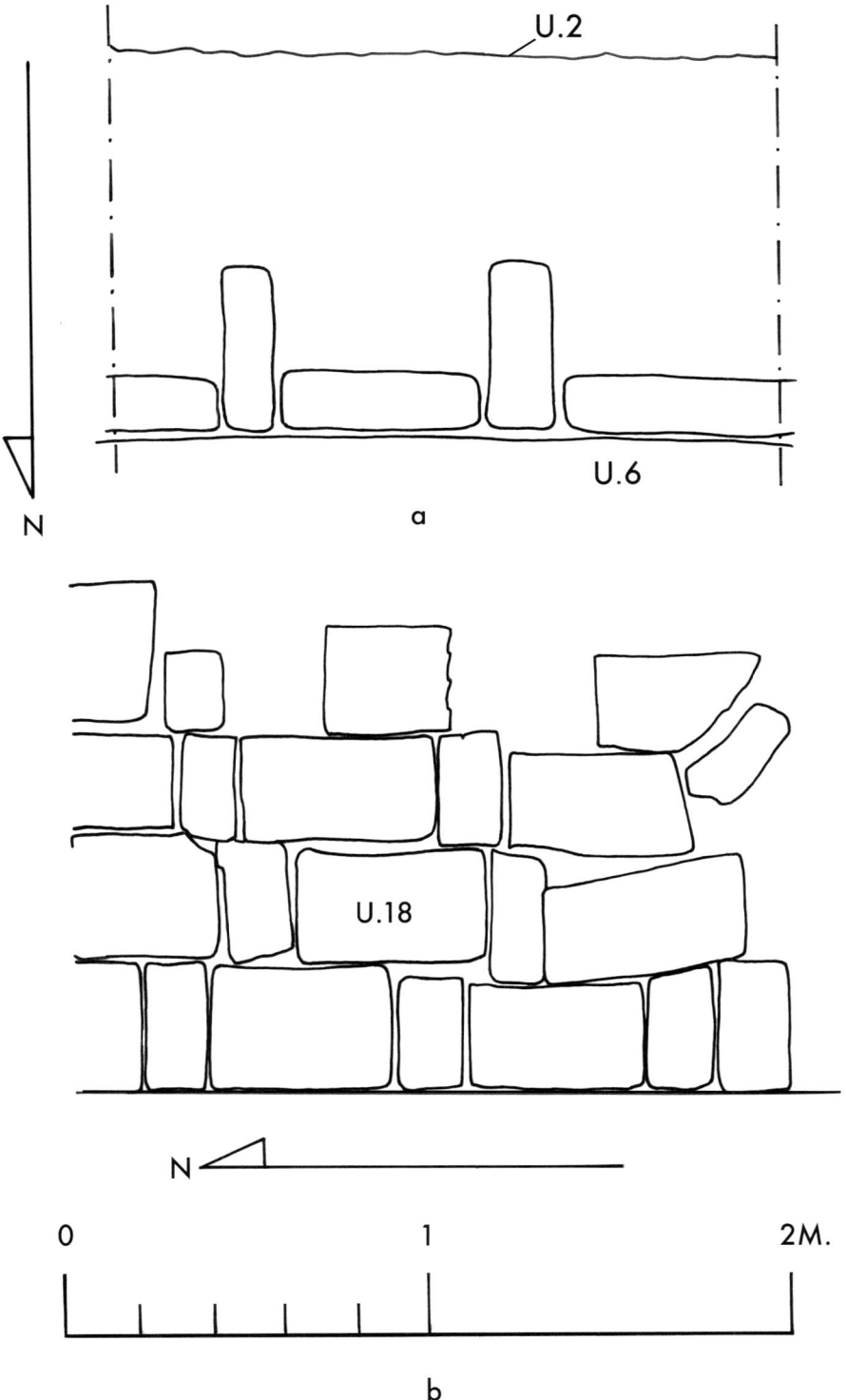

Str. 5D-15: (*a*) Plan showing basal masonry of 3rd rear wall exposed in axial trench. U. 2 is the last construction wall in 3rd core (Fig. 16); U. 6 is the repaving between 5D-15 and Str. 5D-144 (Fig. 16). (*b*) Elevation showing wall masonry (U. 18) exposed in trench into the W end of 3rd (see also Fig. 48b).

FIGURE 20

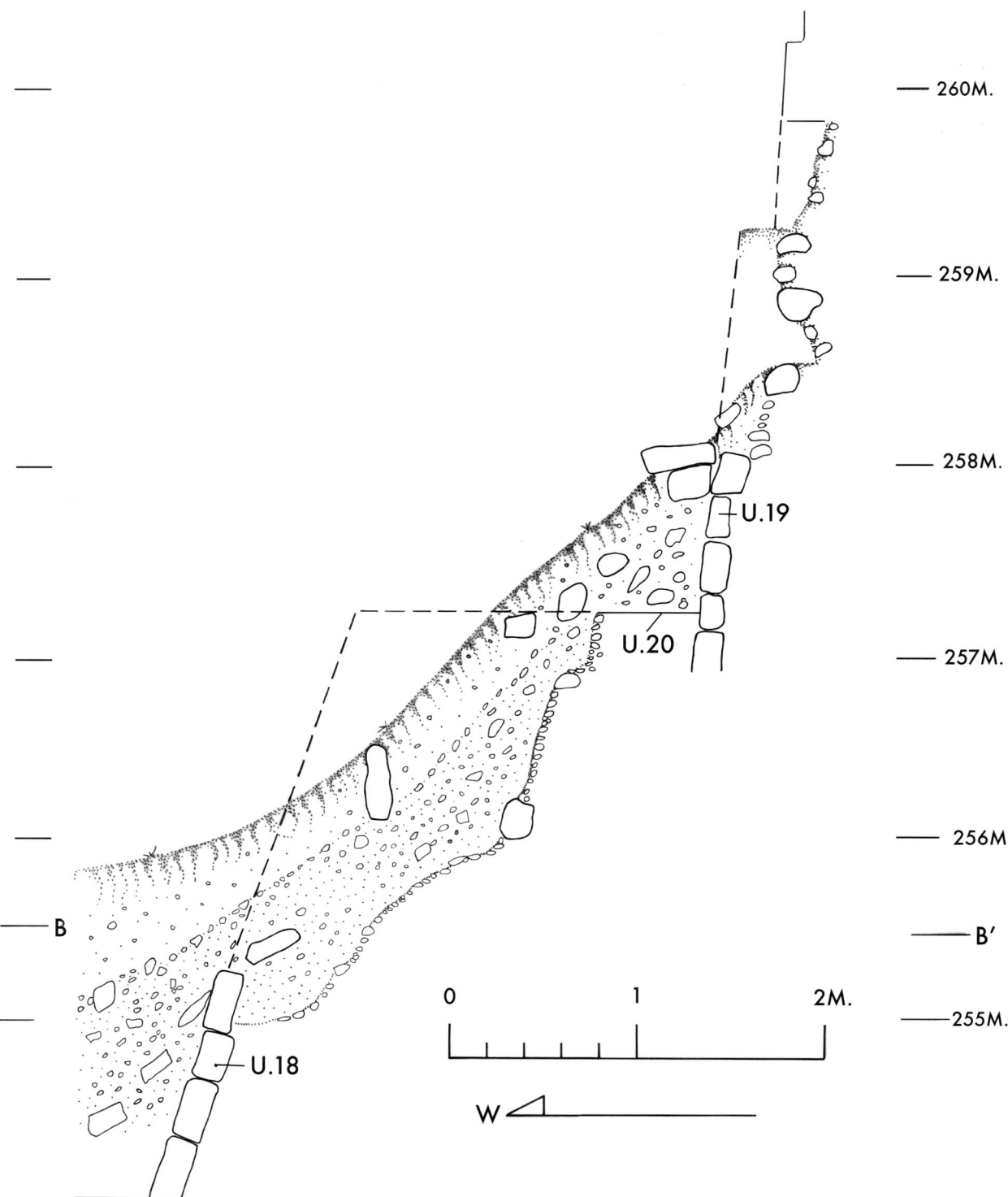

Str. 5D-15: Section B-B′ into W end wall (see Fig. 17 for location). U. 18, Veneer of lower terrace level; U. 19, Outer wall of upper terrace level. U. 20, Remnant of surface of lower terrace level.

FIGURE 21

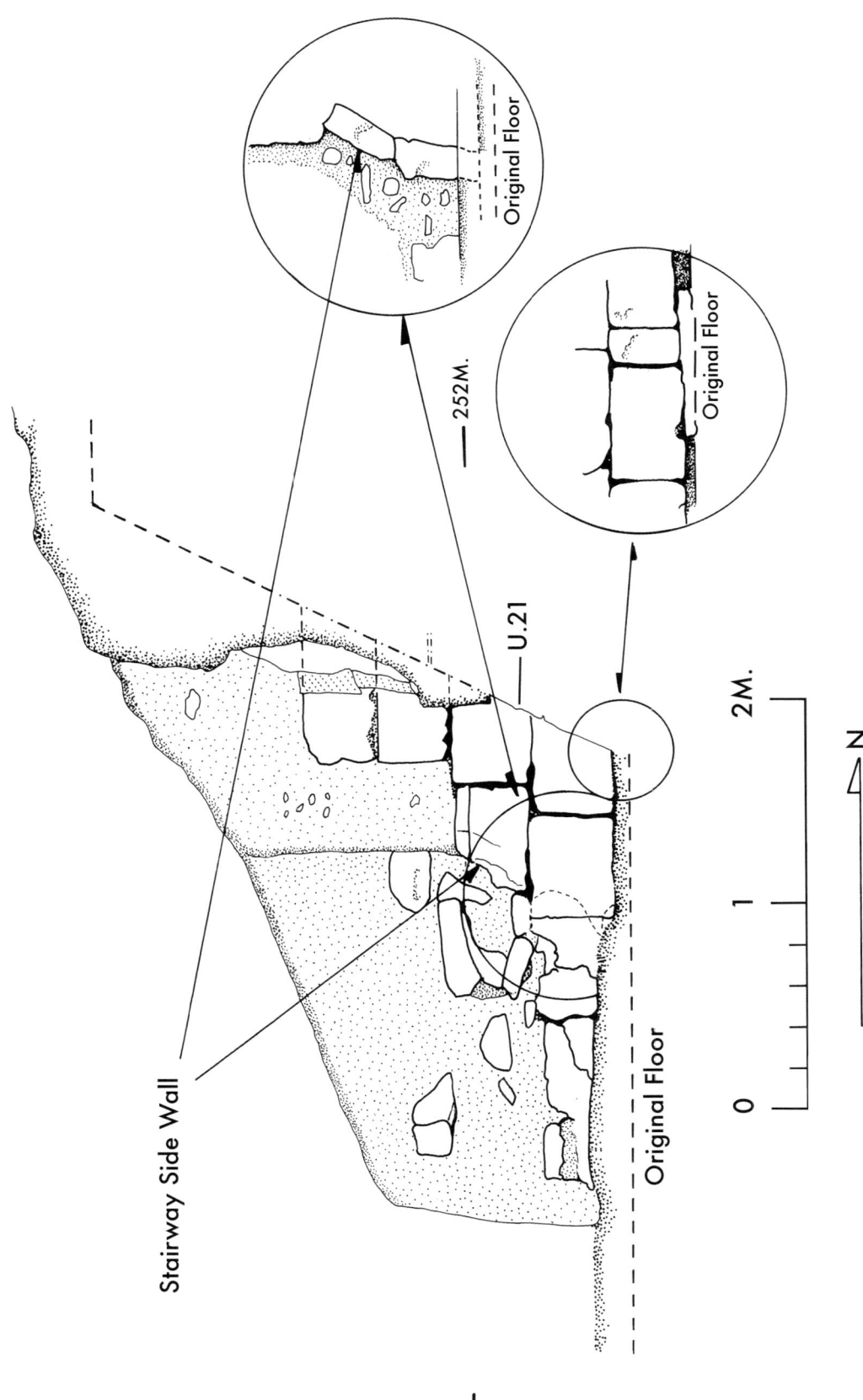

Str. 5D-15: Elevation of E stair wall and profile of U. 21 wall.

FIGURE 22

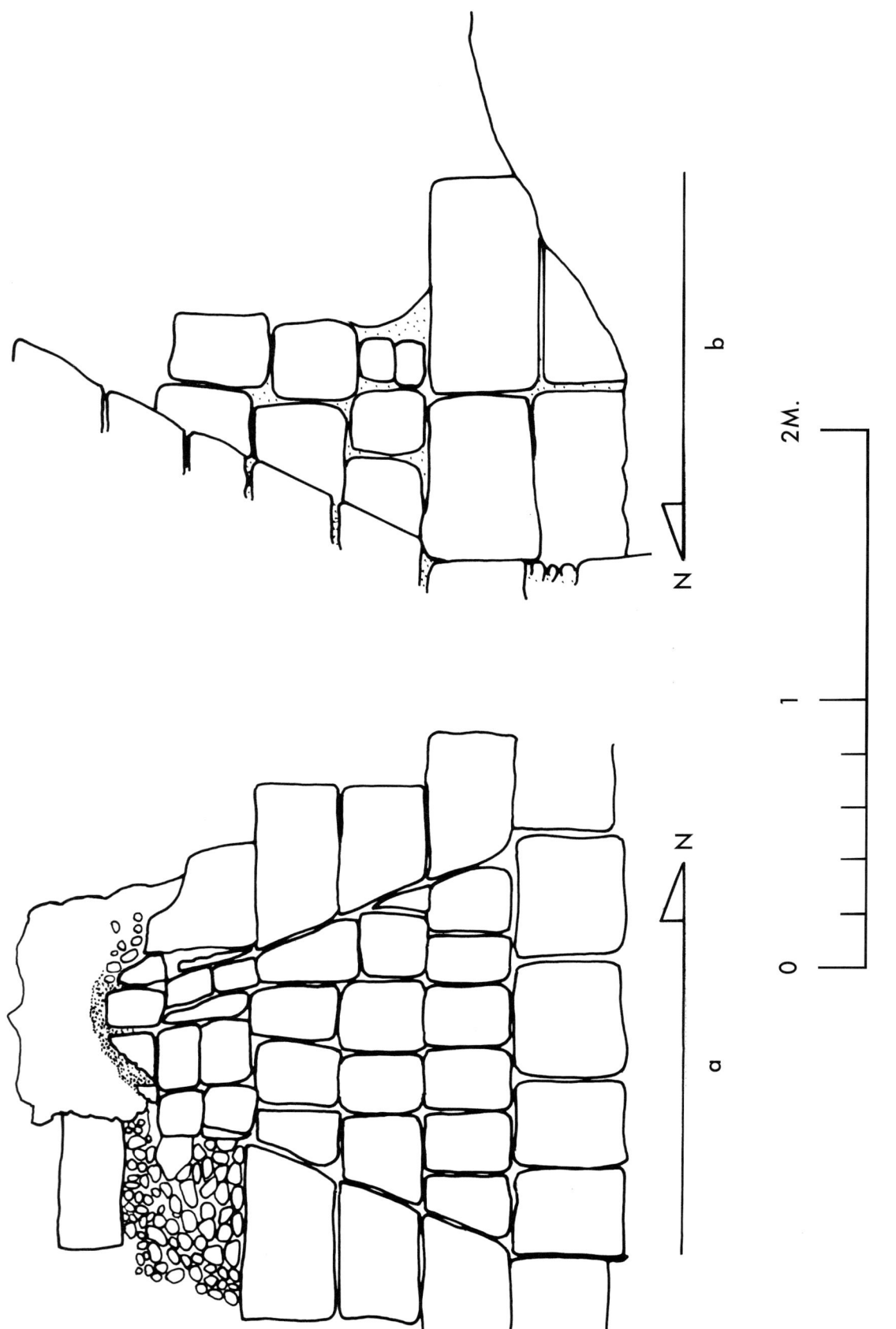

Str. 5D-15: (*a*) W end of front room vault looking W; (*b*) Profile of W end vault, rear room (see also Fig. 49c,d).

FIGURE 23

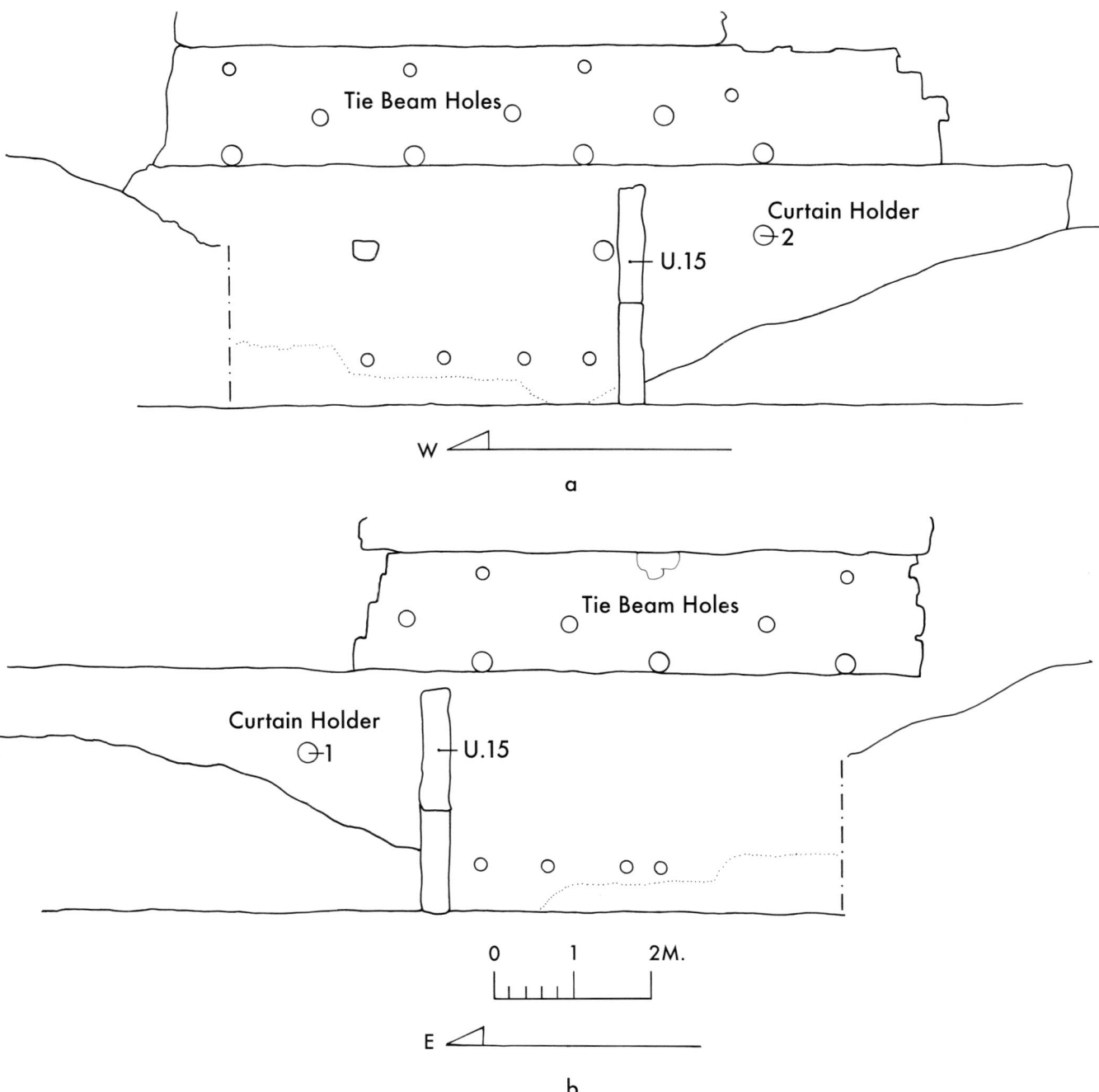

Str. 5D-15-1st: Elevation of N (*a*) and S (*b*) walls in the E end of the rear gallery showing the vault beam holes. *Pertinent to Str. 5D-15*: 1, 2, Curtain-holder holes opposite one another in the walls (not shown in Fig. 17). U. 15, Late partition defining 1st-A (see Fig. 17, 50a).

FIGURE 24

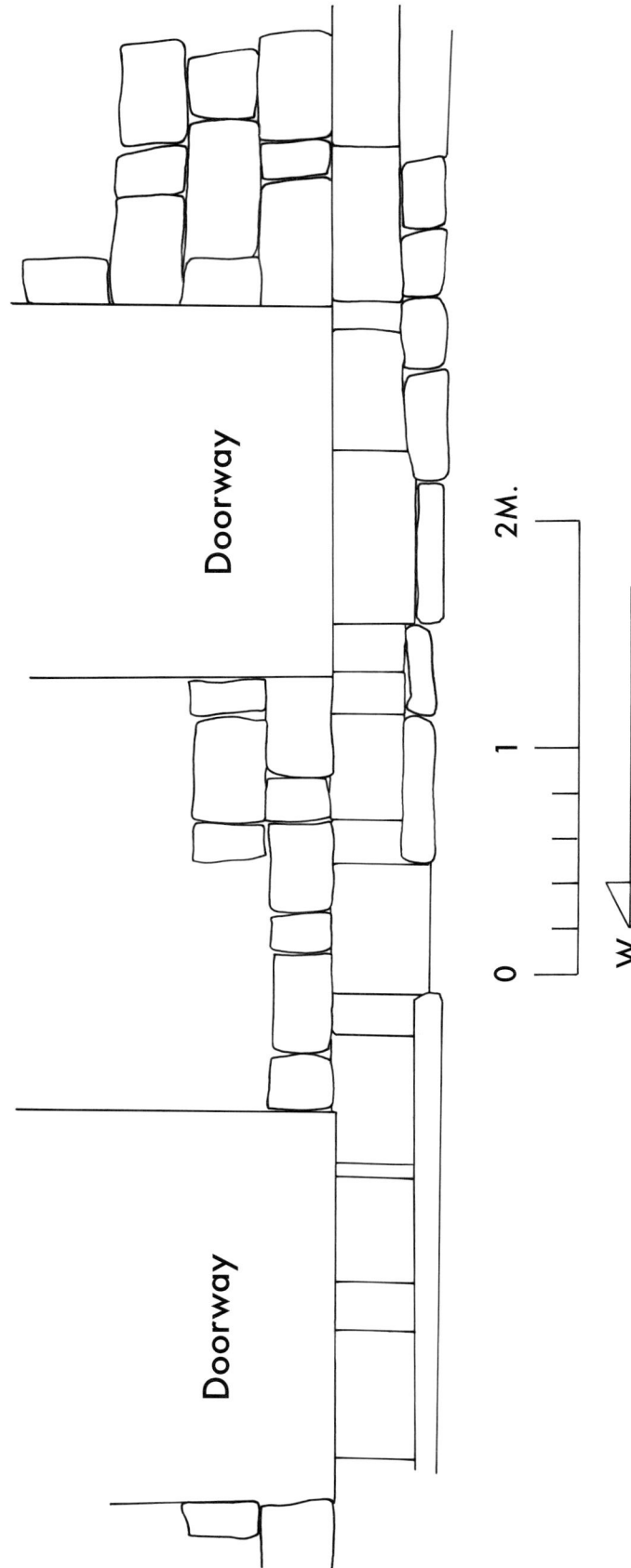

Str. 5D-15: Elevation showing W end of building facade (see also Fig. 49b).

FIGURE 25

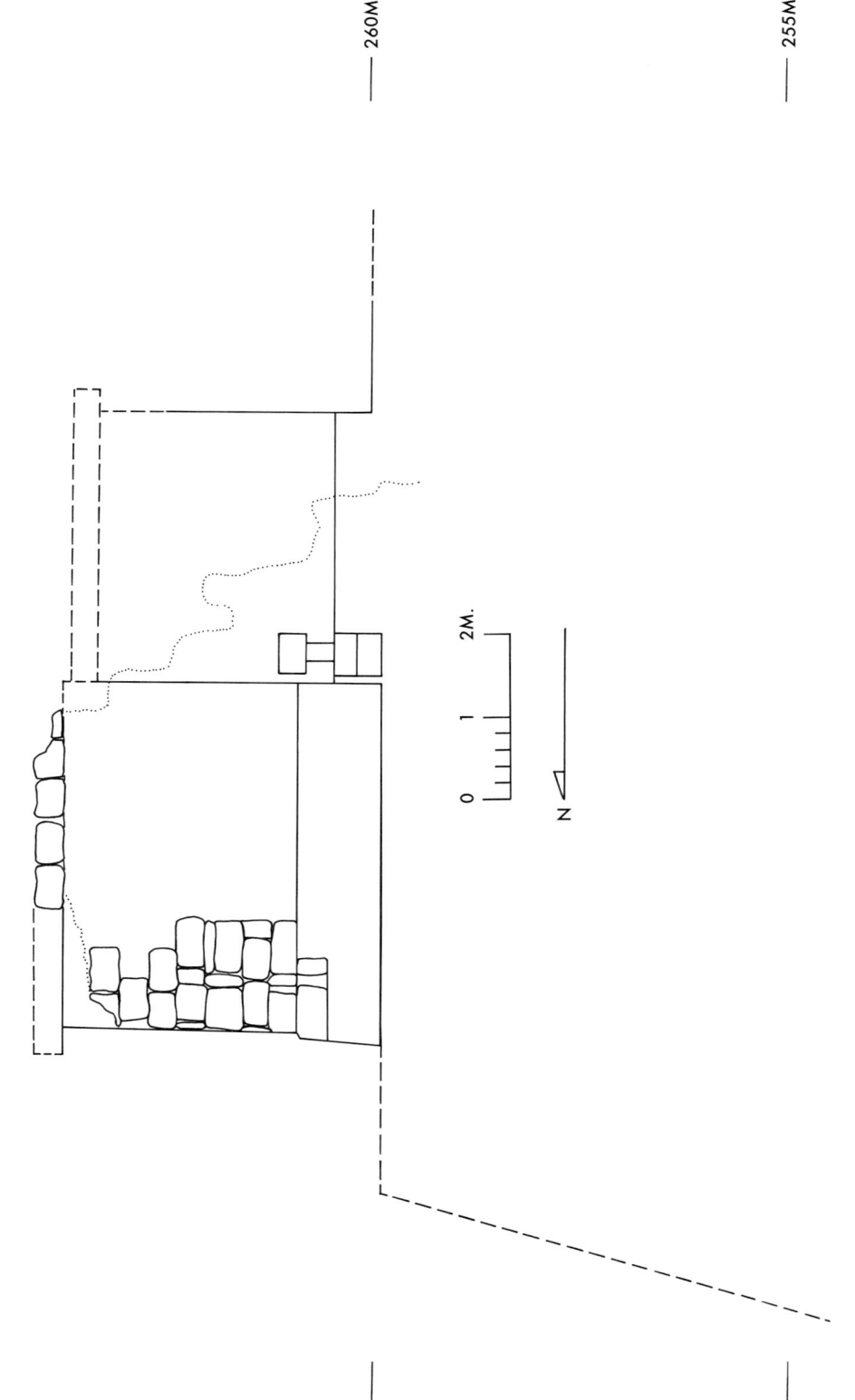

Str. 5D-15: Surviving upper zone masonry, exterior of W wall.

FIGURE 26

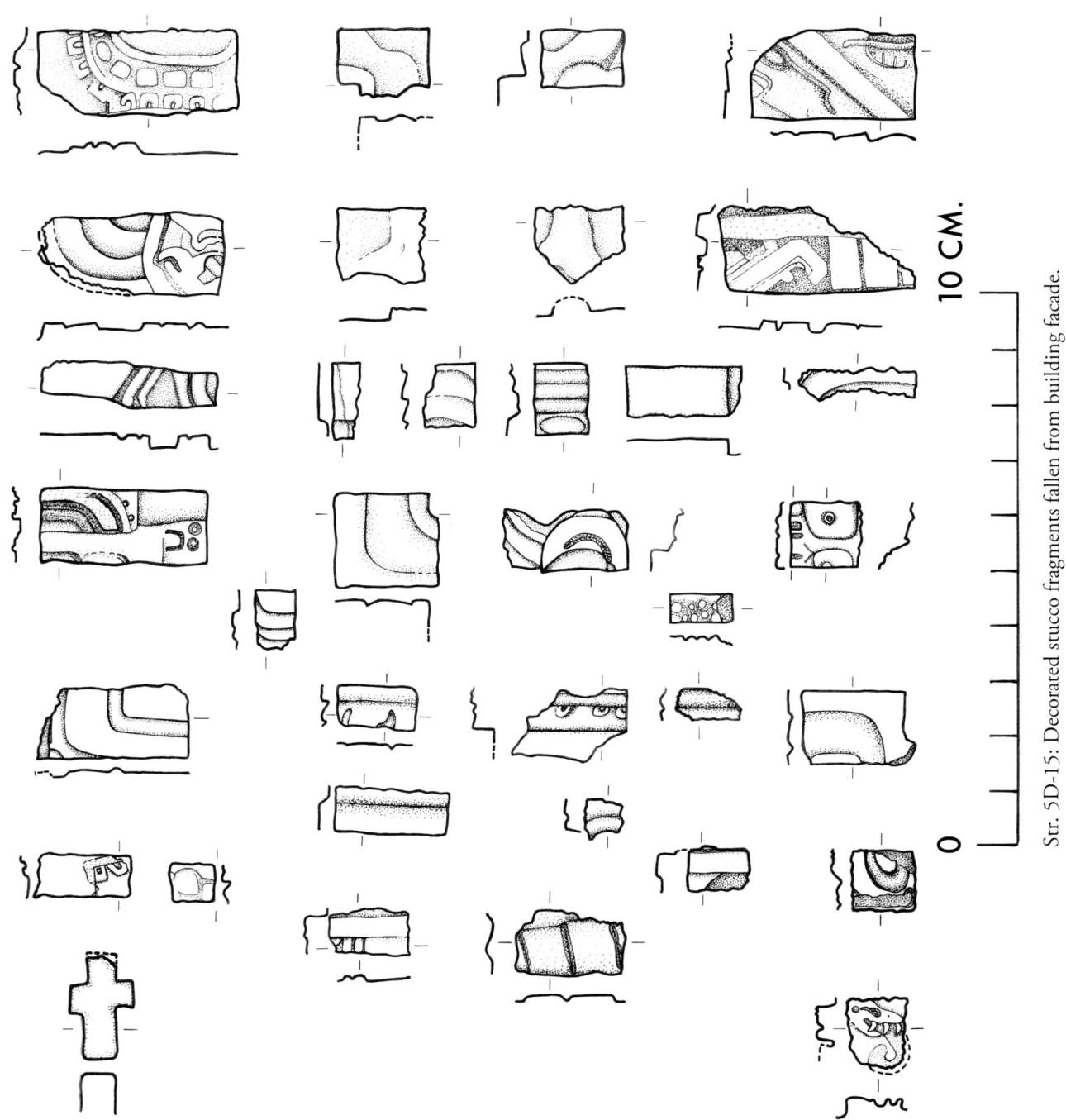

Str. 5D-15: Decorated stucco fragments fallen from building facade.

FIGURE 27

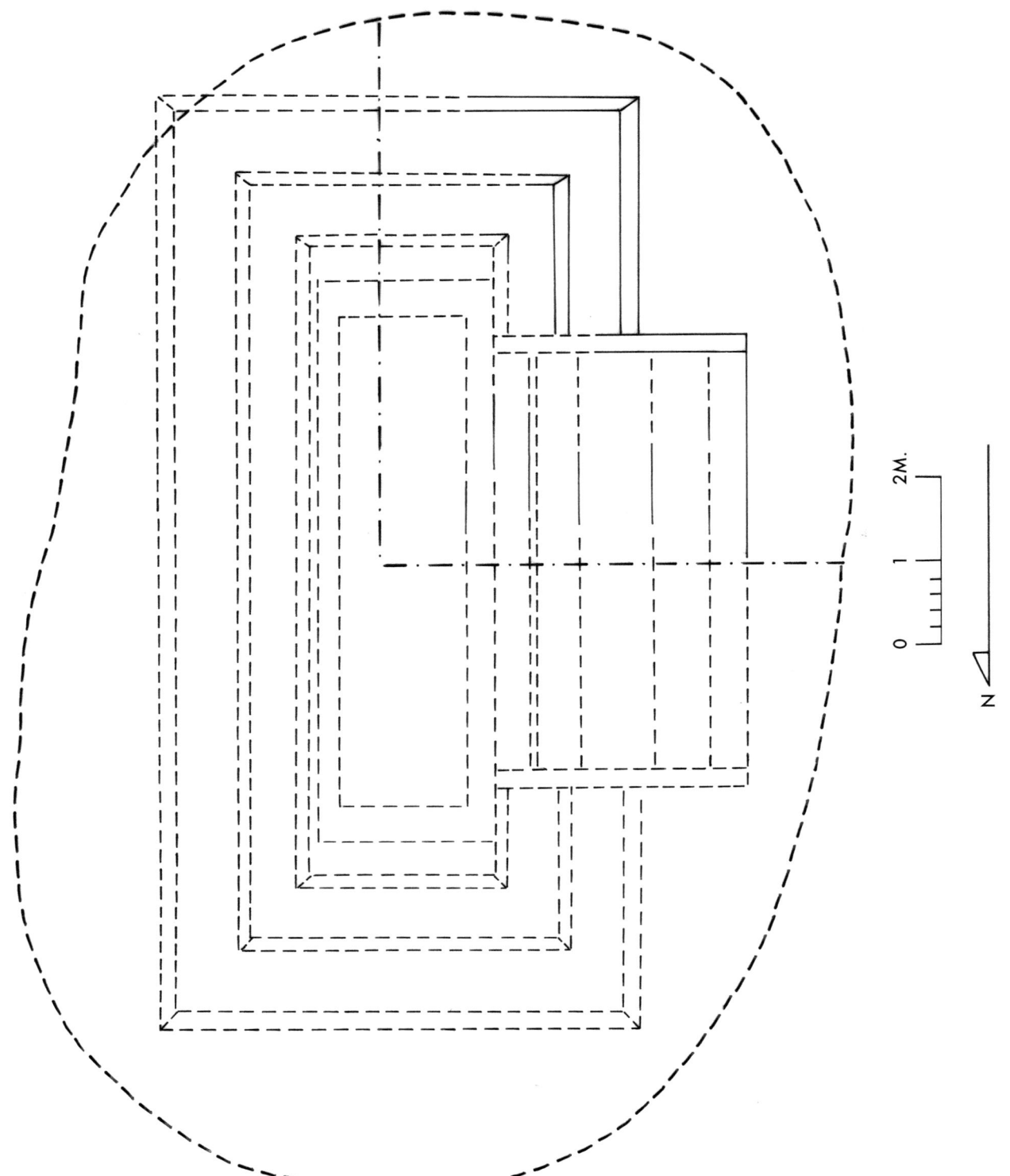

Str. 5D-19: Plan. Broken line surrounding the structure is the base of the ruin mound. For detail of SW quarter, see Fig. 28.

FIGURE 28

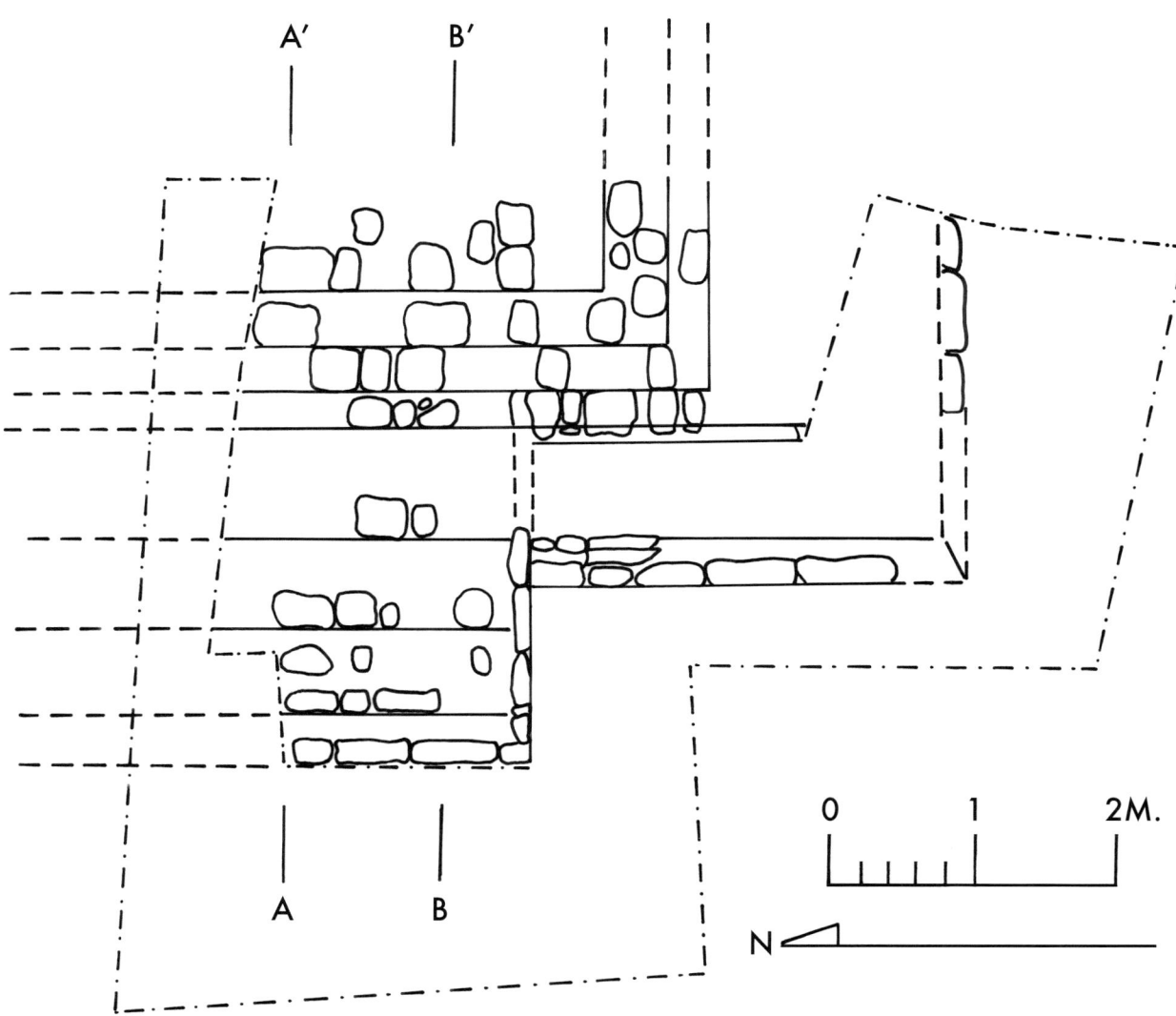

Str. 5D-19: Plan of SW quarter after surface clearing (see also Fig. 50d, 51a).

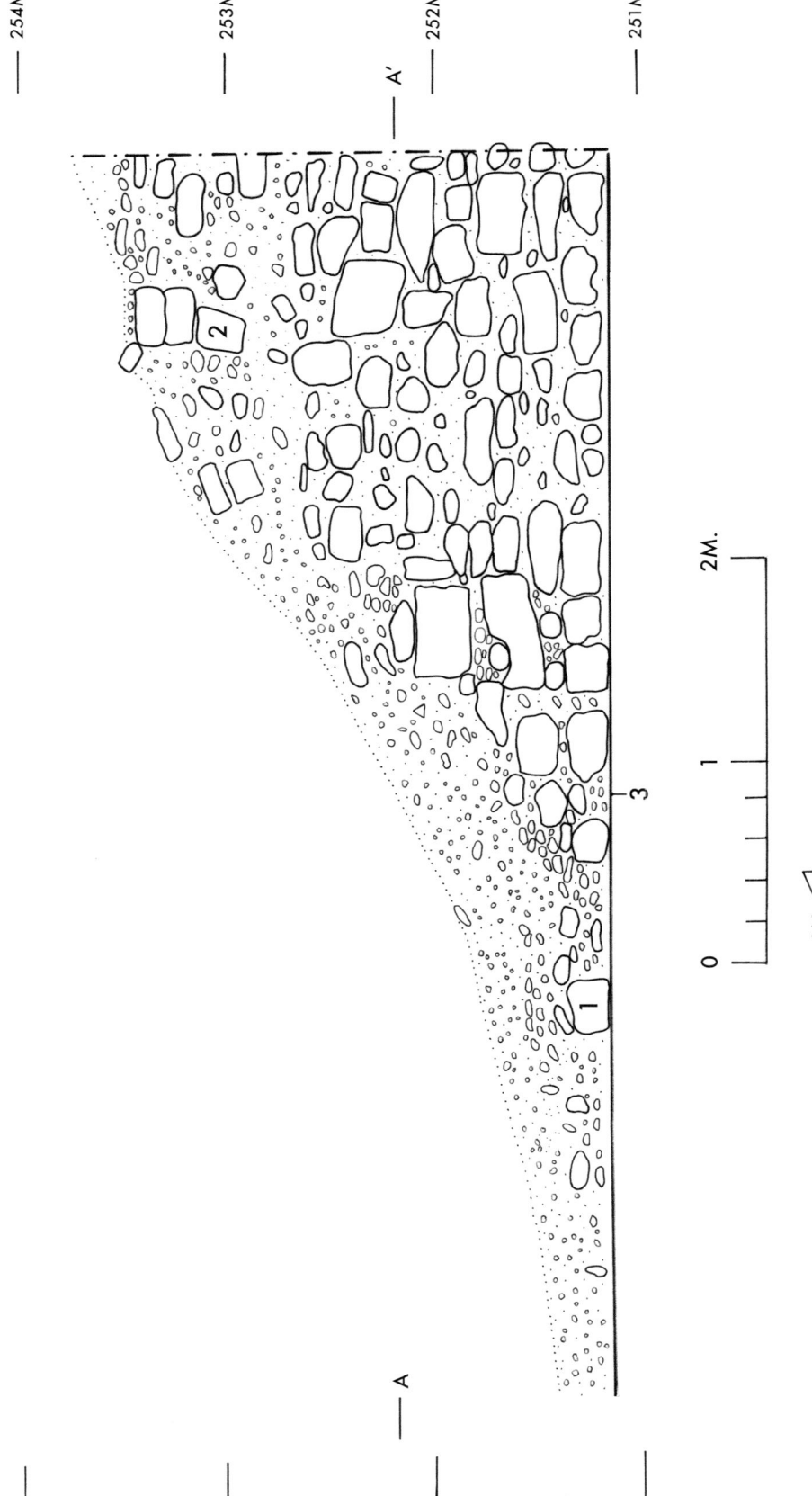

Str. 5D-19: Section A-A'. For location, see Fig. 28. *Pertinent to Str. 5D-11: 1*, First stair riser. *2*, Seventh stair riser with smooth face. *Pertinent to Plat. 5D-5: 3*, Floor of 1st.

FIGURE 30

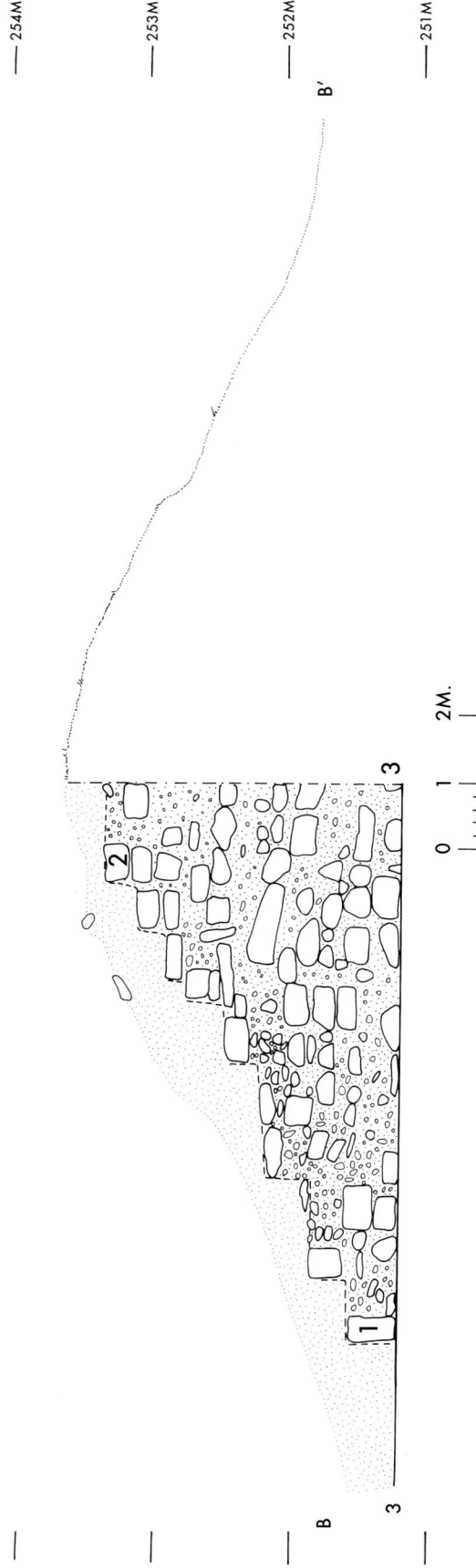

Str. 5D-19: Section B-B'. For location, see Fig. 28. Pertinent to Str. 5D-19: 1, 2, First and seventh stair risers (see Fig. 29). Pertinent to Plat. 5D-5: 3, Floor of 1st (see Fig. 29).

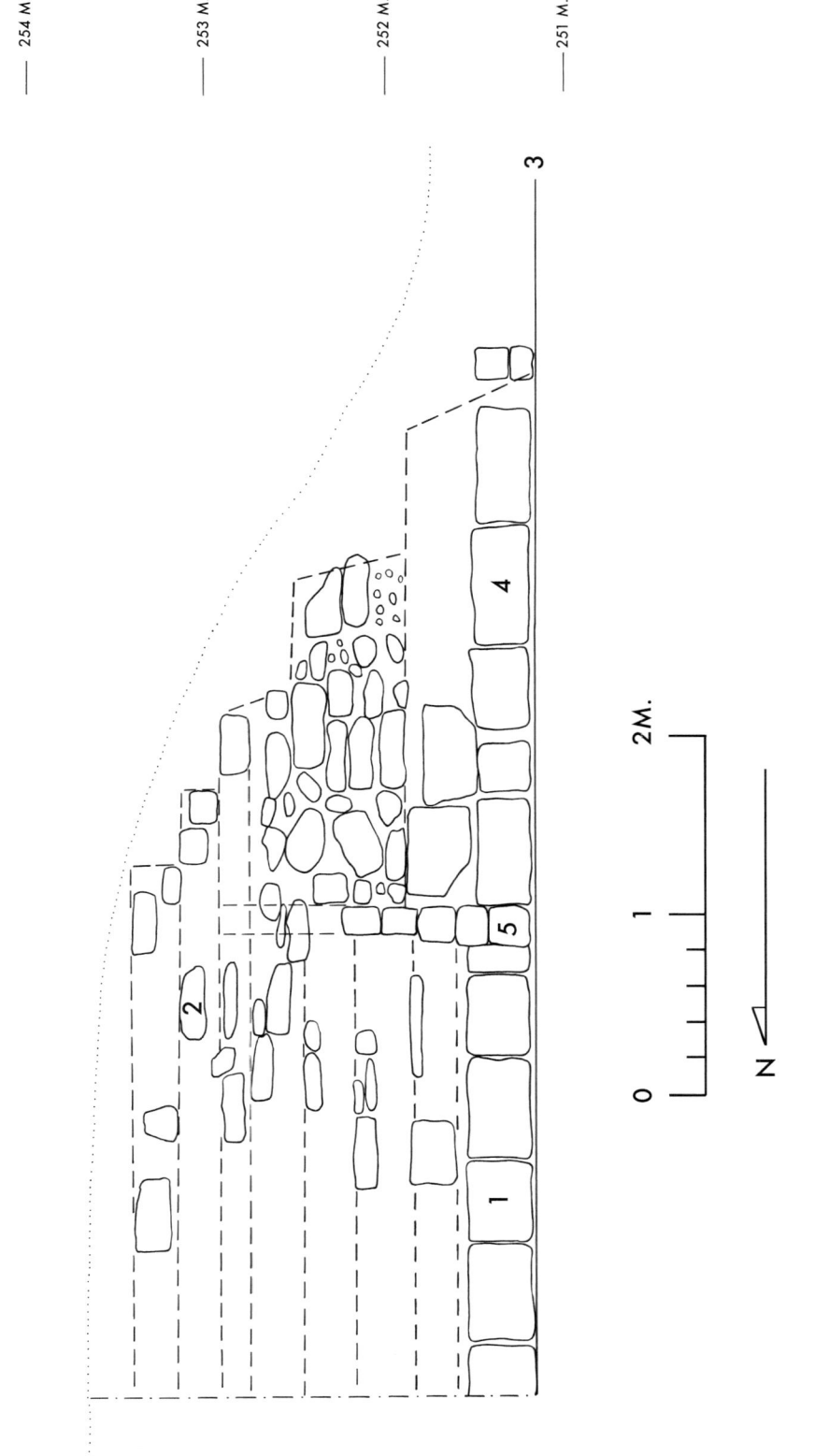

FIGURE 31

Str. 5D-19: Elevation of S half of facade.
Pertinent to Str. 5D-19: 1, 2, First and seventh stair risers (Fig. 29, 30). *4,* Masonry veneer of lowest terrace level of structure. *Pertinent to Plat. 5D-5: 3,* Floor of 1st. *5,* S end wall of stairway.

FIGURE 32

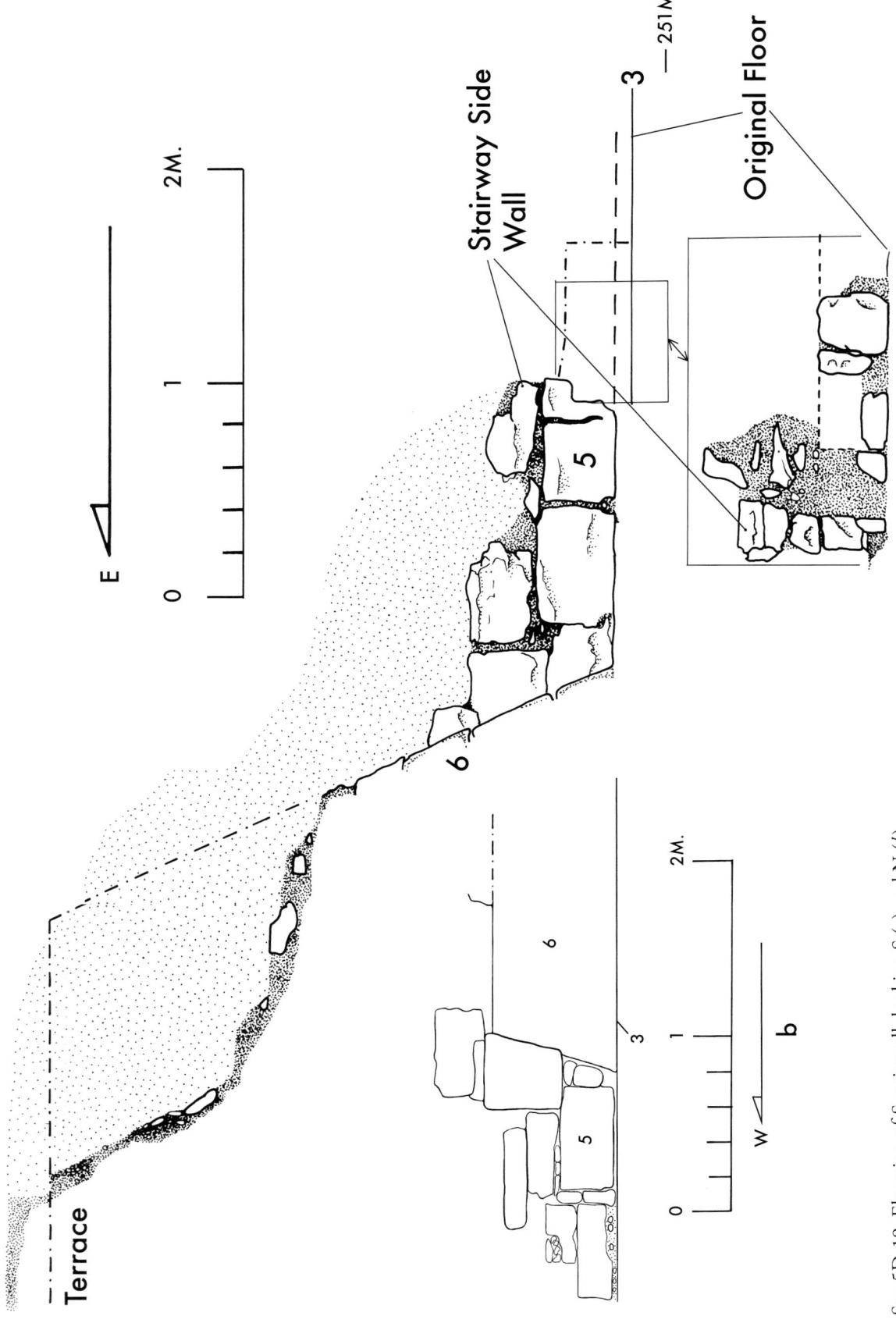

Str. 5D-19: Elevation of S stair wall, looking S (*a*) and N (*b*).
Pertinent to Str. 5D-19: 5, S end of stairs (Fig. 31). 6, Lowest terrace level of structure.
Pertinent to Plat. 5D-5: 3, Floor of 1st.

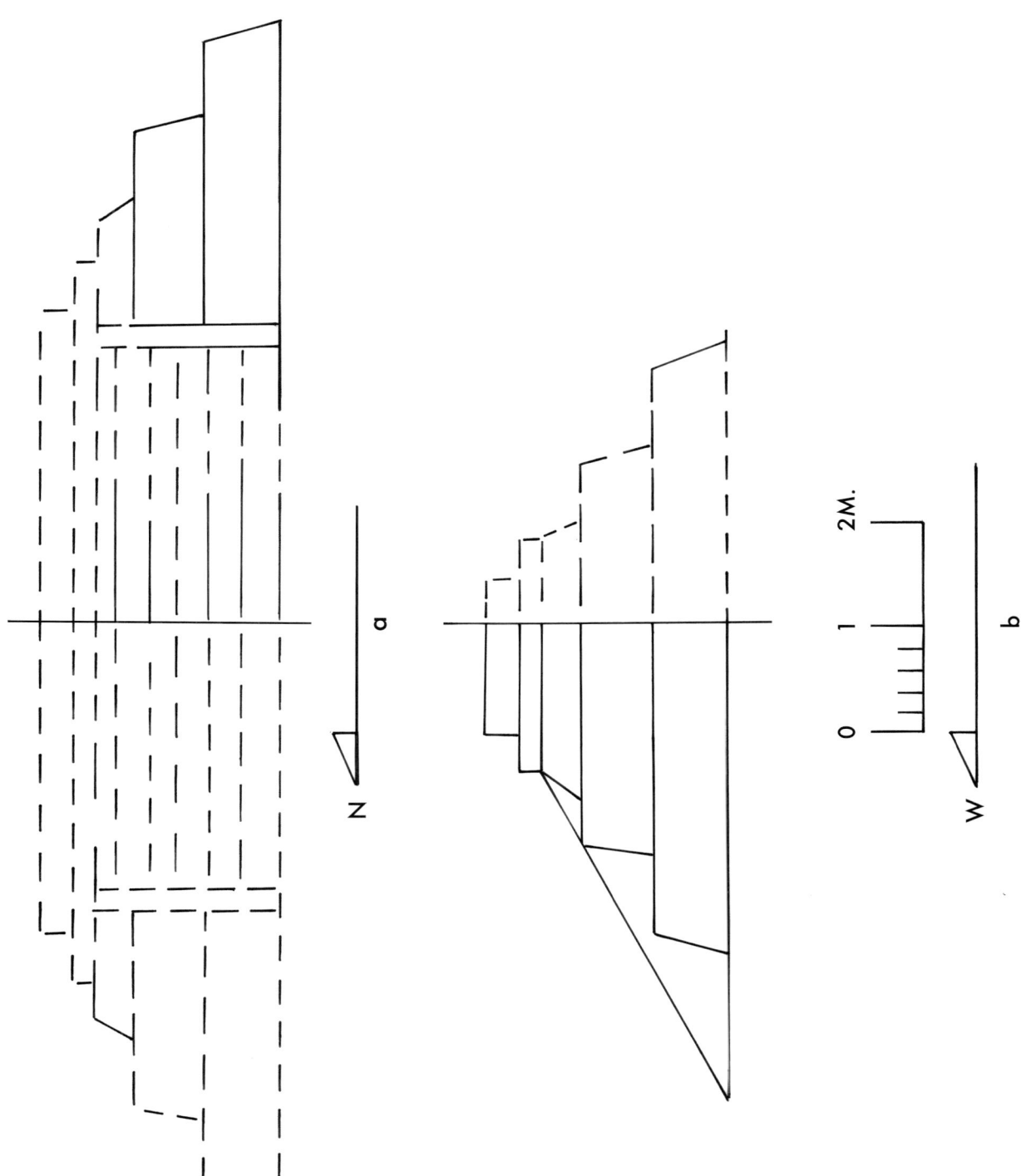

Str. 5D-19: Reconstruction drawings of the front (*a*) and S end (*b*).

Bu. 77 (*a*) and Ca. 167 (*b*): Plans, as located in Fig. 11 and 16.
(*a*) Bu. 77. *1–6*, Pottery vessels; *7*, *Spondylus* shell; *8*, Rectangular bead and pearl; *9*, Jade bead; *10*, Jade pendant; *11*, Jade flares from beneath the skull; *12*, Composite ear ornaments; *13*, Jade and *Spondylus* beads by left wrist. For photos, see Fig. 45b–d, 46a,b. b. Ca. 167. *1*, Pottery vessel; *2*, Masonry block beside jar; *3*, Deep pit beneath cache. Plat. 5D-1:U. 36 is an early wall encountered by the Maya when digging the pit. For photo, see Fig. 50c.

FIGURE 34

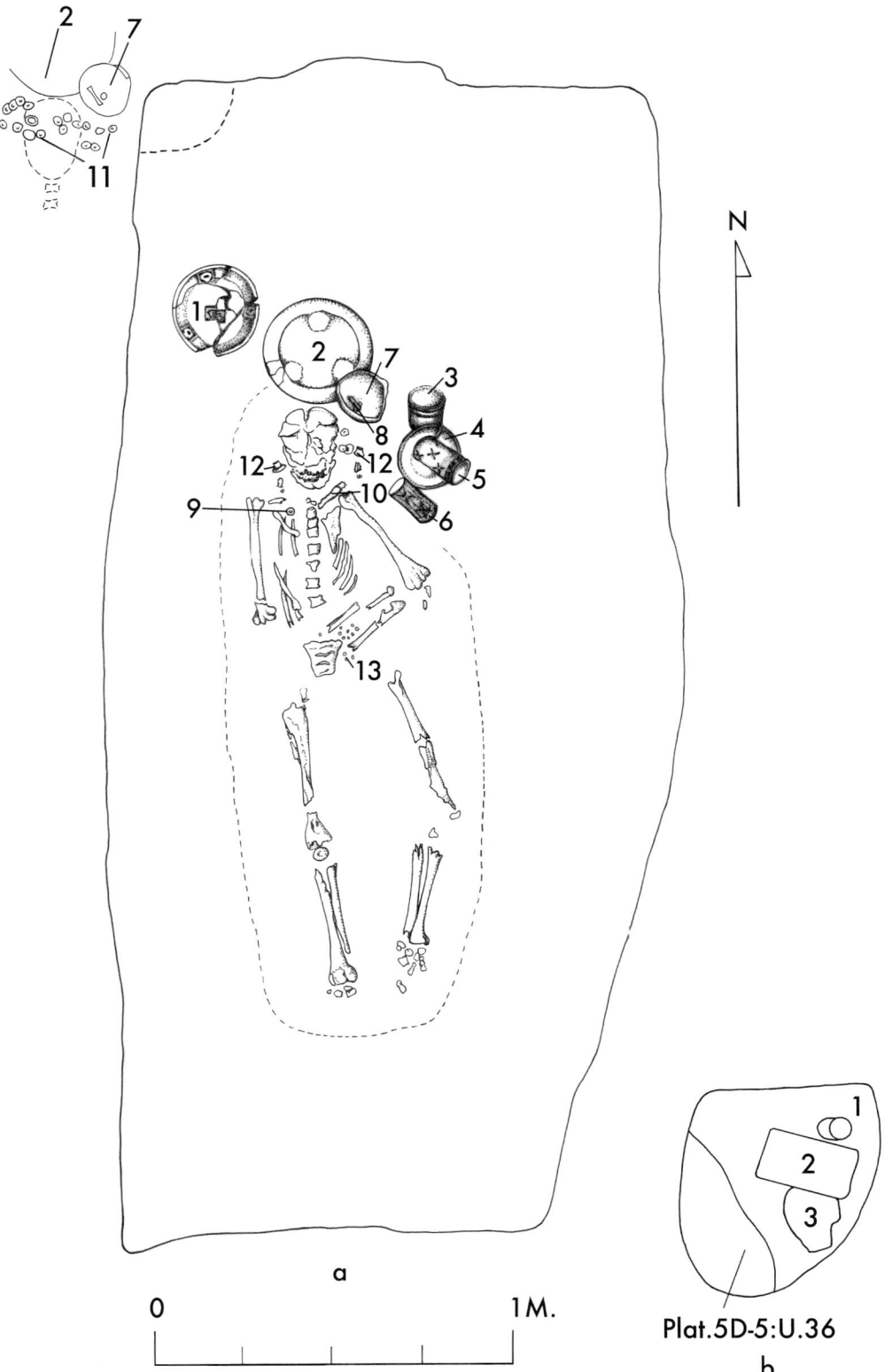

a

0　　　　　　　　1M.

Plat.5D-5:U.36

b

St. P30, P31, and MS. 38 (Frag. 2 of St. P21) and Alt. P26: Plan (*a*) and Section A-A′ (*b*). For sections B-B′ and C-C′, see Fig. 36.
Pertinent to Plat. 5D-5: U. 1, Floor for 2nd; U. 2, Projected level of floor for 3rd; U. 3, 4, Floors for 4th and 5th, respectively. Cache 84 was on and slightly below U. 3.

FIGURE 35

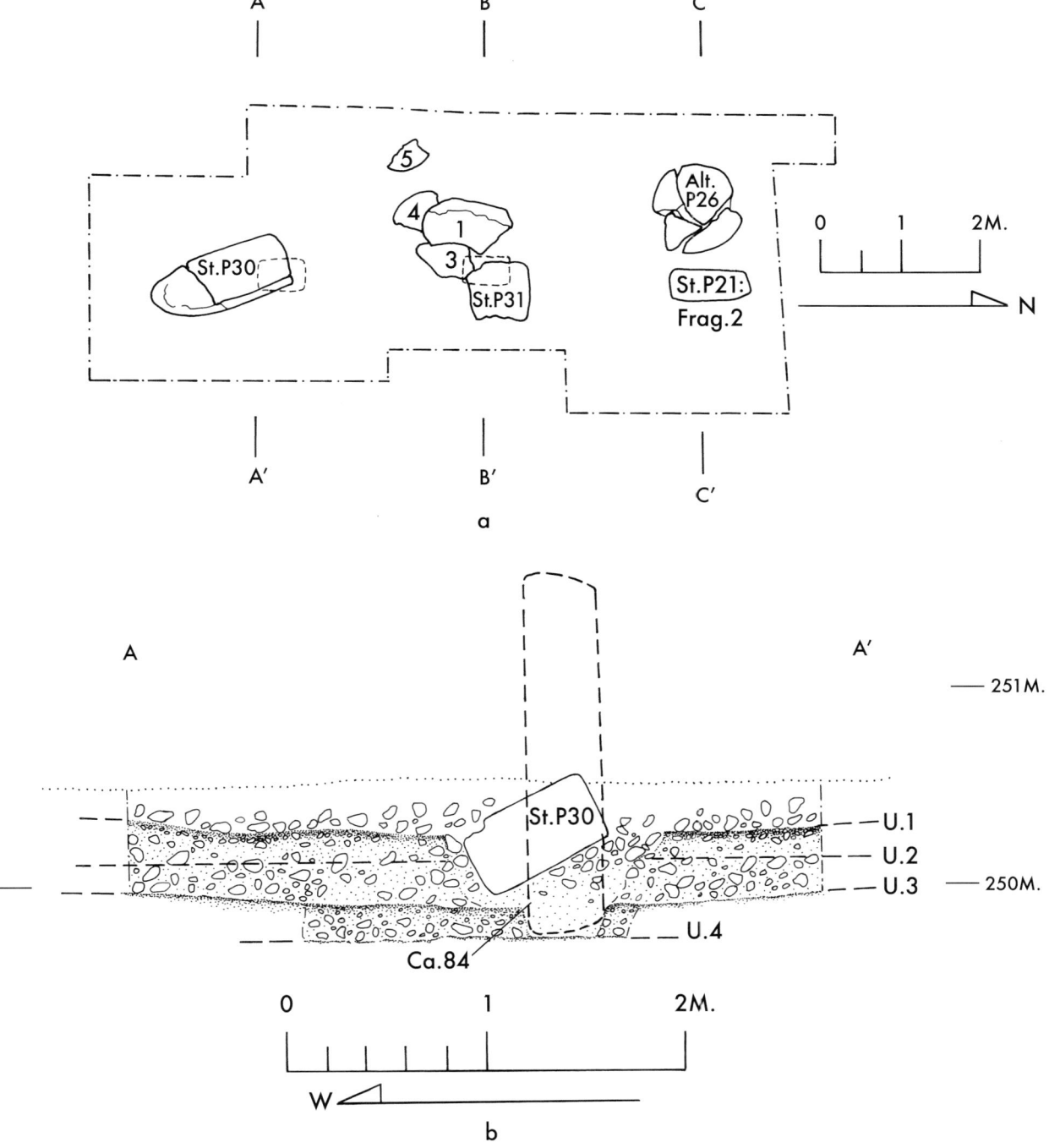

St. P31: Section B-B′ (*a*) and Reconstruction (*b*); MS. 38 (St. P21, Frag. 2) with Alt. P26, Section C-C′ (*c*), as located in Fig. 35a.
Pertinent to Plat. 5D-5: U. 1–4 (see Fig. 35a). Cache 94 was beneath the butt (Frag. 2) of St. P21; Ca. 95 below the rounded butt of St. P31, principally on the N side.

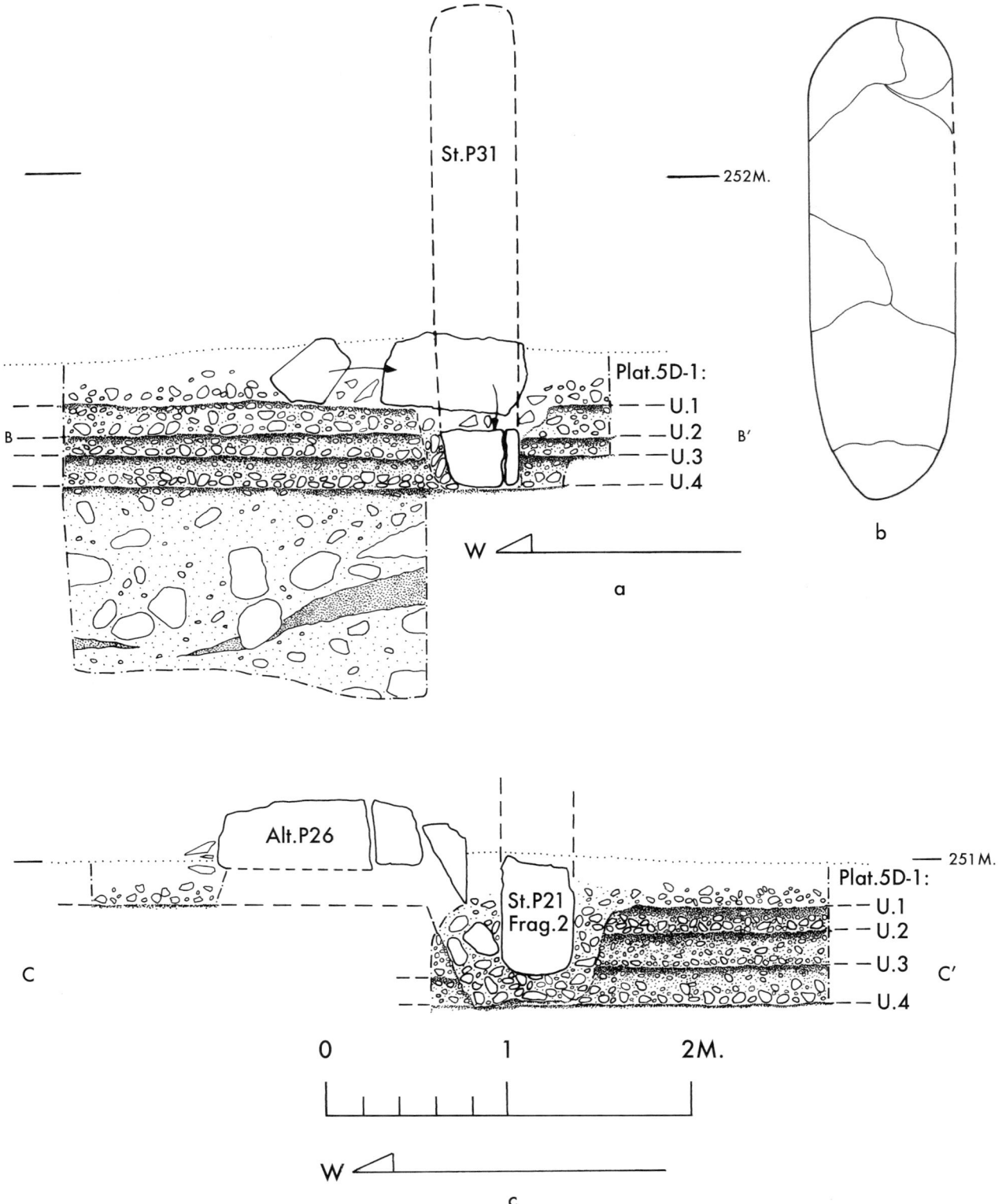
FIGURE 36

St. 15 and Alt. P28: Plan (*a*) and Section (*b*) of excavation; Section of stela (*c*). The stela setting in b is reconstructed.
Pertinent to Plat. 5D-5: U. 5, Floor of 2nd (Fig. 3–8); U. 6, Floor of 3rd (Fig. 4–7); U. 19, Floor of 1st (Fig. 5, 6). The pit shown SW of the one for St. 15 may have been for another monument. For photo of St. 15, see Fig. 51c; for Alt. P28, see Fig. 52c.

FIGURE 37

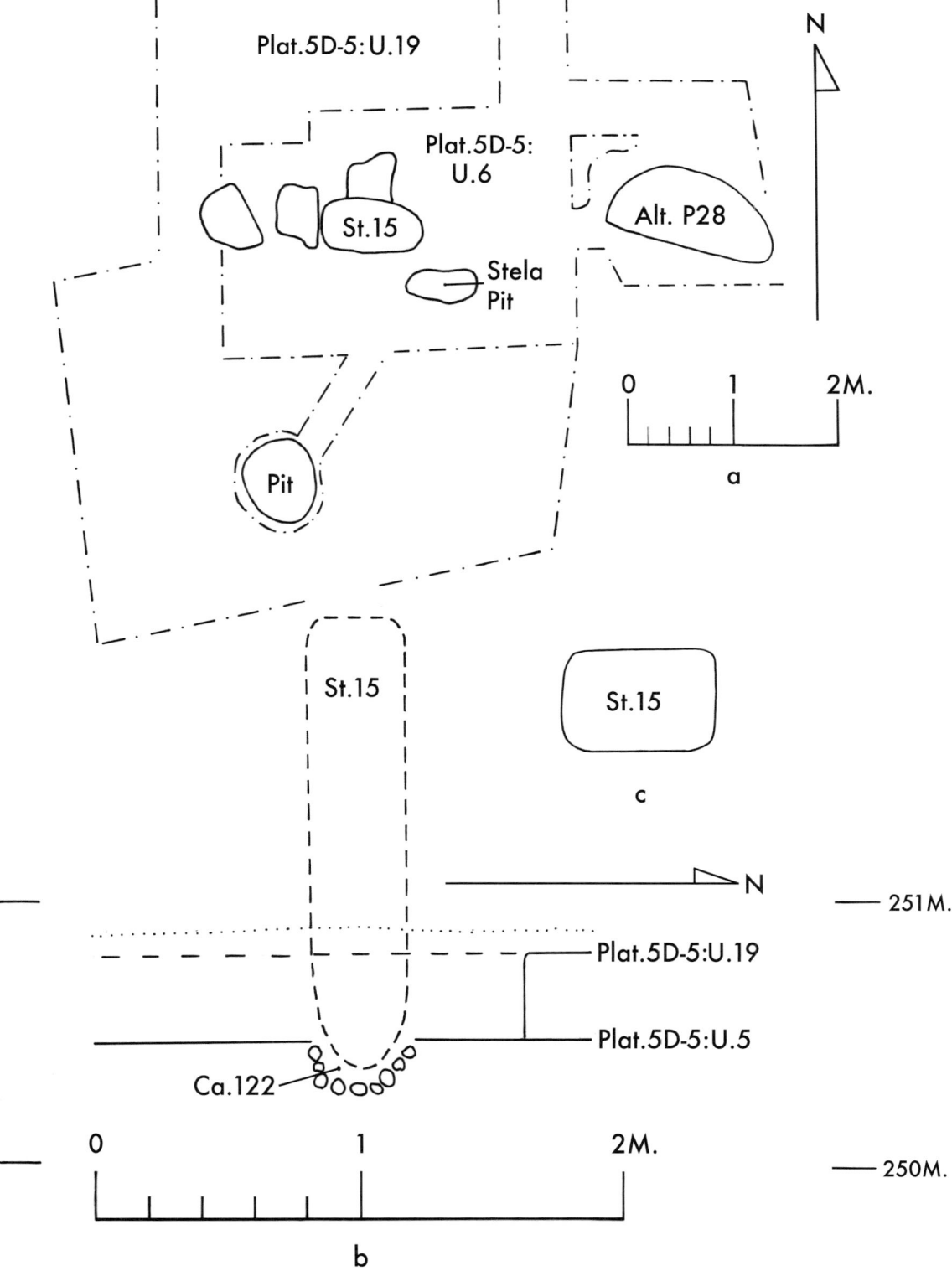

FIGURE 38

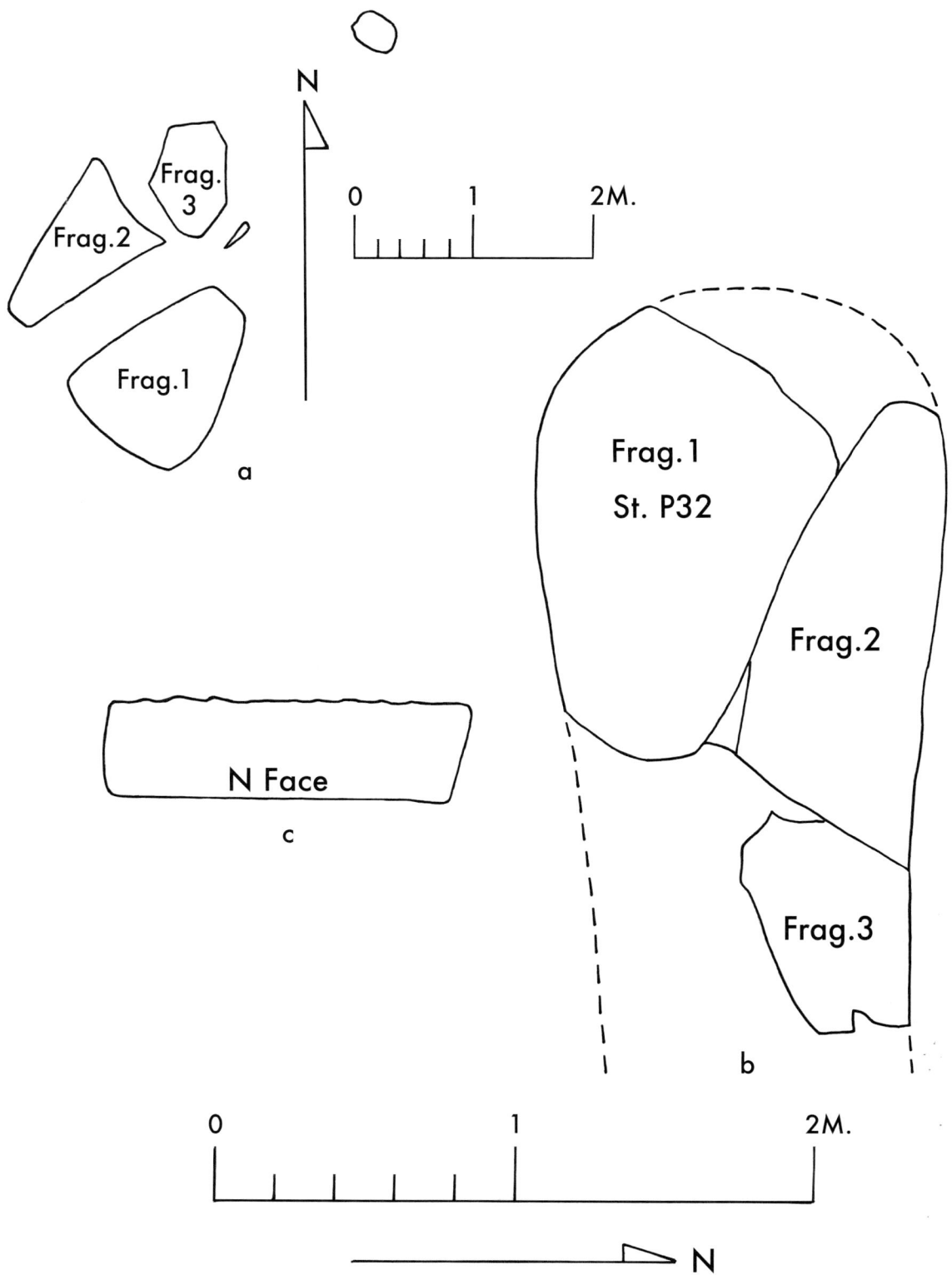

St. P32 fragments as found (*a*) and reconstructed (*b*); section through monument (*c*). For section through excavation, see Fig. 5b, 8a. For photo, see Fig. 51d.

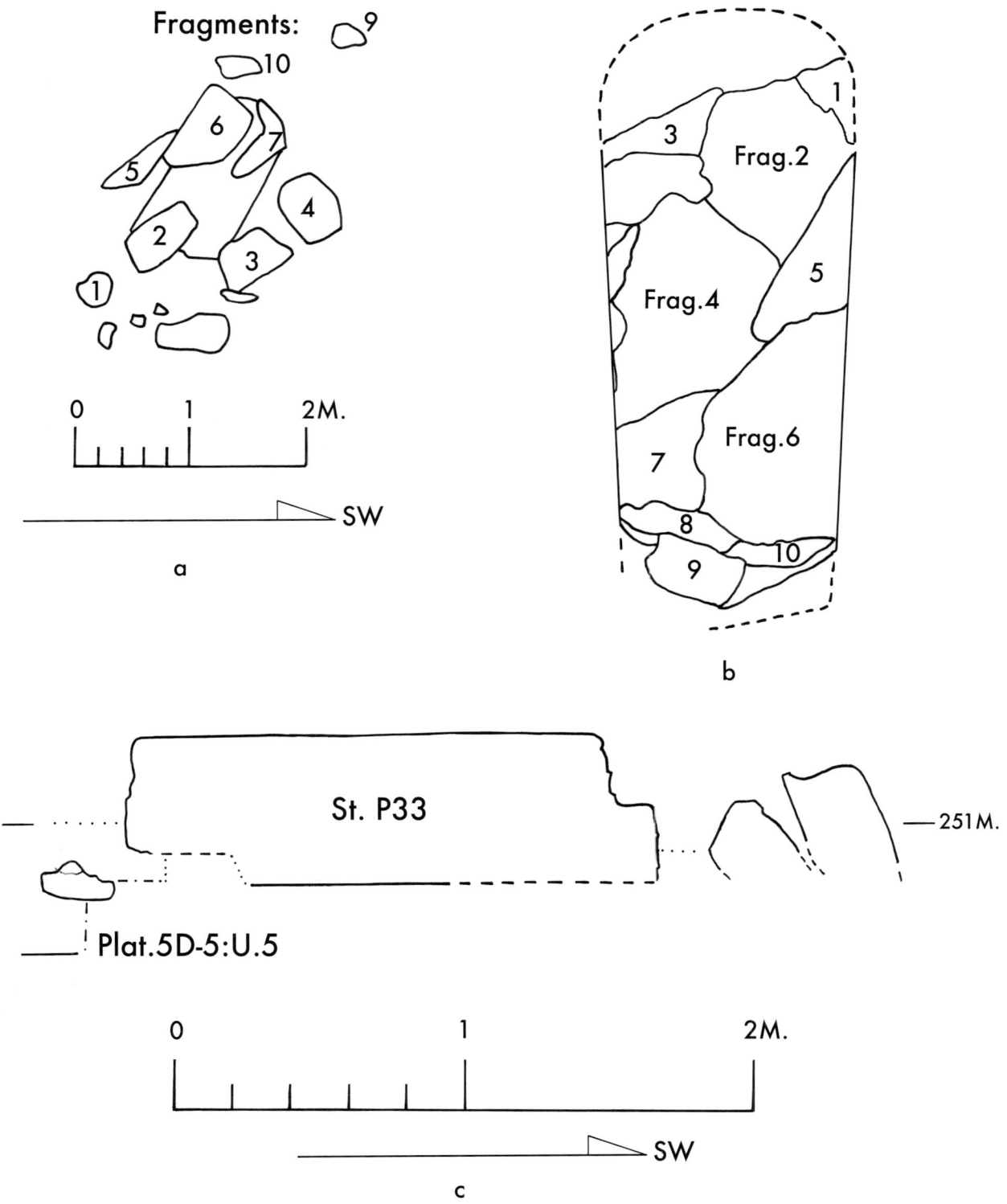

St. P33 fragments as found (*a*) and reconstructed (*b*); section of excavation (*c*).
Pertinent to Plat. 5D-5: U. 5, Floor of 2nd. For another section, see Fig. 7; for photo, see Fig. 52a.

FIGURE 40

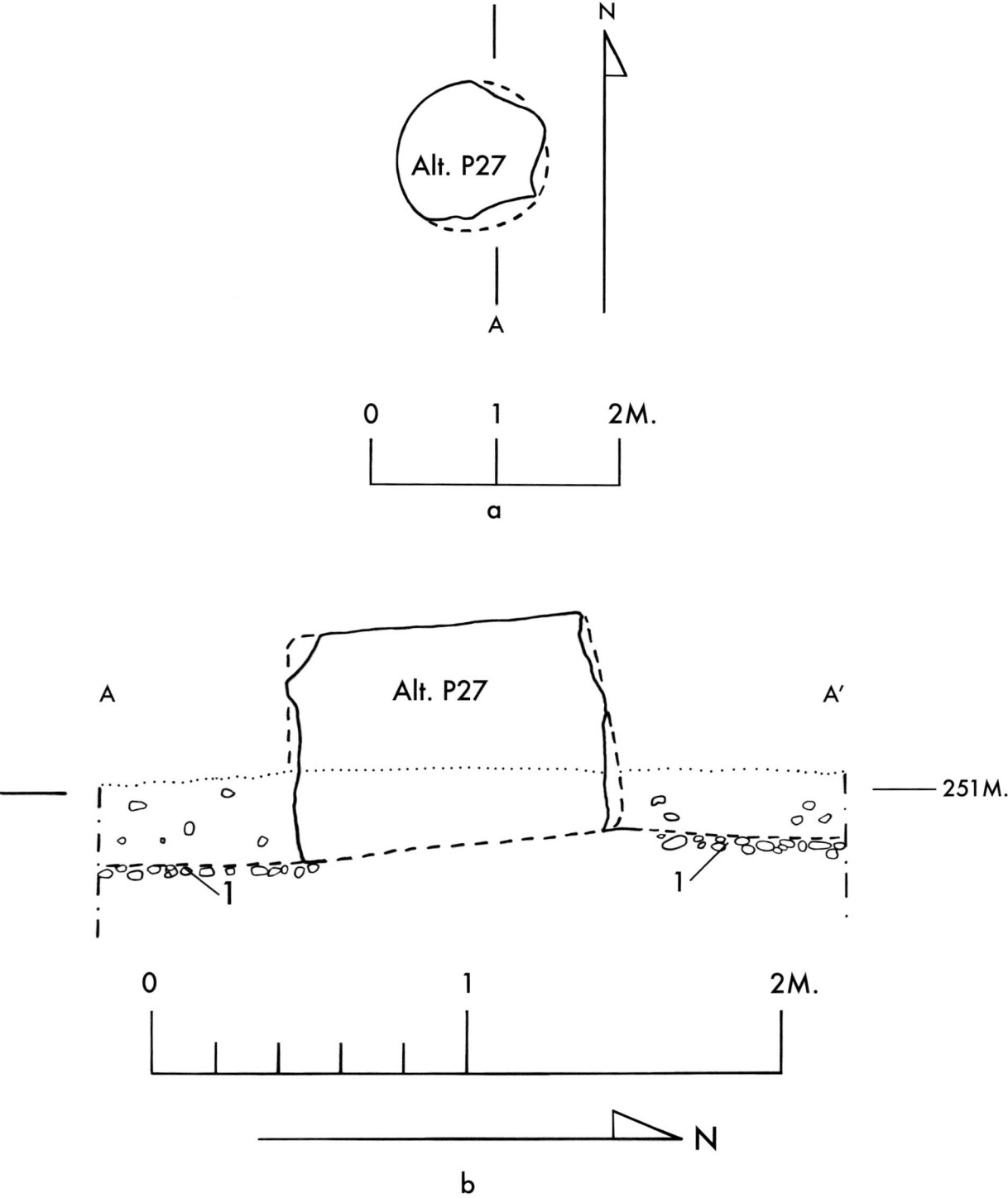

Alt. P27: Plan (*a*) and Section (*b*). See also Fig. 7. *Pertinent to Plat. 5D-5*: *1*, Compact limestone fragments remaining from a floor, probably U. 19. See also Fig. 7; for photo, see Fig. 52b.

FIGURE 41

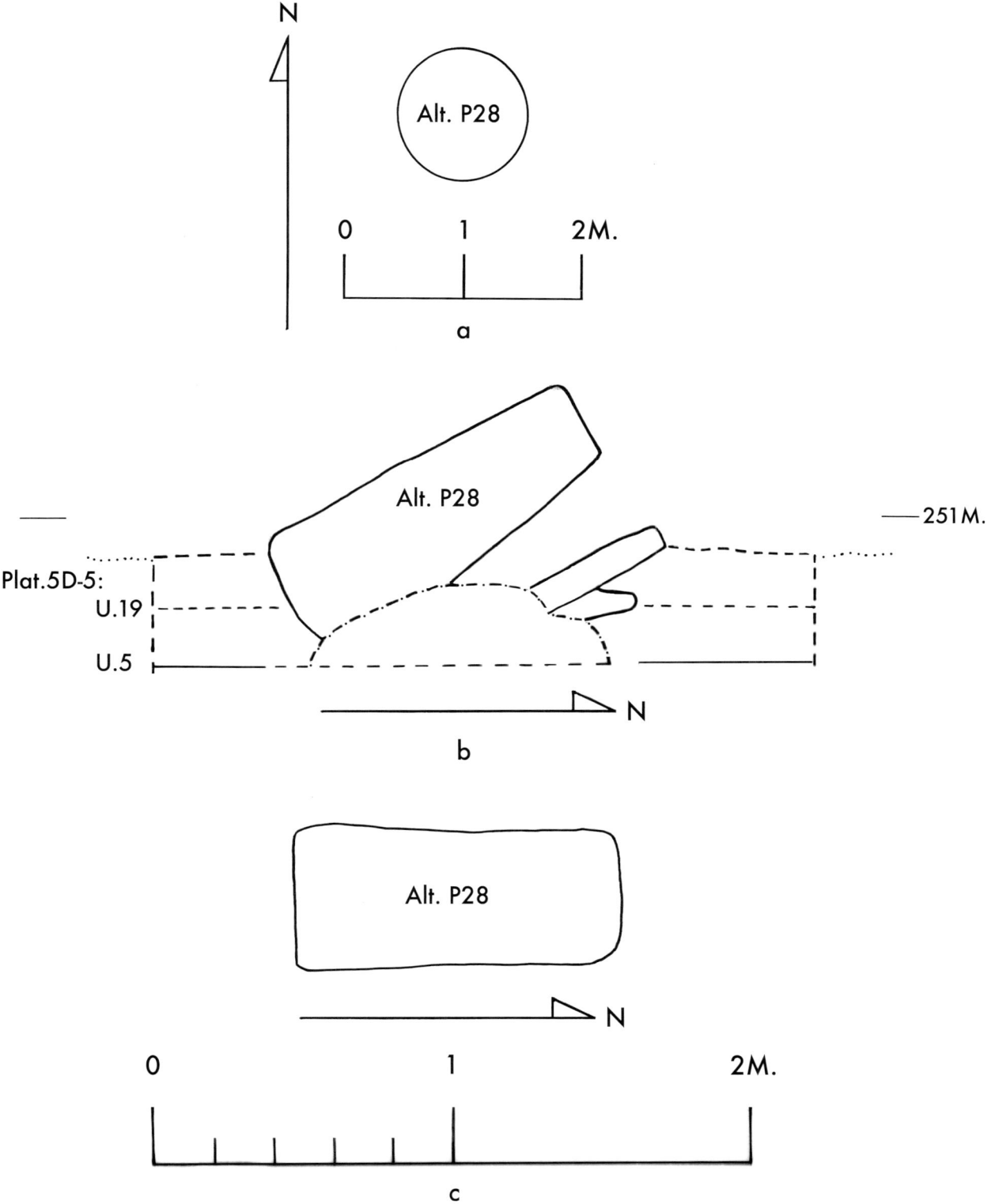

Alt. P28: Plan (*a*), Section of excavation (*b*) and Section of repaired altar (*c*).
Pertinent to Plat. 5D-5: U. 5, Floor of 2nd (Fig. 3–7); U. 19, Floor of 1st (Fig. 5, 6). For photo, see Fig. 52c.

FIGURE 42

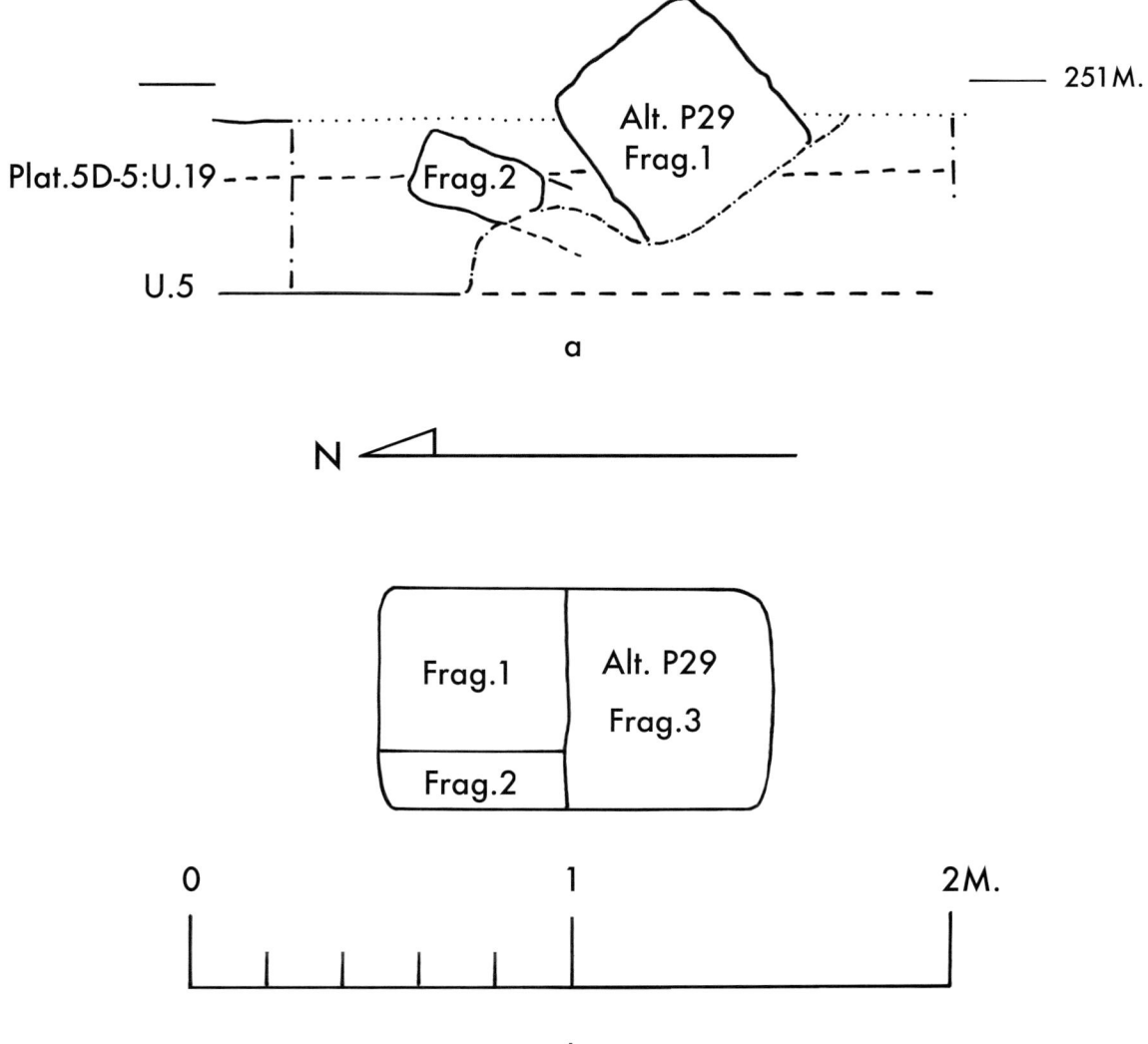

Alt. P29: Section of excavation (*a*), and repaired altar (*b*), as located in Fig. 43.
Pertinent to Plat. 5D-5: U. 5, Floor of 2nd (see Fig. 3–7); U. 19, Floor of 1st (Fig. 5, 6). A tree-fall has driven the altar down through this floor.

FIGURE 43

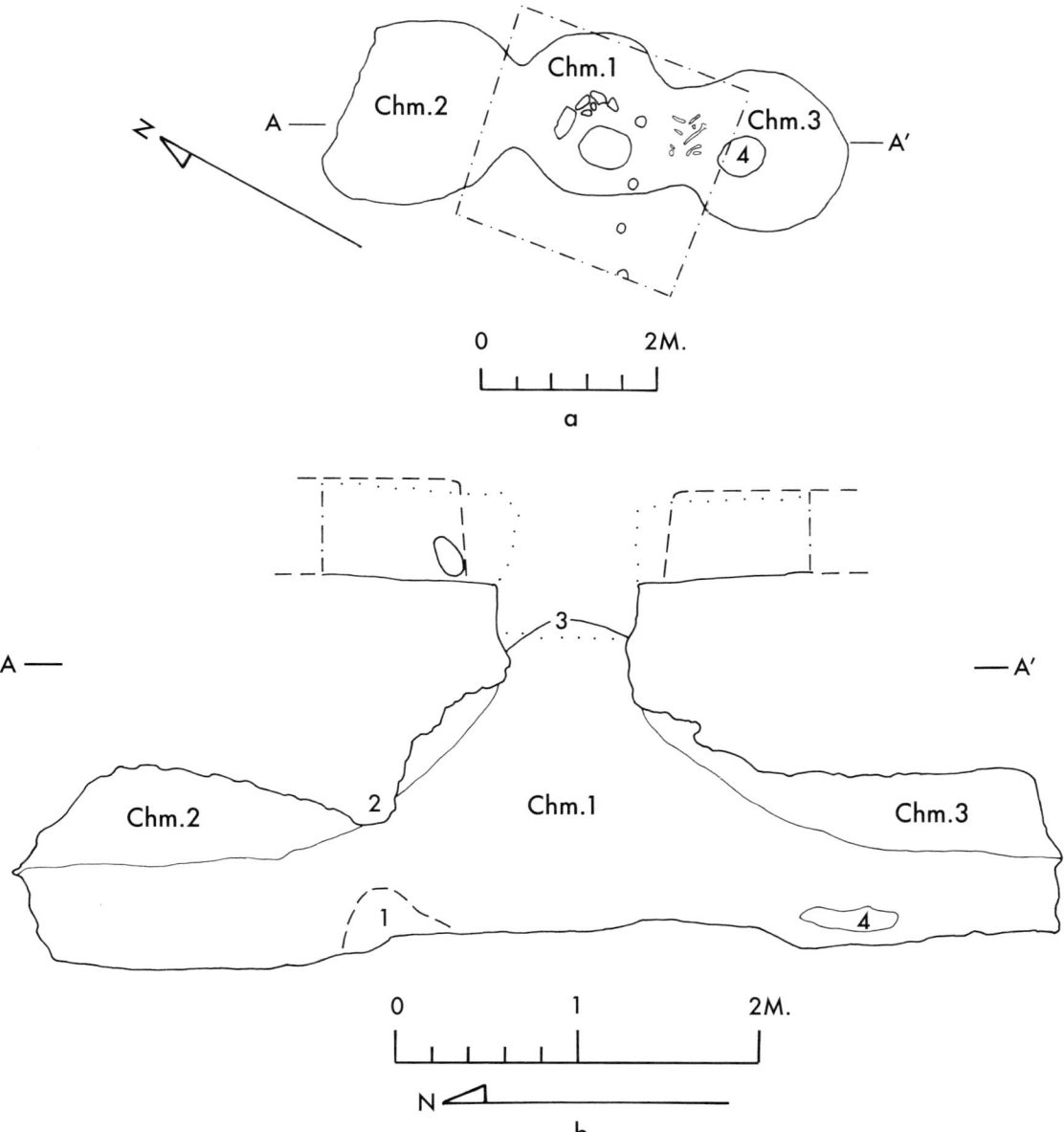

Ch. 5D-2: Plan (*a*) and Section (*b*).
Pertinent to Ch. 5D-2: *1*, Sill in entrance from Chm. 1 to Chm. 2; *2*, Restriction in ceiling of entrance to Chm. 2. Note that water seeping along the ceiling from the shaft would have dripped onto the side of the sill in Chm. 1, preventing its entrance into Chm. 2. *3*, Possible remains of a shelf-like cut to hold a stone cover; *4*, Battered stone cover, dumped into Chm. 3 when the chultun was filled.

FIGURE 44

(*a*) Str. 5D-11 before excavation, looking S; (*b*) Str. 5D-11 looking W into axial trench; (*c*) Str. 5D-11 axial trench, showing the second and third steps of 2nd above sectioned first step; masonry of 1st shows above; (*d*) W wall of Str. 5D-11-1st, stripped of finished masonry.

FIGURE 45

(*a*) Exposed front of Str. 5D-11 S of the axial trench. Visible in the trench is section through Plat. 5D-5:U. 5 and the first three steps of 5D-11-2nd and 1st; (*b*) Clearing rubble from Bu. 77 in the axial trench into Str. 5D-11. Visible behind the workman is a section through U. 7, a construction wall in fill of 5D-11-1st; (*c*) Bu. 77, rubble from above the roof of the grave, collapsed into the chamber; (*d*) Bu. 77, bedrock chamber with skeleton, two tripod plates, and *Spondylus* shell visible on the floor.

FIGURE 46

(*a*) Hattula Moholy-Nagy cleaning the large *Spondylus* shell in Bu. 77. Shown are the six pottery vessels, the skull and upper chest with the jade pendant (Fig. 34a:10) visible above the left shoulder of the skeleton; (*b*) Peter Harrison drawing Bu. 77 (a fallen stone is beneath the corner of the paper). Visible in the *Spondylus* shell is the jade bead, in Fig. 34a; (*c*) Bu. 77, skull and chest of the skeleton. The jade pendant has been removed, but the ear ornaments are visible on either side of the skull; (*d*) Initial clearing operations on Str. 5D-15.

FIGURE 47

a

b

c

d

(*a*) View of Str. 5D-15 after clearing; (*b*) Rear wall masonry of Str. 5D-15-3rd as seen in the trench/tunnel into the N (back) of the substructure; (*c*) Looking S into the tunnel into the back of Str. 5D-15-3rd. Visible in the section are the rear wall, the U. 6 floor, and (on the lower left) the base of the rear (S) wall (U. 7) of Str. 5D-144; (*d*) Trench/tunnel into the back of 5D-15-3rd showing the surviving stairway of 6th.

FIGURE 48

(*a*) Lowest stairs of Str. 5D-15-3rd; the axial trench has cut through the lowest two. Below stairs is Plat. 5D-5:U. 19 (floor of 1st); (*b*) Exposure of W end masonry of 5D-15-3rd above U. 20 in Op. 42C trench; (*c*) NW corner of Str. 5D-15-3rd above U. 22. Note the rounded corner of the masonry; (*d*) Str. 5D-15-3rd looking E along the front of the U. 21 terrace, toward the W end wall of the stairs.

FIGURE 49

(*a*) Inside corner of U. 21 terrace of Str. 5D-15-3rd, between W side of stairs for 2nd and facade; (*b*) W half of the facade of Str. 5D-15-3rd/2nd/1st after clearing; (*c,d*) Str. 5D-15-3rd, section of E end vault of the rear gallery: looking W (*c*) and E (*d*).

FIGURE 50

(*a*) Str. 5D-15-3rd/2nd/1st section of E end vault of the rear gallery looking W; visible in the room is U. 15, the late partition that defines 1st-A; (*b*) Peter Harrison with Col. Alt. 1 as found lying on the ruins of the stairway of Str. 5D-15; (*c*) Ca. 167, showing cache vessel and masonry block beside it; (*d*) Str. 5D-19, cleared prior to excavation.

FIGURE 51

(*a*) Str. 5D-19, showing the SW quarter excavated. Looming in the background is the massive substructure of North Acropolis Str. 5D-35; (*b*) Broken pottery left on the plaza floor in the corner where the S stair wall meets the front of Str. 5D-19; (*c*) St. 15 as reset; (*d*) St. P32 (excavated to U. 6 floor).

FIGURE 52

a

b

c

(*a*) St. P33 from its butt end; (*b*) Alt. P27; (*c*) Alt. P28.